Biological Treatments for Autism and PDD

What's going on?
What can **you** do about it?

William Shaw Ph.D.
The Great Plains Laboratory
9335 W. 75 St.
Overland Park, KS 66204
Phone: 913 341-8949
Fax: 913 341-6207
Email: GPL4U@aol.com
www.greatplainslaboratory.com

D0180333

with contributions by Bernard Rimland Ph.D., Bruce Semon M.D. Ph.D., Lisa Lewis Ph.D., Karyn Seroussi, and Pamela Scott

Disclaimer

This book is a summary of current research and medical therapies in use for the treatment of autism and PDD. The authors have written this book to serve as a guide to therapies and as a reference source for both professionals and nonprofessionals. All of this information is meant to be used under the care of the patient's health care professional and the authors do not intend that the information in this book be considered as a prescription for medical therapy for anyone. Many of the therapies discussed in this book are relatively new and may be associated with risks that may not be known for decades. Every medical therapy has inherent risks. The reader and the medical professional who treats himself or his children are responsible for weighing the risks involved in any of the therapies reviewed in this book before instituting such therapies. Although the authors have exhaustively researched all sources to ensure the accuracy of the information in this book, we assume no responsibility for errors, inaccuracies, or omissions.

Acknowledgements

I would like to thank the following individuals who have assisted me in many different ways in this work: Steve and Sandy Passer, Sidney Baker M.D., Bernard Rimland Ph.D. at the Autism Research Institute, Ellen Bolte and Portia Iversen at the Cure Autism Now Foundation, William Crook M.D. of the International Health Foundation, Kelly Dorfman and Patricia Lemer at the Developmental Delay Registry, my teachers, especially Samuel Rogers Ph.D., D.V.M. for his outstanding instruction in basic biochemistry, and Ellen Kassen for her outstanding work in the laboratory. I would also like to thank the hundreds of other parents and professionals who supported and encouraged my work and offered me additional information that led to me to explore new therapies and theories.

William Shaw Ph.D.

Printed in the United States of America

ISBN 0-9661238-0-8

Table of contents

Preface

The purpose of writing this book is to integrate information from the fields of biochemistry, immunology, genetics, nutrition, and microbiology about autism, ADD, and PDD into a form that could be assimilated by both parents, professionals such as nutritionists and dietitians, and physicians who deal with children with these disorders. Long conversations with hundreds of parents of children with autism and PDD, including many who are themselves physicians, have provided me with many clues to these disorders.

The wealth of information on the abnormalities of the immune system in autism leads me to the conclusion that the genetic factors in autism appear to be primarily those affecting the immune system. In my view, the anatomical abnormalities in the brain that have been documented may be secondary to abnormal metabolic function caused by abnormal microbial metabolites and/or toxic peptides from wheat and milk, which in turn are due to an impaired immune system.

The information in this book may be useful not only for people with autism but also for children with any disorder in which some of the symptoms of autism are sometimes or frequently present including pervasive developmental disorder (PDD), Rett's syndrome, Williams disease, neurofibromatosis, tuberous sclerosis, Fragile X, Down's syndrome, Tourette's syndrome, Prader-Willi syndrome, and attention deficit disorder(ADD). Many of the same abnormalities in autism are also present in these disorders and the therapies suggested in this book for autism may also help children and adults with these other disorders as well. My objectives are to describe the abnormalities in autism and related disorders and to describe some of the therapies that are frequently beneficial for children and adults who have some or all of the symptoms of autism. Although a few children have completely recovered from autism using the therapies outlined in this book (and the parents of two of them include their accounts in this book), I am **not** suggesting that **all** children will benefit but hope that many will benefit to some degree.

I think that the accounts of the two mothers whose children recovered are very important because of the similarities of the therapies they used. Both mothers obtained information and instituted therapy independently. Both children were diagnosed early about the age of two years. Both mothers independently arrived at the use of antifungal therapy, an antiyeast diet low in sugar and free of yeast, treatment of food allergies, and a gluten and casein-free diet as key cornerstones of therapy but also used intensive behavioral interventions as well. You will note that there are significant differences in the nutritional and antifungal approaches presented by different authors in this book. I realize that this may be confusing but this information honestly reflects the fact that there are still many unknowns. You may wish to experiment with several of the different nutritional and antifungal approaches to determine which ones are most beneficial for your patient or your child.

Some of this material may be difficult but I have made every attempt to simplify it without distorting the meaning. Knowledge is power. **Much of this information may not be familiar to parents or to medical practitioners.** The parent who reads this book should assume that their family doctor or even their neurologist or other specialist may not know nearly as much as they do about autism after reading this book. Most of the information has been available in the form of research papers that have been available only to medical research specialists but was essentially unknown by persons outside the narrow specialty. There has been a tremendous increase in the application of knowledge about autism and PDD that was stimulated by a group of physicians and scientists who met in Dallas in January 1995 as a part of Dr. Bernard Rimland's Defeat Autism Now! (DAN!) Conference.

My goal for this book is to allow your child to be healthier and function better so that both you and your child will have a better life. I am sure to be criticized for recommending action based on "incomplete" or "anecdotal" data. While acknowledging the great benefits of antibiotics in treating disease, I think the overuse of antibiotics may have been the single most damaging medical treatment of the last half of this century for some of our children. However, I think the dangers to our children are too great to wait until all data are **perfect**, meaning that we should wait *forever*. The Red Cross refused to act on behalf of the Jews in German concentration camps in World War II despite numerous reports of genocide because the evidence was "anecdotal" rather than "definitive." It has taken nearly 50 years from the time of the first research linking lung cancer and smoking to get restrictions on cigarette use for minors. It took 25 years from the initial discovery that folic acid supplementation prevented a birth defect called spina bifida until extra folic acid supplements were recommended for pregnant women. The stakes for the safety of our children are too high to wait forever. William Shaw Ph.D.

About the authors.
William Shaw received a Ph.D. in biochemistry from the Medical University of South Carolina. He has board certifications in both the fields of Clinical Chemistry and in Toxicology. He worked for six years in nutritional biochemistry, endocrinology, and immunology at the Centers for Disease Control, for twelve

years in a large medical testing laboratory called Smith Kline Beecham Clinical Laboratories involved with specialized medical testing for toxicology (poisons and drugs), chemistry, immunology, and endocrinology. Next, for five years, he was an associate professor at the University of Missouri at Kansas City (UMKC) School of Medicine and Director of Clinical Chemistry, Toxicology, and Endocrinology and the organic acid testing for metabolic diseases at Children's Mercy Hospital, the teaching hospital for the University of Missouri at Kansas City School of Medicine. Dr. Shaw has lectured throughout the world on autism and has been a keynote speaker at the Autism Society of America National Meeting, the National Meeting of the American Association for Environmental Medicine, and the National Meeting of the American College for Advancement of Medicine. He is actively involved with both the Defeat Autism Now(DAN) group and the Cure Autism Now(CAN) foundation. Dr. Shaw is the author of many scientific papers and the co-author of two book chapters dealing with laboratory medicine and nutritional biochemistry. Dr. Shaw can be reached by phone at 913 341-8949 or by e-mail at williamsha@aol.com. The website for the Great Plains Laboratory is www.greatplainslaboratory.com and the mailing address is The Great Plains Laboratory, 9335 W 75 St, Overland Park, KS 66204.

Bernard Rimland Ph.D., a research psychologist, has been the director of the Autism Research Institute since it was founded in 1967. He is the editor of the Autism Research Review International and is the founder of the Autism Society of America. His prize-winning book Infantile Autism: the Syndrome and its Implications for a Neural Theory of Behavior is credited with changing the field of psychiatry from its "blame the mother " orientation to its current recognition that autism is a biological disorder., not an emotional illness. He has lectured on autism and related problems throughout the world, and is the author of numerous publications. He has received many awards for his work on autism. Dr. Rimland served as primary technical advisor on autism for the film Rain Man. Dr. Rimland, who earned his Ph.D. in experimental psychology and research design at Penn State University, has also conducted research on the relationship between nutrition and behavior. He is a past officer of several societies devoted to research in this area, and has lectured and published extensively on this topic, as well as in the field of autism. Dr. Rimland can be reached at the Autism Research Institute, 4182 Adams Ave., San Diego, CA 92116.

Bruce Semon M.D. Ph.D. is both a child psychiatrist and nutritionist practicing in Milwaukee, Wisconsin. He has practiced nutritional medicine since 1991. He received his M.D. from University of Wisconsin-Madison in 1984 and his Ph.D. in Nutrition from University of California-Davis in 1989. He was a Fellow at the National Institute of Health, National Cancer Institute (Laboratory of Nutritional and Molecular Regulation) from 1989-1991. He completed an adult residency in psychiatry at the Medical College of Wisconsin in 1995 and a fellowship in child and adolescent psychiatry in 1997. Dr. Semon has published several academic papers relating to nutrition. Dr. Semon has treated many patients suffering from autism and other disorders in conventional ways, seeing very few positive changes. He has treated many patients for yeast-related illnesses, including eczema, psoriasis, depression and autism, with remarkable results. He is using the nutritional approach in his private practice in Milwaukee, as well as in a Milwaukee based mental health clinic with which he is affiliated. Dr. Semon and his wife, Lori Kornblum, are in the process of publishing a cookbook implementing a diet free of yeast and fermented foods, casein, gluten, eggs, corn, and soy. Dr. Semon can be reached at: 250 W. Coventry Court, Suite 101, Glendale, Wisconsin 53217, (414) 352-6500.

Lisa S. Lewis Ph.D. is the mother of two children, one of whom was diagnosed with autism at the age of three. Her formal academic training is in biological anthropology; while earning a doctorate in that field she studied genetic variation and performed studies of blood proteins in several species of non-human primates. This science background laid the foundation for understanding the theories underlying dietary interventions. The picture was completed by her great interest in baking and has a small catering business which specializes in children's birthday cakes. For the last ten years, Dr. Lewis has been in the computing field. After her son's autism diagnosis, she soon found that doctors had little to offer in the way of information or treatment. She did her own research; this resulted in a dietary intervention that began as a trial and has now become a way of life for her son. Because she have spent so much time and energy trying to understand *why* this has helped him, and how to implement this diet, she put what she found together into an eighteen page brochure that was widely distributed via the Internet, and through the mails. She is the author of the recent book *Special Diets for Special Kids: Understanding and Implementing Dietary Intervention for Autistic Children.*

Karyn A. Seroussi is the co-founder with Lisa Lewis of the Autism Network for Dietary Intervention, and a co-founder of the Rochester, NY chapter of Parents of Allergic Children. She lives with her husband and two children, all of whom have different dietary requirements. She is currently completing a book about her family's experience and her son's recovery from autism.

Pamela Scott is a parent first and an advocate for life. She is currently working as a Parent Training Consultant for The Parent Connection. The Parent Connection is devoted to making broad systems change in the way families access services through Missouri's Division of Mental Retardation and Developmental Disabilities. The Parent Connection offers educational workshops, training, and presentations. These services are available to families, parent groups, and the professionals who work with them.

Foreword

Dr. Shaw has performed a great and much needed service for the parents of autistic children--and the physicians who work with autistic children—by publishing this book.

There are a great many parent guidebooks which offer psychological and educational advice. There are also many books which discuss esoteric medical and scientific issues. There are, however, very few books-like this one-which address the practical, here and now biomedical treatments that can bring about dramatic improvement in many autistic individuals.

The term autism (and the newer, quite confusing term "PDD") are umbrella words which cover a broad array of disorders sharing a number of overlapping symptoms, but having a large variety of different causes. No one knows how many causes of autism there are. But there are some causes we do know about, and about which we have a rudimentary understanding.

Children or adults with autism caused by some of the factors covered in this book can be treated with some success and often with quite dramatic success. And it is to some of these known causes, and their treatments, that this important new book is addressed.

The reader will quickly discover that this book is "user friendly". Its purpose is to clarify, to explain, to guide, and to encourage so that at long last the parents themselves can begin to do what they have always wanted to do—have a real hand in the healing of their autistic child.

Thank you Dr. Shaw.

---------Bernard Rimland Ph.D., November 1997.

Infections, antibiotics, and their relationship to autism and ADD. Alternative treatments.

by William Shaw Ph.D.

Is there an autism epidemic?

Bernard Rimland Ph.D. at the Autism Research Institute asked the question, Is there an autism epidemic? His data in Table 1 show that, between 1965 and 1969, only 1% of parents who contacted him were inquiring on behalf of a child with autism under 3 years old. However, between 1994 and 1995, 17 % of the parents who called him were inquiring on behalf of a child under 3. Presumably the higher percentage of inquiries on behalf of children under three could be attributed to two factors: (1)greater knowledge about autism on the part of physicians and parents, leading to earlier diagnosis of autism and/or (2)higher incidence of autism in the younger age group. Furthermore, a large number of pediatricians and physicians who have large practices in the field of autism have noticed an increase in the incidence of autism. The pediatrician William Crook M.D. who had been practicing since the 1950's and was aware of the symptoms of autism says that he did not see a case of autism until 1973, 24 years after starting his practice of medicine. Then it seemed to him that the incidence of autism accelerated. Many other professionals who are working in this field of autism think that there is an increase in the incidence of autism. This increase in autism is critical for determining whether genetic or environmental factors are most important in causing autism. If autism is mainly due to genetic factors, the incidence of autism would be constant. Furthermore, the percentage of individuals with autism in a particular age group would

Infections, antibiotics, and their relationship to autism and ADD.

be the same. Thus, if the incidence of autism in three year olds is one in a thousand, the incidence of autism in fifty year olds should also be one in a thousand.

Table1.
Is there an autism epidemic?

Year	%under 3 years	Number
1965-69	1	919
1970-79	5	4184
1980-89	5	4018
1990-93	8	6785
1994-95	17	3916

Fortunately, such data has been reported in Iceland(2). Iceland is an ideal country for this evaluation since a single institution confirmed **all** cases of autism in the entire country and since the investigators personally reviewed all cases diagnosed in the entire country so that differences due to different people making the diagnoses are minimized. These investigators found that the incidence of autism had doubled over the last 20 years. Furthermore, the male to female ratio had increased significantly over the same time period. This study is extremely important since it shows that factors other than genetics may be causing autism. What could some of these nongenetic factors be?

Kontstantareas and Homatidis (3) at the University of Guelph in Ontario, Canada found a high correlation between the prevalence of ear infections and the incidence of autism. They found that the earlier the child had an ear infection, the more likely that child had a more severe form of autism. They also found that increased incidence of ear infections was associated with a more severe rather than a mild form of autism. Many similar studies have been conducted in the field of attention deficit hyperactivity (ADHD). These studies also indicate that increased ear infection early on in life results in much greater incidents of hyperactivity (4-8). Roberts and his colleagues (4) reported that recurrent otitis media during infancy was correlated

2

Infections, antibiotics, and their relationship to autism and ADD.

with increased distractibility of the students later in life. Other studies(5-8) correlated recurrent otitis media in infancy with later low IQ scores, poor performance on tests of reading, spelling, and math, increased retention in grade, increased attention deficits, and increased behavior problems in school.

Both the autism and ADHD research groups have assumed that the hearing impairment caused by the ear infection is what caused the abnormal development. My own interpretation of these data is that abnormal byproducts of yeast and drug-resistant bacteria absorbed into the body from the intestine following the excessive use of antibiotics is the cause of these epidemics. Later chapters will deal with the mechanism of this problem in great detail.

The antibiotic revolution
Antibiotics were first produced on a commercial scale around the end of World War II. In 1949, the amount of antibiotic production was very low, about 80 tons per year(9) In addition to the production of antibiotics being fairly low, the kind of antibiotic used was mostly of the injectable type. But by the 1950's, oral antibiotics were increasingly used. The oral antibiotics are taken by mouth rather than being injected intramuscularly. I was a child in grammar school in the 1950's so I got most of my antibiotics injected into the buttocks. By 1954, 250 tons of antibiotics per year were being produced. By 1990, **20,000 tons** (40 million pounds) of antibiotics per year were being produced(9). I think that this explosive growth in the use of antibiotics is a major factor for the increased incidence of autism and other developmental disorders such as ADD as well as a number of adult disorders such as fibromyalgia. In the United States one of the main reasons for antibiotic use in children is for a condition called otitis media or ear infection.

Ear infections
According to a publication (10) by The Panel for Otitis Media, a group of prominent pediatricians and scientists from throughout the United States:

Infections, antibiotics, and their relationship to autism and ADD.

- Ear infections account for one-third of all visits to the pediatrician and 75% of all follow-up visits.
- Between 1975 and 1990, office visits for otitis media increased by 150% to 24.5 million visits per year.
- **Children under age two** had the highest rate per year of office visits to the doctor for evaluation of otitis media and also the **greatest increase in visits per year between 1975 and 1990: 224%** !
- A two year study of children between 2 and 6 years in day-care showed that 53% had at least one episode of otitis media during their first year and 61% during their second year. Thirty percent of the children had recurrent bouts of otitis media.
- A cost analysis in 1991 estimated that the cost *per episode* including direct and indirect costs, prescription drugs, and parents' time lost from work at $406 for a total yearly cost in 1991 of about ten billion dollars.

Otitis media has proven to be a cash cow to both primary care physicians and the drug industry. Now consider another 30 billion dollars a year spent on specialized speech and developmental therapy (11)and billions of dollars more spent to treat ADD, PDD, autism, and other disorders. If, in fact, the overuse of antibiotics is related to the increase in these disorders, then the financial impact of otitis media is very large indeed.

Nonhuman use of antibiotics and the rise of antibiotic-resistant bacteria

In addition to the marked increase in antibiotic use in humans, the use of antibiotics in food animals has also sky-rocketed, not because our animals are sicker than usual but because they gain weight much faster when antibiotics are given with their feed. The animals are supposed to be withdrawn from antibiotic use prior to slaughter so that most of the antibiotics they are exposed to have been eliminated by the time of their death if the feedlot owner follows the regulations. However, the abnormal microbial ecology in the intestines of these animals caused by the use of these products persists; it seems likely

4

that chemical byproducts (such as gliotoxins) produced in the intestines of these animals by yeast, fungi, and antibiotic-resistant bacteria may be absorbed into the bloodstream of these animals and are likely present in their meat as well. It is difficult to know how much of a problem this is for humans who eat this meat. Pamela Scott, who has written a later chapter in this book, was so concerned about this problem that she only fed her son meat from range animals not exposed to antibiotics in feed lots.

According to Stuart Levy M.D. a professor at Tuft's University School of Medicine in his book *The Antibiotic Paradox: How Miracle Drugs Are Destroying the Miracle*(9), the use of antibiotics for fattening animals and other agricultural uses also selects for more drug-resistant bacteria which then enter the ecosystem in the meat and feces of these animals and may infect humans. Dr Levy found that six months after the use of antibiotics in feed for chickens, stool samples from humans in the surrounding community contained the same drug-resistant bacteria that had developed in the chickens. The use of human antibiotics in animal feed has been banned in Great Britain but is still allowed and is widely used in the United States. Antibiotics have even been added to the water in which salmon and catfish are raised; antibiotic-resistant bacteria have been found in the flesh of these catfish. In addition, antibiotics such as Streptomycin and oxytetracycline have been sprayed from airplanes to control diseases in fruit trees and potatoes, allowing the development of drug-resistant bacteria in soils over a wide geographic area. Some pathogenic bacteria may now be resistant to as many as 10 different antibiotics.

Bacteria that cause ear infection
The three most common bacteria causing ear infection are Streptococcus pneumoniae, Haemophilus influenza, and Moraxella catarrhalis. These organisms account for 70-90% of all ear infections(12). These organisms commonly inhabit the nose and throat of children and can easily move into the ear via the Eustachian tube. Streptococcus pneumoniae accounts for 30-40% of all cases.

Infections, antibiotics, and their relationship to autism and ADD.

As many as 28% of strains of this organism have been found to be penicillin resistant. Haemophilus influenza is responsible for about 21% of otitis media; 15-30% of strains of this bacteria are resistant to several types of penicillin. Moraxella catarrhalis accounts for 12 % of all cases. As many as 96% of strains of this organism may be resistant to penicillin such as amoxicillin (12). Moraxella catarrhalis is present at some time in the nose or mouth of 75% of infants before the age of two years.

The Panel for Otitis Media(10) stated:

'It is characteristic of health care providers in the United States to intervene for otitis media with effusion,, but the panel was impressed by data suggesting that otitis media was an effusion usually following a benign course, without treatment. Thus, although such a study might be difficult to implement because it runs counter to prevailing attitudes, research to document the natural course of otitis media with effusion is essential.."

Translated into simple English, this means: doctors and parents are used to using antibiotics for ear infections. The proof that they work over the long run is shaky. However, it is going to be extremely hard to change the way things are done because habits are difficult to change.

A large Dutch study that was done with 1,439 children put the children in two groups. One of them got nothing and one of them got antibiotics and antihistamines. In the untreated children, 60% of the children recovered without medical intervention within three months. This kind of treatment would almost never be done in the United States. To give you some idea of the cultural differences in the two countries, only about 30% of physicians in Holland use antibiotics for treating ear infections. In the United States, you would find close to 99% of physicians use antibiotics on a regular basis to treat ear

6

Infections, antibiotics, and their relationship to autism and ADD.

infections. Parents and employers must also be blamed for this antibiotic overuse because with so many two income families, mothers are under pressure to be at work rather than stay home with a sick child. The parents put pressure on the physicians to use antibiotics even when inappropriate. The physician knows he may lose the patient unless he complies.

In another study of 518 children with ear infection, Cantekin (13) found that six weeks after stopping the antibiotic amoxicillin, the recurrence was 2-6 times higher in the antibiotic-treated children than those in the placebo group. Van Buchem (14) treated one group of otitis media patients with antibiotics, one with tubes in the ears, and a third with neither. The outcome in the three groups was essentially the same.

One of the reasons that I was very interested in otitis media was due to the fact that a very high percentage of children with autism whose medical charts were examined by me had a history of frequent ear infections or other infections treated by antibiotics. In hundreds of medical charts I examined at a hospital, children with seizures, autism, and even psychosis had a history of antibiotic use prior to the development of these conditions. The urine organic acid testing of these children frequently revealed high concentrations of compounds derived from yeast and/or bacteria that are commonly resistant to broad-spectrum antibiotics. The pattern was so prevalent and so striking that there is little doubt in my mind that there is a relationship between the high concentrations of yeast and bacteria byproducts and the resulting disorders.

Exposure to cigarette smoke is also a significant risk factor for otitis media. In a study of seven year old British children, the authors found cotinine, a metabolite of nicotine was present in the saliva of children exposed to secondhand smoke and that the cotinine increased with the number of smokers in the household. The authors

7

Infections, antibiotics, and their relationship to autism and ADD.

(15) found that one-third of the cases of otitis media could be attributed to exposure to secondhand smoke.

Allergies can frequently be the major underlying cause of ear infection because allergic reaction can cause swelling of the tissues of the ears that interferes with proper drainage and allows bacteria to grow more readily. McMahan (16) and Nsouli (17) both found that treatment of underlying allergies greatly diminished the recurrence of otitis media. Because ear infections are such difficult medical problems for both parents and children, I have compiled a list of different approaches for these ear infections which follows on the next page.

Infections, antibiotics, and their relationship to autism and ADD.

Ear infections and other recurrent infections and how to break the cycle or at least reduce the damage.

The following are different techniques that will help break the cycle and minimize the damage. Remember that there are **exceptions to every rule** and antibiotics may **sometimes** be needed.

1. Tough it out or employ watchful waiting. Use ear drops containing benzocaine and a decongestant to stop the pain. A large study conducted in Holland showed no difference in outcome when children receiving antibiotics were compared to a placebo group. Antibiotics are not used nearly as much in Europe as in the United States. Only 31% of general practitioners in Holland use antibiotics to treat ear infections. By not treating immediately, you allow your child's immune system to react and build up a defense against future infections. If infections are treated immediately, the immune system will not have a chance to strengthen itself.

2. Eliminate milk, wheat, and other allergy causing foods from the diet. Milk is the number one culprit in causing food allergies and sinus infections that often cause blockage of the Eustachian tube leading to ear infections. If milk and dairy elimination does not clear up the infections get a complete food allergy work-up for your child from an allergist.

3. Stop any cigarette or other smoking inside the house.

4. Never use antibiotics for colds or flu since antibiotics kill bacteria but not cold or flu viruses.

5. If you have to use antibiotics for your child, have your doctor prescribe the antifungal drug nystatin along with the antibiotic. **There are no adverse reactions between nystatin and any other antibiotic because nystatin is not absorbed into the bloodstream from the intestine in an appreciable amount.** If your doctor won't prescribe nystatin, give one of the natural antifungal products such as garlic, caprylic acid, or grapefruit seed extract along with the antibiotic. The beneficial bacteria

Infections, antibiotics, and their relationship to autism and ADD.

Lactobacillus acidophilus may not help while the antibiotics are being given since the antibiotics may kill the acidophilus bacteria as well. Penicillin, chloramphenicol, erythromycin, tetracycline, oxacillin, vancomycin, and ceftriaxone all will kill the acidophilus bacteria. After antibiotics are completed, give supplements of Lactobacillus acidophilus for at least 30 days after completing the antibiotic. As a matter of fact, consider giving acidophilus supplements on a daily basis all the time to maintain a healthy intestine.

6. Get a throat culture done if your child has frequent infections. The most common organisms causing ear infection commonly inhabit the nose and throat. There is a vaccine available for Streptococcus pneumoniae which is the most common cause of ear infections. If your child has a positive throat culture for Streptococcus pneumoniae, ask your pediatrician about getting vaccinated against this organism. The vaccine is termed the 23-type pneumococcal polysaccharide vaccine.

7. Consider if one of the parents can stay home at home with the child until he is at least two years old and avoid preschool and day care centers. Day care is a breeding ground for germs.

8. Breast-feed your child for as long as possible since breast-milk contains antibodies against the bacteria that cause ear infections and other infections as well. Children who are breast-fed were much less likely to get frequent infections during the first six months of life(18,19).

9. Echinacea, the corn flower was used extensively by the Plains Indians of the United States to treat infections and this knowledge was transferred to the settlers. Echinacea is a stimulant of the immune system and is available in pediatric doses in many health food stores such as Wild Oats and others. It can also be ordered over the phone(800 494-WILD) if a store is not nearby. (I have no financial interest in any of the products mentioned in this book.) This therapy is even more effective if drops of garlic and mull(also called mullein) oil are placed **in the ears** while giving the Echinacea.(My son used this method and resolved his earache overnight.) Three days of this therapy will

clear up most ear infections. If this doesn't work, you still have the option of using antibiotics. Echinacea is a general immune system stimulant and will help to decrease the incidence and severity of colds and flu as well. This product has been used extensively in Germany for many kinds of illnesses and much of the literature documenting its use is written in German but some of the articles in English are listed in the references(20-23). Echinacea works the best if it is given for 10 days and then is discontinued for two weeks before started again.

10. Ask your doctor to give your child a "shot" of penicillin in the buttocks instead of the oral penicillin. I got these as a child in the 1950's all the time and so did millions of other people. The main benefit of the injection is that it will not kill the beneficial bacteria in the intestinal tract and lead to an overgrowth of the intestinal tract with yeast and harmful bacteria like Clostridia. The antibiotic will reach the human cells in the intestine but will not reach the bacteria in the cavity inside the intestine.

11. If your child has four or more infections in one year, consider an evaluation of their immune system. Many children with autism have an inborn weakness of the immune system called an immunodeficiency. The best person to consult about this is called a clinical immunologist, which is a physician (M.D. or D.O.) who specializes in these diseases. Usually these physicians are also part-time researchers and are associated with a medical school. If your child has a significant immunodeficiency, ask your physician about the possibility of using antibody infusions (called IVIG or intravenous immunoglobulin) to help your child's immune system fight off new infections. Sudhir Gupta M.D. at the University of California at Irvine has obtained complete remissions of some cases of autism(24) using IVIG therapy. See the chapter on the immune system for more detailed information..

12. Consult a health practitioner trained in homeopathy. The technique called homeopathy was shown to be more effective (25) than conventional antibiotic treatment in a German study of 103 children between 1 and 11 years. Homeopathy drops are also available at most health food stores. After one year, 70.7% of the

Infections, antibiotics, and their relationship to autism and ADD.

children treated with homeopathy had no relapses compared to 56.5% of children treated with antibiotics. The average number of relapses was also much higher in the children treated with antibiotics than in those treated with homeopathy.

13. Consider tubes in the ear (tympanotomy tubes) if all else fails.

Infections, antibiotics, and their relationship to autism and ADD.

References
1. Rimland B. Is there an autism epidemic? Autism Research Review International 9: 3, 1995.
2. Magnusson P and Saemundsen E. A study of prevalence of autism in Iceland. Proceedings of the 5th European Congress of Autism. Barcelona, Spain, 1996.
3. Kontstantareas M and Homatidis S. Ear infections in autistic and normal children. J Autism and Dev Dis 17:585,1987.
4. Roberts J, Burchinal M, and Campbell F. Otitis media in early childhood and patterns of intellectual development and later academic performance. J Ped Psychol 19:347-367,1994.
5. Hagerman R and Falkenstein A. An association between recurrent otitis media in infancy and later hyperactivity. Clin Pediat 26:253-257, 1987.
6. Teele D, Klein J, Rosner B, and The Greater Boston Study Group. Otitis media with effusion during the first years of life and development of speech and language. Pediatrics 74: 282-287,1984.
7. Silva P, Chalmers D, and Stewart I. Some audiological, psychological, educational, and behavioral characteristics of children with bilateral otitis media with effusion: a longitudinal study. J Learning Disabilities 19: 165-169, 1986.
8. Sak R and Ruben R. Effects of recurrent middle ear effusion in preschool years on language and learning. Developmental and Behavioral Pediatrics 3: 7-11, 1982.
9. Levy S. The Antibiotic Paradox. How Miracle Drugs Are Destroying the Miracle. Plenum Press, New York,1992.
10. Stool SE et al. Otitis media with effusion in young children. Clinical practice guideline. Number 12. AHCPR Publication No.94-0622.Rockville, M.D.: Agency for Health Care Policy and Research, Public Health Service, US Department of Health and Human Services. July 1994.
11. Nsouli T. Serous otitis media and food allergy. Clinical Pearls News 5: 1, 1995.
12. Barnett E and Klein JO. The problem of resistant bacteria for the management of acute otitis media. Pediatric Clinics of North America 42: 509-517,1995.
13. Cantekin E et al. Antimicrobial therapy for otitis media with effusion. JAMA 266: 3309-3317,1991.
14. Van Buchem F and Dunk J. Therapy of acute otitis media: myringotomy, antibiotics, or neither? Lancet 2: 883-887,1981.

Infections, antibiotics, and their relationship to autism and ADD.

15. Strachah D et al. Passive smoking salivary cotinine concentrations and middle ear effusion in seven-year-old children. Brit Med J 298:1549-1552, 1989.
16. Mc Mahan J et al. Chronic otitis media with effusion: modified RAST analysis of 119 cases. Otolaryngol Head Neck Surgery 89: 427-431,1981.
17. Nsouli T et al. Serous otitis media and food allergy. Ann Allergy 73:215-219,1994.
18. Teele, D et al. Epidemiology of otitis media during the first seven years of life in greater Boston: a prospective cohort study. J Infect Dis 160: 83-94, 1989.
19. Williams E. Breast feeding attitudes and knowledge of pediatricians-in-training. Amer J of Prev Med 11:26-33,1995.
20. Luettig B et al. Macrophage activation and induction of macrophage cytotoxicity by purified polysaccharide fractions from the plant Echinacea purpurea. Infection Immunity 46: 845-849,1984.
21. Roesler J et al. Application of purified polysaccharides from cell cultures of the plant Echinacea purpurea to mice mediates protection against systemic infections with Listeria monocytogenes and Candida albicans. Int J Immunopharmacol 13: 27-37,1991.
22. Wacker A and Hilbig W. Virus inhibition by Echinacea purpurea. Planta Medica 33:89-102,1978.
23. Vogel V. American Indian Medicine. University of Oklahoma Press, Norman, OK, 1970 pp 356-357.
24. Gupta S, Aggarwal , and Heads C. (1995). Dysregulated immune system in children with autism. Beneficial effects of intravenous immune globulin on autistic characteristics. J. Autism Develop Dis 26:439-52,1996.
25. Friese KH et al. Otitis media in children: A comparison of conventional and homeopathic drugs. Head and Neck Otorhinolaryngology 44:462-466, 1996.

The microorganisms in the gastrointestinal tract

by William Shaw Ph.D.

Bacteria in the intestinal tract
In order to understand how the widespread use of antibiotics may have such devastating effects, it is necessary to understand the role of microorganisms in the intestinal tract.

There are two main kinds of bacteria in the intestinal tract: aerobic and anaerobic. The aerobic bacteria need oxygen while the anaerobic bacteria don't need oxygen to live and even may be killed if oxygen is present. Some bacteria grow faster with oxygen but can adapt to a low oxygen environment. Another major group of organisms in the intestine are the yeast and fungi. In the intestinal tracts of some individuals there may be single-celled animals called protozoa as well. These organisms in a normal intestinal tract are found in a natural balance that is healthy. It is estimated that there are 500 or more different species of bacteria in the average human intestinal tract(1). Because there is not much oxygen in the intestinal tract, the anaerobic bacteria that don't need oxygen predominate. Of the 500 species, there are perhaps 30 or 40 species that constitute the majority of the bacteria present. It's estimated that there are about 10-100 trillion cells of bacteria in the intestinal tract at any one time(1). To give you an idea of the size of that number, there are about a 100 trillion human cells in the entire human body. Thus, 10-50 % of your total cells are due to bacteria in a normal individual who is not on antibiotics.

There are very few bacteria in the stomach because the stomach acid kills them. But, in the colon there are tremendous numbers: about a million times more in the colon compared to the stomach. The

stomach acid kills most bacteria but the stomach acid is neutralized
with bicarbonate from the pancreas in the normal individual as food
passes into the small intestine. Bacteria constitute about 50% of the
content of feces. These residents of the intestinal tract are always in a
state of flux : new bacteria are continuously being produced and old
bacteria are continuously being flushed out in the moving intestinal
contents and later as feces.

In a study that was reported in the Journal of Infection and
Immunology   (2), it was found oral penicillin administered to
experimental animals   reduced the total population of anaerobic
bacteria by a factor of 1,000 including beneficial bacteria which are
called Lactobacilli. These bacteria are present in yogurt. As the good
bacteria are killed off, the potentially harmful bacteria   increase
rapidly. This study reported translocation of the harmful bacteria out
of the intestinal tract and into the lymph nodes surrounding the
intestinal tract. From these lymph nodes, these bacteria were then
strategically placed to cause new infections throughout the body.

Yeast overgrowth of the intestinal tract
Another harmful effect of antibiotics is that killing off all the normal
bacteria results in the proliferation of yeast. There are hundreds of
articles in the scientific and medical literature indicating yeast overgrowth is associated with antibiotic use. Some of the most important
are included in the references at the end of this chapter (3-13). There
are two reasons for it. First, when the normal bacteria in the intestine
are killed off, the yeast have no competition so they are able to get
the lion's share of all the food that passes through the intestinal tract
after a meal. Second, the yeast may actually be stimulated by many of
the antibiotics (12,13).

Scientific work on animals is relevant to yeast infection in humans.
Infant mice were much more susceptible to Candida infection than
older mice and, once exposed to Candida at an early age, developed
persistent candidiasis(3). If these mice were given antibiotics at an
early age, the Candida in the intestinal tract increased an average

130-fold. Exposure of infant mice to the hormone cortisone increased Candida in the intestine 8-fold. Similar results are found in humans(5-11). Largely because of the overuse of antibiotics, the incidence of disseminated candidiasis has changed from a rare occurrence prior to 1960 to the fifth most common organism encountered in infections acquired at a hospital in Southern California (14).The reason these bacteria and yeast are important is because they produce chemical byproducts that are normally only present in very low concentrations. When yeast and bacteria, normally present in small quantities, reach extremely high numbers, they produce these byproducts in much higher concentrations. These byproducts of yeast and bacteria are then absorbed from the intestinal tract into the blood. From there, they circulate throughout the body to all the tissues and are eventually filtered out of the body into the urine.

In addition to the production of these byproducts, the yeast cells may convert to their more invasive colony form. The yeast in this hypha form imbed themselves into the lining of the intestinal tract like ivy climbing a brick wall. This attachment is facilitated by the secretion of yeast digestive enzymes at the point of attachment. The intestinal lining is thus digested by a variety of yeast enzymes including phospholipase A2, catalase, acid and alkaline phosphatases, coagulase, keratinase, and secretory aspartate protease(15-17). The secretory aspartate protease is of especial importance; it may destroy the lining of the intestinal tract and may also digest the IgA and IgM antibodies produced by the body to attack the yeast (15). The destruction of this gastrointestinal lining may be the reason for the abnormal secretin response discussed in the chapter on the digestive system.

Some of the intestinal cells probably die as a result of this attack. As a result of multiple yeast attaching to the intestinal lining, the lining may appear like Swiss-cheese on a microscopic level. Ordinarily, undigested food molecules would not be able to pass through this

17

intestinal lining. However, because of the holes in the intestinal lining, undigested food molecules pass through. This phenomenon is called the leaky gut syndrome. A major consequence of the leaky gut syndrome is much greater susceptibility to food allergies. The undigested food is recognized as an invader by the immune system and as a consequence, antibodies of both the IgE and IgG types may start to be produced. After a while both behavioral and allergic reactions may occur after eating these foods. Many times patients with multiple allergies will be retested after antiyeast therapy and find that their allergies have disappeared. When the yeast overgrowth has been eliminated, the intestinal lining heals, the intestine is no longer leaky, and the immune system diminishes its attacks against the offending foods. If your child has multiple food allergies in addition to milk and wheat sensitivity, you may find it nearly impossible to implement a suitable diet. Therefore, I usually recommend that an underlying yeast problem always be treated at least 60 days **before** allergy testing is done.

Evidence for abnormal bacterial byproducts in autism

One of the chemical compounds in urine that I initially suspected was due to a yeast overgrowth of the intestine is called dihydroxyphenylpropionic acid-like compound (DHPPA). Several years ago, I began a collaborative study with Dr Walter Gattaz, a research psychiatrist at the Central Mental Health Institute of Germany in Mannheim to evaluate urine samples of patients with schizophrenia. These samples were very valuable since they were obtained from patients who were drug-free. Thus, any biochemical abnormalities would be due to their disease and not a drug effect. Five of the twelve samples contained a very high concentration of a compound identified by GC/MS as a derivative of the amino acid tyrosine which is very similar to but is not identical to 3,4-dihydroxyphenylpropionic acid. I have termed this compound dihydroxyphenylpropionic acid-like compound (DHPPA-like compound). This compound is an isomer of dihydroxyphenylpropionic acid but I have not yet identified the exact isomer.

Figure 1. Comparison of DHPPA-like compound in urine samples of infants, normal children, and children with autism.

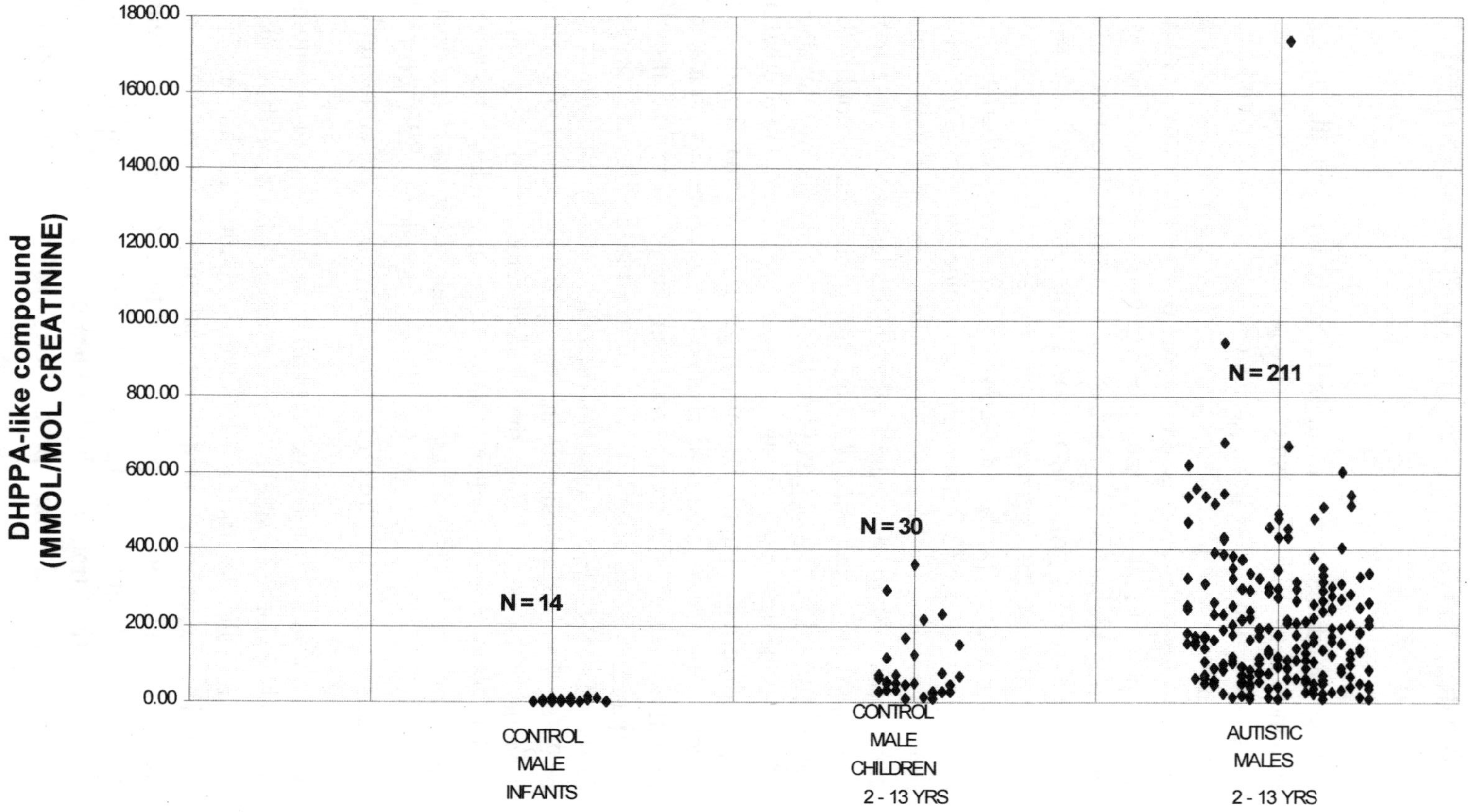

THE MICROORGANISMS IN THE GASTROINTESTINAL TRACT

Newborns infants tested at approximately one month of age had extremely low values of this compound in urine since newborns are not colonized with intestinal germs (Figure1). In older children, the values are much higher. In children with autism, values may be extremely high. There is some degree of overlap in the normal and autism population but the median and the mean values are significantly higher in the children with autism. (The median is the middle value of a group of numbers while the mean is the average value of the group.)The mean value for all infants is 3.7 mmol/mol creatinine with a standard deviation of 3.6 mmol/mol creatinine and a range from 0.3 - 12.7 mmol/mol creatinine. In normal male control children, the mean value is 91.5 mmol/mol creatinine with a standard deviation of 90.4; the median value in this group is 51.1 mmol/mol creatinine. In autistic male children, the mean value is double that of the controls: 192.4 mmol/mol creatinine with a standard deviation of 90.4; the median value in this group is 143.5 mmol/mol creatinine, nearly triple the value of the control group. In normal female control children, the mean value is 85.5 mmol/mol creatinine with a standard deviation of 55.9; the median value in this group is 74.5 mmol/mol creatinine. In autistic female children, the mean value is double that of the controls: 182.4 mmol/mol creatinine with a standard deviation of 200.6; the median value in this group is 111 mmol/mol creatinine, a value 49% greater than the control females. In all groups the median values are smaller than the corresponding mean values indicating that the values are not normally distributed and that the populations are skewed by some samples with very high concentrations of dihydroxyphenylpropionic acid-like compound.

What was surprising to me was that there was not a significant decrease in DHPPA-like compound after antifungal drug therapy. The mean value for the DHPPA-like compound actually increased a little. This increase indicated to me that this compound could not be due to the yeast but was probably due to a different microorganism Since several children and adults with Clostridium difficile infection of the intestinal tract had high values of DHPPA-like compound in their urine and the production of a similar compound,

20

THE MICROORGANISMS IN THE GASTROINTESTINAL TRACT

monohydroxyphenylpropionic is characteristic of different species of Clostridia(18,19), I suspected that one or more species of the bacteria genus Clostridium were producing this compound.

Some of the common species of Clostridium are Clostridium tetani that causes tetanus, Clostridium botulinum that causes the food poisoning botulism, and Clostridium perfringens and Clostridium difficile that cause diarrhea(20). Clostridium perfringens, Clostridium novyi, Clostridium bifermentans, Clostridium histolyticum, Clostridium septicum, and Clostridium fallax may all cause gangrene(20). Many other species of Clostridium are normal inhabitants of the intestinal tract but may not even be scientifically described and are not even named as a species. The major reason for a lack of knowledge about these organisms is that they are strict anaerobes that cannot tolerate oxygen. Since they must be processed in an oxygen free environment, many hospital laboratories do not have the capability to identify these organisms. The exception is Clostridium difficile which is identified by the toxin it produces in the stool rather than by the isolation of the organism itself. Clostridium difficile overgrowth of the intestinal tract causes a severe potentially fatal disorder called pseudomembranous colitis(21). This overgrowth is frequently associated with the use of oral antibiotics, indicating that this organism is resistant to many of the common antibiotics such as penicillin, ampicillin, tetracyclines, cephalosporins, chloramphenicol, and others(22). This organism is usually treated with either metronidazole (Flagyl) or vancomycin followed by a replenishment of the intestine with Lactobacillus acidophilus(23). Since many bacteria can genetically transfer drug resistance to other similar species and even unrelated species, it seems likely (to me) that multiple species of Clostridia may now be resistant to the most common drugs.

Another reason that I was interested in this compound was due to the theory of Ellen Bolte (Autism and Clostridium tetani: a hypothesis, Medical Hypotheses, In Press) that the tetanus bacteria (Clostridium

tetani) might be responsible for some cases of autism. Her child
developed autism after a DPT immunization which is a multiple
immunization (Diphtheria, pertussis,and tetanus) which includes a
tetanus toxoid. She was concerned that her child may actually have
contracted tetanus from a contaminated vaccine. When the antibodies
to tetanus were checked several years after this vaccination, the
antibodies to tetanus were very high. Her child was extremely
developmentally delayed and also had a high value of DHPPA-like
compound in the urine.

There are some interesting parallels between autism and tetanus.
Individuals with tetanus have extreme sensory sensitivity and may
need to be placed in dimly lighted rooms(24,25). Loud noises had to
be avoided. In addition, patients with this disorder might have
difficulty chewing and swallowing; lockjaw is the other name for
tetanus. Thus, Ellen's idea was that perhaps her child had a
"subacute" tetanus that caused many of the symptoms of autism
related to sensory sensitivity but would not be lethal because her
child was immunized. Such cases of subacute tetanus have been
reported even in individuals who had been immunized and had high
levels of antibodies to the tetanus toxin(24,25). Although I thought it
was highly unlikely that her child contracted tetanus from the
vaccine, I thought it possible that he might have a Clostridium tetani
overgrowth of the intestinal tract or an overgrowth of another
species of Clostridium that might also be producing toxins similar to
that of tetanus that might have caused the high antibody levels in her
child. Clostridium tetani overgrowth of the intestinal tract has been
demonstrated in rats(26). The toxins produced by several different
species of Clostridia (tetani, botulinum, barati, and butyricum) are
very similar biochemically(27) and therefore antibodies produced
against one Clostridium toxin would also probably react against the
tetanus toxin. Also the gene for the tetanus neurotoxin is located on
a plasmid(28), a piece of "naked" DNA that can be easily passed on
to different species of Clostridia and perhaps even other species of
bacteria and which would confer on the new species the ability to
make tetanus toxin.

Table 1

Effect of Flagyl therapy on urinary excretion of DHPPA-like compound

Diagnosis Age(yr.)and sex	Length of Time(Days) from start of Flagyl Therapy	Urinary DHPPA -like compound mmol/mol creatinine
autism, male, 4 yr	0	435
	6	184
	16	1
	21(stop Flagyl)	5
	24	2
	43	236
	93	274
female 54 yr C. difficile infection and uncontrolled diarrhea	0	396
	13	1
autism, male, 3 yr	0	549
	19	1
	30	3
autism, male, 4 yr	0	1362
	11	28
	15	3

Several of the patients with high urine concentrations of DHPPA-like compound had positive stool immunoassay tests for Clostridium difficile, leading me to suspect that Clostridia species were responsible for the production of this compound. Treatment of a number of patients with elevations of this compound with drugs that kill Clostridia such as Vancomycin and Flagyl resulted in nearly complete elimination of this compound in urine samples.

There is a marked decrease in the urinary concentration of dihydroxyphenylpropionic acid-like compound following the administration of standard age-appropriate doses of the antibiotic Flagyl (metronidazole). In all four patients, the concentrations of dihydroxyphenylpropionic acid-like compound decreased 99% or more after two to three weeks on this drug(Table 1). In the first patient in the above series, dihydroxyphenylpropionic acid-like compound rapidly increased following the cessation of metronidazole treatment. I suspect that this increase after stopping the drug was due to the fact that Clostridia are spore-forming organisms. Spores are extremely resistant forms of the bacteria that are difficult to kill and "hatch out" when drug therapy ends and then repopulate the intestinal tract. The first patient improved after Flagyl treatment but then regressed when the drug was discontinued. The same child was retreated with a six-week course of Vancomycin. A developmental specialist estimated that the child had gained six months of development after the six weeks of therapy. Again, the child regressed after discontinuation of therapy.

Elevated DHPPA-like compound is not found only in autism. Patients with values of DHPPA-like compound greater than 500 mmol/mol creatinine in the urine almost always have severe neurological, psychiatric, or gastrointestinal disorders such as autism, severe depression, psychotic behavior or schizophrenia, partial muscle paralysis, severe colitis, or sometimes a combination of these disorders. One young woman with an acute psychosis had the highest value I have found, nearly 7500 mmol/mol creatinine, a value approximately 100 times the normal median value! Treatment of psychotic individuals who have elevated DHPPA-like compound in urine with vancomycin has resulted in remission of symptoms without the use of neuroleptic drugs according to the patients' physicians.

THE MICROORGANISMS IN THE GASTROINTESTINAL TRACT

How important is this compound in autism? A number of children with very high values(greater than 400 mmol/mol creatinine) of DHPPA-like compound have responded favorably to treatment with Flagyl or vancomycin. I would estimate that perhaps 20% of children with autism may have these very high values. However, in some cases Flagyl or vancomycin therapy might not even be needed and just a supplement with the Lactobacillus acidophilus may be able to control the overgrowth especially if the DHPPA value is less than 400 mmol/mol creatinine If the DHPPA-like compound value is above 400 mmol/mol creatinine, then drug therapy may be needed and should be discussed with the child's physician. At this time, remember that this compound is **probably** produced by Clostridia species but additional research is needed to prove this idea conclusively.

A herbal product called Biocidin has been effective in controlling bacteria, yeast, and parasites according to Kelly Dorfman, the founder of the Developmental Delay Registry. She indicates that two drops of Biocidin liquid in fruit juice once a day at dinner has normalized the urinary excretion of this compound in children with PDD and autism. This product is a mixture of a herbal ingredients including Chlorophyll, impatiens pallida, hydrastis canadensis, ferula galbanum, hypericum perforatum, villa rubris, fumaria, frasera carolensis, gentiana campestris, sanguinaria, allicin, and garlic and can be obtained from Bio-Botanical Research at 800 775-4140. Literature from the company indicates that this product kills yeast as well as bacteria such as harmful bacteria such as Pseudomonas aeruginosa, Escherichia coli, Klebsiella pneumoniae, and Staphylococcus aureus. No formal research studies of the effectiveness of any of these therapies have been completed but several different studies to determine the exact species of bacteria that may be important in autism are underway.

I want to emphasize that **the die-off reaction** with the Flagyl, Biocidin, or vancomycin may be **very severe**. The die-off reaction appears to be a release of toxins by the Clostridia as they die that may last 3-7 days after drug therapy. A child getting this particular therapy should be under very close medical supervision because the side effects may be much more severe than those associated with the yeast die off reaction and can include symptoms such as heart palpitations, fever, extreme tiredness: some children may not even move during the first several days of therapy. The severity of the die-off reaction indicates to me the potency of the toxins produced by these organisms. However, the die-off reaction may be minimized by the concomitant use of materials such as bentonite or powdered charcoal which are available in health food stores to adsorb the toxins.

Although Clostridium difficile appears to be one of the organisms that produce the DHPPA, there are as many as 100 different species of Clostridium that may inhabit the intestinal tract according to Sidney Finegold MD, one of the world's leading experts on anaerobic bacteria (Personal Communication). There is an immunological test for the toxin produced by Clostridium difficile that can be done on stool to confirm this organism. **A negative test for Clostridium difficile does not rule out all species of Clostridium, only Clostridium difficile.** There is no convenient method to confirm the identity of the other 99 species of Clostridium in the intestinal tract that may also produce this compound.

Relationship between the immune system, early use of antibiotics and the microorganisms in the gastrointestinal tract.
It has been found that injection of an animal's own fecal matter which is about 50% bacteria by weight only causes a mild immune response(1) indicating that the normal flora (germs) of the intestine are given tolerance by the immune system, that is the immune system does not mount an attack against these organisms. It has been found that the immune system takes an "inventory" of all the cells present in the body during fetal development and shortly after birth.(I have relied on material by Teresa Binstock Ph.D.(29) at the University of Colorado School of Medicine as the primary source of this

information.) In addition to the immune system taking inventory of its own cells, it seems increasingly likely that the immune system also takes an inventory of bacteria and yeast cells present in the intestinal tract. This inventory is performed by a group of cells called the CD5+ B-cells, which are among the very first immunological cells to appear in the developing embryo and appear to play a role in tolerance to intestinal microorganisms in postnatal life. These cells may play a role in regulating the secretion of IgA, the antibody class that is secreted into the intestinal tract and which may select which microorganisms are tolerated in the intestinal tract. Furthermore, the eradication of normal flora by repetitive antibiotic use during infancy may cause the CD5+ B-cells to reject normal organisms as foreign invaders at a later age. Any cells that are on this early inventory may be given immune tolerance and will not be attacked later on by the immune system.

I have been impressed by numerous reports from parents of children with autism who indicate that their children used antibiotics at a very young age. I suspect that yeast and undesirable bacteria resulting from antibiotic therapy during early infancy have been "granted" immune tolerance; this immune tolerance may be one of the reasons why the yeast overgrowth in autism is so difficult to control and tends to recur even after months of antifungal therapy. Such an immune tolerance to yeast in the developing fetus may also occur if the mother has yeast infections during pregnancy. The daughter of a mother with severe vaginal yeast infections during pregnancy had severe yeast infection of the mouth called thrush at birth and was later diagnosed with autism. Such cases may explain children who appear to behave abnormally even as young infants. Thus, a new direction for future research might be to find a way to reprogram CD5+ B-cells or to replace them with more suitable cells from a donor.

Secretory IgA, an antibody produced by the immune system to fight intestinal germs, was found to react with harmful organisms but not those of the normal flora. The secretory IgA coats the harmful bacteria and seems to prevent them from binding to the mucosa cells.

THE MICROORGANISMS IN THE GASTROINTESTINAL TRACT

Bacteria that cannot implant are more quickly flushed out of the intestine. Since a high percentage of children with autism are deficient in the production of IgA, their immune systems may have more difficulty in excluding overgrowths of harmful yeast and bacteria.

References

1. Conway P. Microbial ecology of the human large intestine. In: Human Colonic Bacteria. Role in Nutrition, Physiology, and Pathology. CRC Press. Ann Arbor. Gibson and MacFarlane, editors. pgs 1-24.
2. Berg R. Promotion of enteric bacteria from the gastrointestinal tracts of mice by oral treatment with penicillin clindamycin, or metranidazole. Infection and Immunity 33:854-61, 1981.
3. Guentzel M and Herrera C. Effects of compromising agents on candidosis in mice with persistent infections initiated in infancy. Infection and Immunity 35: 222-228,1982.
4. Kennedy M and Volz P Dissemination of yeasts after gastrointestinal inoculation in antibiotic-treated mice. Sabouradia 21:27-33, 1983.
5. Danna P, Urban C, Bellin E, and Rahal J. Role of Candida in pathogenesis of antibiotic-associated diarrhoea in elderly patients. Lancet 337: 511-14, 1991.
6. Ostfeld E , Rubinstein E, Gazit E, Smetana Z. Effect of systemic antibiotics on the microbial flora of the external ear canal in hospitalized children. Pediat 60: 364-66, 1977.
7. Kinsman OS, Pitblado K. Candida albicans gastrointestinal colonization and invasion in the mouse: effect of antibacterial dosing, antifungal therapy, and immunosuppression. Mycoses 32:664-74,1989.
8. Van der Waaij D. Colonization resistance of the digestive tract-- mechanism and clinical consequences. Nahrung 31:507-17, 1987.
9. Samonis G and Dassiou M. Antibiotics affecting gastrointestinal colonization of mice by yeasts. Chemotherapy 6: 50-2, 1994.
10. Samonis G, Gikas A, and Toloudis P . Prospective evaluation of the impact of broad-spectrum antibiotics on the yeast flora of the

human gut. European Journal of Clinical Microbiology & Infectious Diseases 13:665-7, 1994.

11. Samonis G, Gikas A, and Anaissie E. Prospective evaluation of the impact of broad-spectrum antibiotics on gastrointestinal yeast colonization of humans. Antimicrobial Agents and Chemotherapy 37: 51-53, 1993.

12. Kasckin P. Some aspects of the candidosis problem. Mycopathologia et Mycologia applicata 53:173-181,1974.

13. Mattman L. Cell Wall Deficient Forms. Stealth Pathogens. Second Edition. CRC Press. pg 245-246,1993.

14. Shepherd M et al. Candida albicans: biology, genetics, and pathogenicity. Ann Rev Microbiol 39: 579-614,1985.

15. Banno Y, Yamada T, and Nozawa Y. Secreted phospholipases of the dimorphic fungus, Candida albicans; separation of three enzymes and some biological properties.

16. Pugh D and Cawson. The cytochemical localization of phospholipase A and lysophospholipase in Candida albicans. Sabouraudia 13: 110-115,1975.

17. Hauss R. Gastrointestinal mycoses. New laboratory diagnostic tests for pathogenicity. Proceedings of the American Academy of Environmental Medicine Annual Meeting pgs 282-285,1996.

18. Elsden S et al. The end products of the metabolism of aromatic amino acids by Clostridia. Arch Microbiol 107: 283-8, 1976.

19. Bhala A, Bennett M, McGowan K, and Hale D. Limitations of 3-phenylpropionylglycine in early screening for medium chain acyl dehydrogenase deficiency. J Ped 122:100-3,1993.

20. Sande M and Hook E. Other Clostridial infections. In: Principles of Internal Medicine. Tenth Edition. Petersdorf R et al., editors. McGraw Hill, NY, pgs 1009-1013,1983.

21. Afghani B and Stutman H. Toxin related diarrheas. Pediatric Annals 23: 549-555, 1994.

22. Finegold S. Anaerobic infections and Clostridium difficile colitis emerging during antibacterial therapy. Scand J Infect Dis Suppl 49: 160-164, 1986.

23. Gorbach S et al. Successful treatment of relapsing Clostridium difficile colitis with Lactobacillus GG. Lancet ii: 1519,1987.

24. Crone N and Reder A. Severe tetanus in immunized patients with high anti-tetanus titers. Neurology 42:761-764,1992.

25. Ogunyemi A. The clinical recognition of subacute tetanus. J Tropical Medicine and Hygiene 89: 131-135.1986.

26. Wells C and Balish E. Clostridium tetani growth and toxin production in the intestines of germfree rats. Infection and Immunity 41: 826-828,1983.

27. Montecucco C and Schiavo G. Mechanism of action of tetanus and botulinum neurotoxins. Molecular Microbiology 13:1-8,1994.

28. Finn C et al. The structural gene for tetanus neurotoxin is on a plasmid. Science 224:881-884,1984.

29. Binstock T. Hypothesis: Intestinal microflora and CD5+ B cells: their possible significance in some cases of autism. Internet source: Bit.listserv.autism. January 14, 1997.

Organic acid testing, byproducts of yeast and their relationship to autism.

by William Shaw Ph.D.

Metabolic disease testing: the history of organic acid testing

My discovery about abnormal organic acids in autism began as many discoveries do, as an accident. In the 1960's, a great deal of progress had been made in discovering the biochemical abnormalities that caused a number of diseases called inborn errors of metabolism using a technology called gas chromatography-mass spectrometry. It seemed possible that this new technology might be applied to any disease. However, thirty years later, very little progress had been made in solving the mystery of a number of diseases like autism, schizophrenia, and Alzheimer's disease.

In 1991 I had accepted the job as Director of Clinical Chemistry, Endocrinology, and Toxicology at a children's hospital because I wanted to do a better job than what had been done previously in the field of metabolic diseases. I wanted to extend the existing technology to other diseases with unknown causes.

In the field of metabolic diseases, urine samples are analyzed for their chemical constituents after extracting the chemical compounds from the urine using organic solvents such as ether and ethyl acetate. Urine is preferentially tested instead of blood because urine is a filtrate of blood in which much of the water has been removed so that the concentration of a compound in urine might be 100 times more concentrated than it was in blood. A very high concentration of characteristic abnormal chemical compounds would indicate the likely presence of a genetic disease. For example, in the genetic disease PKU or phenylketonuria, very high concentrations of chemical compounds called phenylketones appear in the urine

ORGANIC ACID TESTING, BYPRODUCTS OF YEAST AND BACTERIA, AND THEIR RELATIONSHIP TO AUTISM.

because the child with PKU has a genetic mutation. This mutation in DNA codes for an abnormal form of the enzyme phenylalanine hydroxylase that converts phenylalanine to tyrosine. Since the enzyme is defective, phenylalanine is not converted to tyrosine and phenylalanine builds up in the blood just as a logjam begins in a narrow part of a stream. If a child with PKU is treated with a diet low in phenylalanine as an infant, the child will develop normally. However, if the diagnosis of PKU is not made until the child is much older, the child may be significantly impaired with significant mental retardation(1).

As a biochemist I thought that diseases which had very devastating effects on the individual were bound to change that particular individual's biochemistry. The presumption was that, if a person had a severe disease like autism, seizures, or cerebral palsy, there would have to be some change in one or more of the chemicals processed in the body. All of the body's chemical processes proceed by particular metabolic routes or pathways. Allow me to use an analogy to the Los Angeles freeway system. If an accident happens in Anaheim(a suburb of Los Angeles), traffic may back up in downtown Los Angeles. After a while, alternate roads begin to be utilized and the traffic begins to move again but at a much slower rate. If you measured the number of cars taking different alternate routes, you could pinpoint exactly where the accident had occurred. Using this analogy, the chemicals we eat as food are the traffic which proceeds along well-marked major highways called metabolic pathways until an accident occurs. The accident might be a mutation, an infectious disease, or a vitamin deficiency. As a result of the accident, the traffic flow of molecules is diverted onto the slow alternate routes instead of the twelve lane expressway. The person with the slow traffic of molecules is alive but may not be functioning as well as individuals in which all the metabolic highways are open. The problem I was faced with, using the highway analogy, was "What if certain highways were

not even listed on the highway map because the people who
compiled them were from out of town and didn't know about them
or knew about them but didn't include them on the map?"

In laboratories using the old organic acid technology, certain
abnormal compounds in urine samples might be noted but the amount
of the chemical compound would not usually be quantitated. In
essence, the record of the analysis called a chromatogram would be
visually examined or eyeballed to determine if a markedly abnormal
substance was present. I didn't think this method of examination was
the very best system. It was adequate when this field was starting off
about 20-30 years ago, but I didn't think it was up to date with the
best current technology.

Let me give another analogy: You go into a bank, open an account
and make deposits for several weeks. After about a month you go
back into the bank and you say, "I'd like to know my account
balance." The teller looks at you and says with a straight face, "A
lot". You feel concerned about this lack of information and press her
for more information, and she says, "You really have more than most
people do". That is still not satisfactory but no manager is on duty
so you walk away feeling confused and decide to go back later when
a different teller is on duty. The next time you come in, you ask for
the manager and again ask for your balance and this time the
manager says, "Not much." This type of accounting may be adequate
for comparing the assets of Bill Gates and a person who is collecting
cans out on the street. But this type of accounting is not good for
much the in-between: the middle class. Now I think that after a
while   you   would   stop   going   to   that   bank.

ORGANIC ACID TESTING, BYPRODUCTS OF YEAST AND BACTERIA, AND THEIR RELATIONSHIP TO AUTISM.

In essence, the majority of metabolic disease testing that was performed five years ago and perhaps 50% of the testing done today was the "a lot or not so much" kind.

I suspected that there were many subtle changes in the metabolism of the body that were being overlooked by using the kind of technology that resulted in the "not much and a lot" kind of interpretations. What I set out to do was to quantitate the changes in the different molecules in the urine just as the bank accountants in a bank balance the money transactions. I was able to do that because of new computer software that allowed for the rapid quantitation of very complex data. If it was not for this particular software, my work would not have been possible.

This computer software had originally been designed for the environmental field. In our drinking water, our sewage and in our ground water there may be many kinds of pesticides, herbicides, and industrial chemicals. Testing for all of these chemicals requires very sophisticated computer software. This software was ideally suited for

ORGANIC ACID TESTING, BYPRODUCTS OF YEAST AND BACTERIA, AND THEIR RELATIONSHIP TO AUTISM.

doing metabolic disease testing. I set about achieving several goals including being able to quantitate everything that I possibly could, as accurately as I could, and to be able to identify every chemical that I could.

If we knew every single possible thing about an individual and if we knew what kind of chemical compounds were normal, then we would be able to easily say what was going on in the metabolism of a patient that had a particular disease. Prior to beginning testing, we sent samples out to a another laboratory performing the "a lot, not so much" kind of testing and I was very surprised to see that about 98% of the samples came back with an interpretation of normal. It was very surprising and confusing to me how devastating diseases would not alter metabolism in some way.

I continued the development of my own, more elaborate testing. I found that, indeed, there was some increased detection (perhaps 5-10%) of certain of the known genetic diseases. However, this was a smaller increase than I had anticipated. I also noticed that in many different diseases that there were abnormal elevations of certain compounds that nobody seemed to know too much about or care too much about. When I talked to colleagues in the field of metabolic disease all over the United States and even in other countries, they would say that these particular chemical compounds that you are finding are probably due to microorganisms in the intestinal tract and, therefore, they are not important.

And so I filed that kind of information away in my mind but continued to be skeptical of the non-importance of microbial products The body did not have a metabolic segregation system in which human metabolites were allowed into certain areas of the body

ORGANIC ACID TESTING, BYPRODUCTS OF YEAST AND BACTERIA, AND THEIR RELATIONSHIP TO AUTISM.

while microbial products were shunted into other compartments. All of these products were intermixed throughout the body. Several months after initiating my new laboratory service, a colleague of mine from the University of Kansas Medical School, Enrique Chaves MD, a pediatric neurologist who was also interested in biochemistry(a rather rare occurrence in physicians as a group) referred to me a woman who had two children with severe muscle weakness. Dr Chaves had also been using the old technology in his laboratory for genetic diseases and could find nothing unusual in the two brothers. The muscle weakness was so severe that sometimes, for several hours, they could not stand up. There had been an intensive search for the cause of this muscle weakness. When Dr. Chaves analyzed the samples, he found no evidence of any genetic disease. Since I had this new technology, I was very interested in trying to find out what was going on. I told the mom that we would test samples of her children's urine and see if we could help her out in finding out what was happening to her children.

Evaluation of two brothers with autism
In the field of metabolic diseases it is well known that some disease abnormalities only show up at the time the child is severely ill, i.e. if the child has a severe cold or the flu or chicken pox. The biochemical pattern may be close to normal while the child is well. So when I spoke to the mom, I emphasized that we should get multiple samples rather than just a single one. Several months later the mom came back with a whole armful of samples saved in her freezer which were actually more samples than we usually tested in an entire month. I talked to my technologist Ellen Kassen and told her we would have to bite the bullet and get these tests under way as best we could. We began to test the samples. In each sample, I would see that, indeed, there were no chemical compounds characteristic of any of the known inborn errors in metabolism. But my overall impression was that these samples were still abnormal. When the samples were all tested, there was not any consistent abnormality in any of the known

36

ORGANIC ACID TESTING, BYPRODUCTS OF YEAST AND BACTERIA, AND THEIR RELATIONSHIP TO AUTISM.

genetic diseases which are called inborn errors in metabolism. However, there was a marked difference in the kinds of chemical compounds that were present in the urine samples of the two brothers with the muscle weakness and normal children.

These compounds were the same ones that my colleagues said were not important because they were from microorganisms in the intestinal tract. I was now very curious about what was going on. By this time my colleague from across town Dr Chaves had moved into the same institution. I just had to walk across the hall and ask him some more about what might be going on with these brothers that might explain why they had these abnormal concentrations of chemicals that are characteristic of microorganisms. At that time, he also mentioned that, in addition to the profound muscle weakness, the brothers also had autism. When I looked at their medical charts, I saw that they had a history that is similar to many children with autism which is that they had a history of frequent ear infections. A brief description of the technology used for testing the samples is appropriate at this point.

Figure 1 illustrates an instrument called a gas chromatograph-mass spectrometer. Samples are loaded on this module. The sample is injected into this instrument. The different molecules in the sample go around and around in a large circle called a column just like a group of horses going around a race track and then come out at the finish line. At the finish line the sample is bombarded by a beam of electrons that break the molecules into pieces of different sizes and shapes. The molecules are able to be identified because each molecule has a characteristic way of breaking up or fingerprint. The data from this fingerprint is then transferred into a computer. Then the computer analyzes all that data, makes sense out of it, identifies it and quantifies how much of each kind of molecule is in the

37

Gas chromatography-mass spectrometry

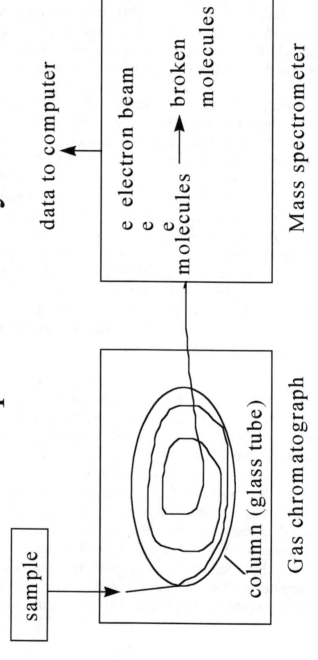

Figure 1.

urine sample. The increase in the capability of this technology is phenomenal. When I first started in this field, the analysis of a single chemical compound would have taken most of the day. Now we can identify a thousand different compounds in a single afternoon.

Figure 2 shows a typical chromatogram for the analysis of the urine sample of a normal child. This profile is called a total ion chromatogram. Each one of these blips that you see is called a peak by people who work in the field. A peak is detected when identical molecules in the sample are swept by the pressure of an inert gas around the circular column and finish at a particular time. The size of this peak is proportional to how much of a particular kind of molecule there is. Small fast molecules cross the finish line faster than big slow molecules just as fast horses have the fastest race times. Fast molecules have the smallest transit time which is called a retention time by people in the field. The bigger the peak, the more of a compound is there. Conversely, the smaller the peak, the smaller the amount of compound is there.

A urine chromatogram of a normal child has many peaks, some of which are small and some of which are large. Contrast this chromatogram of a normal child with the child that has autism (Figure 3). An examination of this figure reveals that there are many more chemical products present in the urine sample of the child with autism. In retrospect, it was lucky that the children I initially tested were more abnormal than the average child with autism since it helped me to notice the marked differences. There is both more of certain molecules (higher concentrations) indicated by larger peaks as well as more peaks. In addition, some of the peaks found in the urine sample of the child with autism are nearly absent in the normal child.

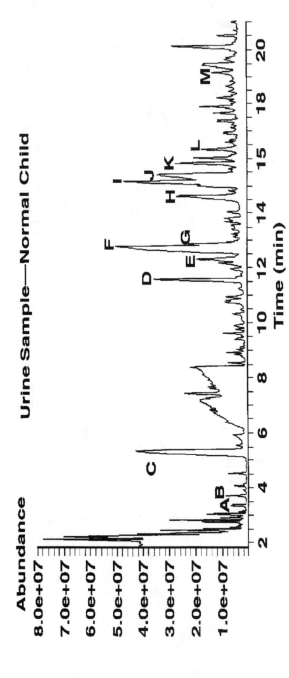

Figure 2. GC-MS chromatogram of urine extract of a normal child. Chemicals in urine derived primarily from gastroin-testinal organisms are written in italics. Each peak is a different chemical product identified as follows: A,pyruvic; B,oxalic; C,urea; D,undecanoic; E,3-hydroxyphenylacetic; F,2-oxoglutaric; G,4-hydroxyphenylacetic; H,aconitic; I,J, hippuric; K,citric; L,vanillylmandelic; M,3-hydroxyhippuric.

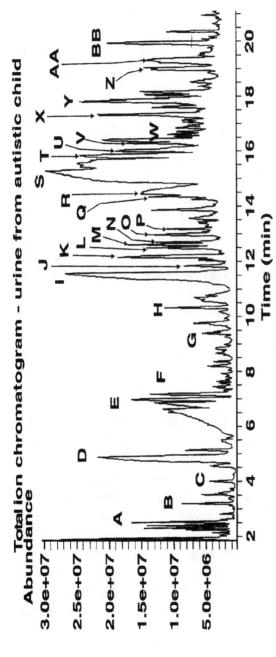

Figure 3. GC-MS chromatogram of a urine extract of a child with autism. Chemicals derived primarily from gastroin-testinal organisms are written in italics. Each peak is a different chemical product identified as follows: A,glycolic; B,oxalic; C,3-hydroxyisobutyric; D,urea; E,phosphoric; F,succinic; G,deoxytetronic; H,citramalic; I,undecanoic; J,?; K,3-hydroxyphenlacetic; L,2-oxoglutaric; M,4-hydroxyphenylacetic; N,furandicarboxylic; O,furancarbonylglycine; P,tartaric; Q,arabinose; R,aconitic; S,hippuric; T,citric; U,dihydroxyphenylpropionic-like compound; V,vanillylmandelic; W,3-indoleacetic; X, ascorbic; Y,citric acid analog; Z,uric; AA,?; BB,4-hydroxyhippuric.

ORGANIC ACID TESTING, BYPRODUCTS OF YEAST AND BACTERIA, AND THEIR RELATIONSHIP TO AUTISM.

What I found is that there was a consistent pattern of abnormally elevated chemicals in the urine samples of the two brothers with autism that were known to be derived from the intestinal microorganisms or later on proved to be due to intestinal microorganisms. So virtually all of the big changes that you see in the chromatogram of the child with autism (2) were due to the fact that they had much higher concentrations of the chemicals that were produced by microorganisms that were residing in their intestinal tracts.

Evaluation of a third child with autism
Based on all the information that I had gathered, I reasoned that if abnormal compounds from the intestinal tract had something to do with causing autism, then treatment of the microorganisms that produced these byproducts should improve the behavior of the child. I only had to wait a short time before I got the opportunity to test out my hypothesis. A child had been referred to the Neurology Dept of the hospital to confirm a case of autism and the organic acid testing had been requested. This child had the kind of history that is very frequent in autism.

The child was developing completely normally when the child began to have ear infections. The ear infections continued. They came one after another. The child developed a thrush or yeast infection of the mouth which occurs because antibiotics have killed off the normal bacteria that keep the yeast population in check. Prior to the recurrent ear infections, the child had a vocabulary of about 150 - 200 words. Following the antibiotics and the yeast infection, the child's development began to slow and then regressed. The child no longer spoke any words. The child became extremely hyperactive, was no longer social, no longer made eye contact, and had a very disruptive sleep pattern. I have seen this particular pattern in many children with autism, but not in all. In some cases, the child may have

42

been treated with antibiotics for recurrent streptococcal throat infections, urinary tract infections, or recurrent bronchitis.

I explained my theory to the mother of the child whom I'll call Bruce. She was a nurse at another nearby hospital and understood about thrush and antibiotics and wanted to give the antifungal drugs a try. The patient "belonged to" the chief of neurology and his approval would be necessary to get a prescription for the drug. He declined. I explained the situation to the child's mother . Since she was a nurse and knew that the antifungal drug nystatin had no serious side-effects, she decided to obtain a prescription for nystatin from her family doctor in private practice who was not associated with the hospital.

Within a couple of days of starting the antifungal drug nystatin, Bruce who had lost most of normal development began to improve and eye contact came back. Bruce's extreme hyperactivity began to go away and he began to have a greater amount of focus. The sleep pattern improved as well and Bruce slept through the night for the first time in months.

At day zero, the day that Bruce first came in and had the organic acid test done, the tartaric acid value in urine was 300 mmol/mol creatinine, a very abnormal value that was about twenty times the median normal value. (Most chemicals measured in urine are divided by the urine creatinine concentration to compensate for different amounts of fluid intake in different individuals.) Following the treatment with the nystatin, the level of the tartaric acid which was one of the compounds that I suspected was derived from the microorganisms decreased considerably and continued to decrease as the nystatin was continued(Figure 4). Nystatin is an antifungal drug

43

which indicated to me that a yeast or fungus (these terms are somewhat interchangeable in that these they are very closely related biologically) was causing the secretion of this compound in the intestinal tract.

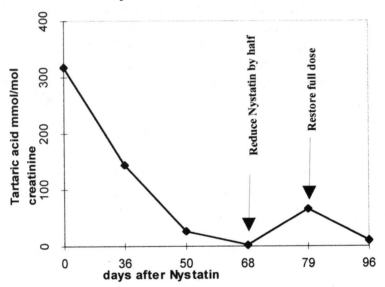

Figure 4

After 68 days Bruce's mother started running out of nystatin and began giving only 1/2 doses so that she didn't run out of it completely. During that time the tartaric acid starting going back up. When she got the nystatin prescription refilled, the tartaric acid went back down. What this indicated to me was the fact that the nystatin was causing a marked reduction in this urine tartaric acid. The other significant finding was that even after two months of nystatin, the biochemical abnormality would reappear within a short time of stopping the antifungal drug. I have now received reports of this same phenomenon in hundreds of other cases. Even after six months and sometimes even after two or three years of antifungal treatment, there is often a biochemical "rebound" and loss of improvements after discontinuing antifungal therapy. Several explanations are possible for this phenomenon:

- Because of one or more defects in the immune system(See chapter on the immune system.), the yeast which are everywhere in our environment including the food we eat repopulate the intestinal tract very rapidly. Early antibiotic use may alter the normal microorganisms in the intestinal tract into an abnormal pattern that the immune system recognizes as normal and will not attack these organisms. (See chapter on gastrointestinal microorganisms.)

- The yeast are very resistant and have not been completely eliminated even after six months of antifungal therapy. Some of these resistant yeast might be the cell-wall deficient yeast described in the chapter on yeast.

- The yeast have genetically transformed some of the human cells that line the intestinal tract so that some of the human cells now contain yeast DNA. These genetically transformed human cells produce both yeast and human products and are somewhat sensitive to antifungal drugs but are not killed by them and produce yeast products whenever antifungal drugs are absent.

- Some of the yeast are hidden in recesses of the intestinal tract or in the deeper layers of the mucosa that lines the intestine where they are relatively safe from the drug. Although their numbers are

45

small, they readily repopulate the intestine after antifungals are stopped.

Properties of tartaric acid

What is tartaric acid and what is known about this product? A toxicology manual (3) indicates that tartaric acid is a highly toxic substance. As little as 12 g has caused human fatality with death occurring from 12 hours to 9 days after ingestion. Gastrointestinal symptoms were marked (violent vomiting and diarrhea, abdominal pain, thirst) and followed by cardiovascular collapse and/or acute renal failure(3). A gram is approximately the weight of a cigarette. This compound especially damages the muscles and the kidney (4,5) and may even cause fatal human nephropathy(kidney damage)(6) which was of interest to me since the two brothers with autism initially evaluated had the extreme muscle weakness as well as evidence of impaired renal function.

Interestingly, I have found that tartaric acid is also elevated in urine samples of adults with the disorder fibromyalgia, a debilitating disease associated with muscle and joint pain, depression, foggy thinking, and chronic fatigue. (Dr Kevorkian has assisted in the suicide of two people with this disorder, which is tragic since a simple antiyeast treatment(7,8) may help relieve the symptoms of this disorder.) Values for tartaric acid in urine may be extremely elevated in autism. A young Korean child with autism had a value of 6000 mmol/mol creatinine, a value that is about 600 times the median normal value. (The child's value returned to normal after a few weeks of antifungal treatment.) Assuming that the yeast in the intestine of the child were producing tartaric acid at a constant rate, **this child would be exposed to 4.5 grams per day of tartaric acid, over one-third of the reported lethal dose of tartaric acid!** Proponents of the theory that wheat gluten sensitivity is the main biochemical abnormality in autism would have difficulty in explaining this case since rice was the only grain in this child's diet.(Gluten and

casein restriction is a very important therapy in most cases of autism
and is dealt with in the chapters by Lisa Lewis, Pamela Scott, and
Karyn Seroussi, as well as in the chapter on the digestive system.)

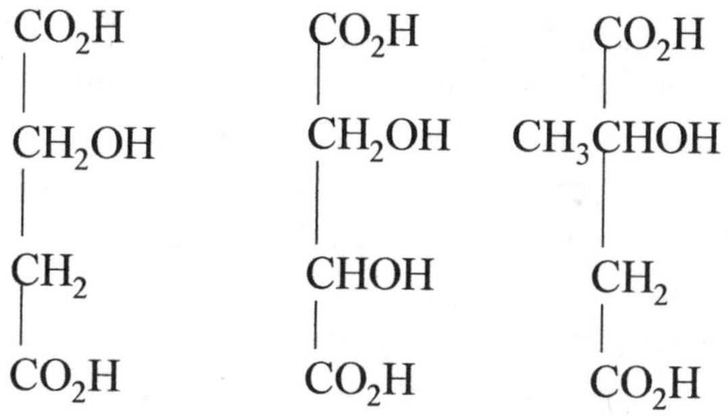

$$CO_2H \quad\quad CO_2H \quad\quad CO_2H$$
$$|\quad\quad\quad\quad\quad |\quad\quad\quad\quad\quad |$$
$$CH_2OH \quad\quad CH_2OH \quad\quad CH_3CHOH$$
$$|\quad\quad\quad\quad\quad |\quad\quad\quad\quad\quad |$$
$$CH_2 \quad\quad CHOH \quad\quad CH_2$$
$$|\quad\quad\quad\quad\quad |\quad\quad\quad\quad\quad |$$
$$CO_2H \quad\quad CO_2H \quad\quad CO_2H$$

Malic acid   Tartaric   Citramalic
                   acid   acid

Figure 5

Surprisingly, the Food and Drug Administration lists tartaric acid in
the **G**enerally **R**ecognized **A**s **S**afe or **GRAS** category(9) which
means this product can be freely used as an additive in processed
foods. Unless a food additive is put on the GRAS list, the food
company using the product may have to spend thousands or even
millions of dollars to prove its safety. Therefore, the political
pressure to get a product on this GRAS list is intense. Tartaric acid is
a byproduct of the wine industry since a tremendous amount of
tartaric acid sludge has to be removed from the wine after yeast
fermentation of the grape juice. This sludge is the primary source of
tartaric acid used as a food additive.

ORGANIC ACID TESTING, BYPRODUCTS OF YEAST AND BACTERIA, AND THEIR RELATIONSHIP TO AUTISM.

Tartaric acid has not yet been found by me in Candida culture media. It may actually be due to plain baker's yeast (Saccharomyces cerevisiae) rather than Candida. Tartaric acid may only be formed in the absence of oxygen. It is also available as a food additive in baking powder, grape and lime flavored beverages, and poultry. It may also be found in grapes and grape products. Cream of tartar which may be used for baking is nearly pure tartaric acid. Its purposes in the food industry include firming agent, flavor enhancer, flavoring agent, humectant, acidity control agent, and sequestant (9). There is no evidence that any mammals can produce it, so it is probably purely a yeast by-product. Tartaric acid is an analog of the Krebs cycle compound malic acid (Figure 5). An analog is a chemical compound that closely resembles but is not identical to another chemical compound. The atoms that differ in the two molecules are shaded in gray. The reason an analog is important is that the analog may prevent the normal biochemical from completing its normal biochemical function.

An analogy I would use to explain the analogs is this. You live in a neighborhood in which many of the houses were built by the same builder who also used the same locksmith for all those houses. The locksmith was a good locksmith and he didn't put the same lock in everyone's house. He put a lock in each house that is just a little different. You have had a few burglaries in your neighborhood recently and you go to visit your neighbor next door. Ordinarily, you would just have left your key there, but because of the burglaries, you decide to lock your door before going to get a cup of coffee at your neighbor's house.

You lock your door, go to your neighbor's house and your neighbor gives you a cup of coffee at the kitchen counter. Your key is in your hand and you put your key on the kitchen counter; your neighbor's key is right there beside yours. You drink the cup of coffee and you move around the counter to the opposite side. You chat for a while and then you decide to go home and you reach down for your key and unknowingly pick up your neighbor's key. Then you take your neighbor's key which looks almost exactly like yours and you go back to your house and stick it in the lock. It goes in and then you start to turn it and nothing happens. Then, if you are a man, you will keep on turning it until the key breaks off. If you are a woman, more than likely what you will do is see that it doesn't fit and go back to your neighbor's and get the right one.

On a molecular level the same kind of thing happens. Probably in some of the cases the analog or false copy of the molecule breaks off and is stuck in the biological keyhole which may be the critical part of an enzyme or cell receptor. These analogs then prevent the biochemical functioning from occurring. In some cases the key eventually comes out and the right one is able to perform its biochemical function. However, your metabolism has experienced some degree of inconvenience and delay and lack of efficiency. This lack of efficiency can be very important if a high percentage of your metabolic processes are being affected simultaneously. Organs like the brain with a high rate of metabolism may be affected more than other organs. Think of how your TV set runs during a brownout when the supply of electricity is too low. If your metabolic processes are not efficient and are not producing sufficient energy, the brain may not process information efficiently.

Let's return to tartaric acid and its specific role as an analog. Tartaric acid inhibits the enzyme fumarase(10) which is important in the function of the Krebs cycle, the biochemical process that produces most of the body's energy. In addition, the inhibition of fumarase also decreases the supply of malic acid for other functions of the cell.

49

ORGANIC ACID TESTING, BYPRODUCTS OF YEAST AND BACTERIA, AND THEIR RELATIONSHIP TO AUTISM.

The proper function of the Krebs cycle depends on a continuing supply of malic acid. If malic acid is not provided in sufficient quantities, the Krebs cycle is short-circuited.

A large percentage of patients with the disorder fibromyalgia who have high amounts of tartaric acid in the urine respond favorably to treatment with malic acid (11-13). I presume that supplements of malic acid are able to overcome the toxic effects of tartaric acid by supplying deficient malic acid. Fifty percent of patients with fibromyalgia who also frequently have elevated yeast metabolites also suffer from hypoglycemia (low blood sugar) even though their diet may have adequate or even excessive sugar(14). The reason may be due to the inhibition of the Krebs cycle by tartaric acid. The Krebs cycle is the main provider of raw materials such as malic acid that can be converted to blood sugar (Figure 6) when the body uses up its supply. (The technical name for this process is gluconeogenesis or "new formation of glucose".) If sufficient malic acid cannot be produced, the body cannot produce the sugar glucose which is the main fuel for the brain. The person with hypoglycemia feels weak and their thinking is foggy because there is insufficient fuel for their brain. If adults with elevated values of tartaric acid in the urine have foggy thinking, have little energy, and are so depressed that they may seek out Dr Kevorkian, imagine what a young child who has some of the same toxins and who has yet to form a clear concept of the world must feel like.

Citramalic acid, like tartaric acid, is another analog of the normal compound malic acid. Citramalic acid is exactly the same(Figure 5) as malic acid except it has an extra CH_3 group called a methyl group on it. Presumably citramalic acid acts like tartaric acid in inhibiting the production of malic acid. There are two different type of

50

citramalic acid called isomers. Both types of citramalic acid are
probably in the urine of children with autism(2).

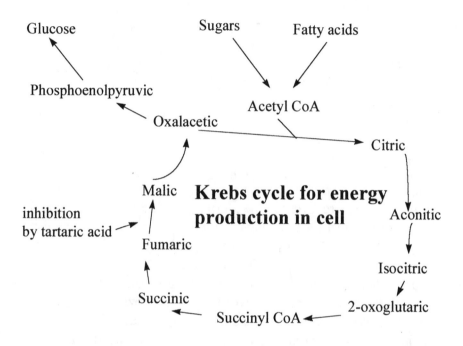

Figure 6

Arabinose and Candida

Figure 7 shows the chemical structure of a compound called
arabinose which is a sugar. (Arabinose is not an organic acid but is a
chemical that we detect with our test.) This is not the same kind of
sugar that is on your kitchen table. But, like the sugar on your
kitchen table, it is sweet. That is what makes it a sugar. It is
chemically very closely related to table sugar even though it is not
the same thing. I found that in the two brothers with autism some of
the values were much higher than in normal children.

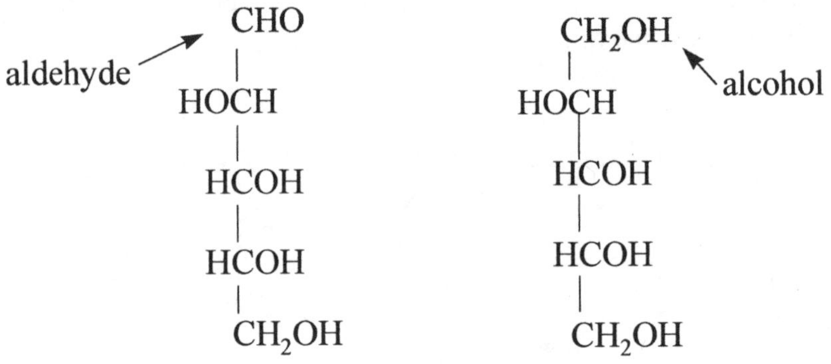

ORGANIC ACID TESTING, BYPRODUCTS OF YEAST AND
BACTERIA, AND THEIR RELATIONSHIP TO AUTISM.

```
                      CHO                      CH₂OH
aldehyde  ──────▶      |                        |        ◀── alcohol
                     HOCH                      HOCH
                       |                         |
                     HCOH                      HCOH
                       |                         |
                     HCOH                      HCOH
                       |                         |
                     CH₂OH                      CH₂OH
                  D-Arabinose                 D-Arabitol
```

Figure 7

In a study that was reported in the journal (a journal is a magazine in which experts report their findings to one another in highly technical language) Science, Kiehn(15) reported information about a very closely related sugar called arabitol. In normal individuals there were very low values of arabitol in the blood serum. But, as people got sicker with the yeast, or in other words were colonized, the values of the arabitol value increased. As the colonization worsened to a state called invasive candidiasis, the arabitol values could get extremely high: over a 1000 times the values found in the normal or control individuals. Many other papers have confirmed that high levels of this compound in both humans and animals were associated with Candida overload(16-18).

Figure 8 shows the distribution of arabinose values in different groups. Each dot represents a different individual value for the urine concentration of this product. In children with autism the values can be extremely high. Although there is some degree of overlap between the children with autism and the control normal children of the same age range, the mean and median values of urine arabinose for children with autism are much higher than those of normal children.

ORGANIC ACID TESTING, BYPRODUCTS OF YEAST AND BACTERIA, AND THEIR RELATIONSHIP TO AUTISM.

The mean arabinose concentration in the urine samples of males with autism was over five times that of the normal male controls and the median value six times that of the normal male controls. In infants (data not shown), arabinose values are extremely low, presumably because the intestinal tracts of newborn babies are nearly free of yeast.

This particular yeast sugar called arabinose is a type of sugar called an aldose that it is not know to be produced by humans. The arabitol (the alternative name for it is arabinitol) is a closely related yeast carbohydrate that is produced by Candida. I suspect that humans may possess the ability to convert arabitol to arabinose. Bacteria in the intestine may also convert arabitol to arabinose. We find a compound that is identified as arabinose in very high levels in urine of autistic children. An autistic child with the highest level of urine arabinose(over 40 times the upper limit of normal) had chronic hypoglycemia almost continuously following antibiotic treatment for a throat infection as an infant(see chapter on gastrointestinal tract).

Women with vulvovaginitis due to Candida were found to have elevated arabinose in the urine(20); restriction of dietary sugar brought about a dramatic reduction in the incidence and severity of the vulvovaginitis. Thus, one of the mechanisms of action of antifungal drug therapy for autism might be to reduce the concentration of an abnormal carbohydrate produced by the yeast that can not be tolerated by the child with defective pentose metabolism. Arabinose tolerance tests should be able to rapidly determine if such biochemical defects are present in children with autism.

Elevated protein-bound arabinose has been found in the serum proteins of schizophrenics (21) and in children with conduct disorders(22) and alteration of protein function by arabinose might be

53

another mechanism by which arabinose might effect biochemical
processes in autism and other diseases.

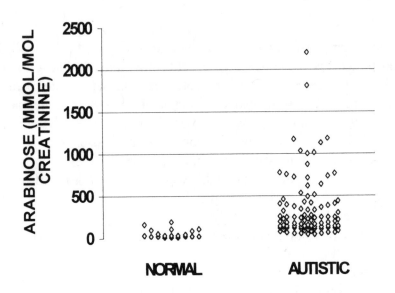

Figure 8

Other sources of arabinose
Arabinose may be found in some other foods in small quantities but
the most significant source of dietary arabinose appears to be apples.
Arabinose values may be very elevated after drinking apple juice or
products such as applesauce(Figure 9).Therefore, apple products
should be restricted for a couple of days prior to testing. Several
parents have reported to me severe worsening of the symptoms of
autism within a short time after their children ate apples. I suspect

that the arabinose from apple products is responsible for this
reaction.

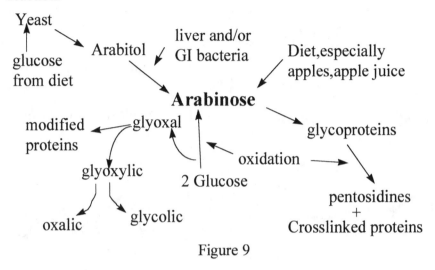

Figure 9

Arabinose may also be formed from the breakdown of the sugar
glucose(23) and antioxidants such as glutathione may inhibit this
conversion(24). The breakdown of glucose also results in the
formation of an aldehyde called glyoxal which can also react with and
modify protein structure and function. Glyoxal may be converted in
the body to glycolic acid, glyoxylic acid, or oxalic acid.

Arabinose, pentosidine, and protein crosslinks
The aldehyde group of arabinose can react with the extra amino
chemical group(called an epsilon amino group) of an amino acid
called lysine that is present in a wide variety of proteins. This
combined arabinose-lysine molecule may then form cross-links with
an amino acid called arginine in an adjoining protein(25), forming a
compound called a pentosidine(Figures10 A,B,C). The formation of
a pentosidine may cross-link different proteins (Figure 11) and may
alter both the biological structure and function of a wide variety of

proteins(25).The effect on all of the body's functions may be devastating.

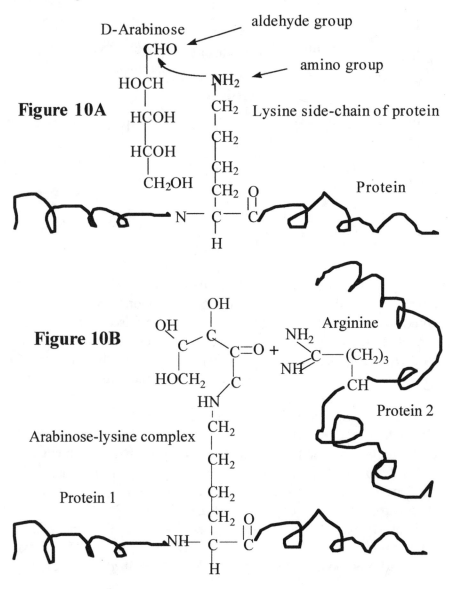

Figure 10A

D-Arabinose

aldehyde group

amino group

Lysine side-chain of protein

Protein

Figure 10B

Arginine

Arabinose-lysine complex

Protein 2

Protein 1

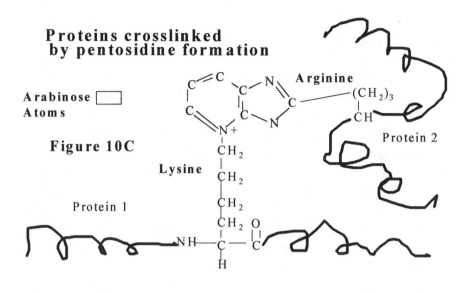

**Proteins crosslinked
by pentosidine formation**

Arabinose
Atoms

Figure 10C

Lysine

Protein 1

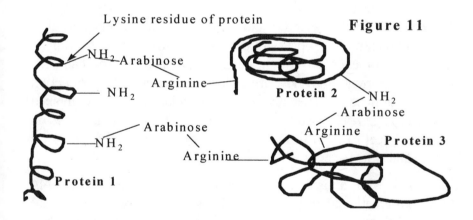

Lysine residue of protein

Figure 11

Protein 1

Let's use the LA freeway analogy again to understand. Suppose that on a very foggy day during the rush hour Gremlins hiding under your moving car and those of your neighbors took strong steel bars and welded them to the frames of the moving cars. The steel bars stick out at a perpendicular angle for about three feet from the side of your car without you or any other driver noticing because of the fog. Arabinose would be like the steel bar and the proteins would be like the cars. Suppose the gremlins welded the other end of the steel bars to the frames of neighboring cars. Then suppose they welded a bar between that neighboring car and a third car and so forth. Furthermore, some cars might be welded to each other by their bumpers in addition to their sides. Now imagine what will happen when one or more of the drivers wanted to exit or change lanes. Chaos and carnage would ensue. The combined molecule of arabinose, lysine, and arginine is called a pentosidine and is like the two cars welded together. The undoing of these cross-links will become a major challenge in the future for treating older individuals with autism in which many of these cross-links have already been established.

I suspect that autism was reversed in the children of Pam Scott and Karyn Seroussi because they started therapy at a very young age. However, I have received reports of some improvements after antifungal therapy in people with autism in their twenties. Antifungal therapy cannot undo any of the cross-links; such therapy can only prevent the formation of new cross-links by reducing the production of yeast arabinose. The tissue concentration of this combined molecule is almost linearly related to age (25); the increase in crosslinks(steel bars) in this molecule is one of the main reasons we lose flexibility as we age.

One child with autism with a very high urine arabinose(1144 mmol/mol creatinine) was examined by MRI (a type of brain scan) and found to have diffuse demyelination (loss of myelin) of the white matter of the brain.(Values as high as 4000 mmol/mol creatinine have been found in children with autism who have not been eating apple products.) It is possible that pentosidine formation could account for this demyelination. Myelin is the material that covers the axons of the

Table 1
Effects of pentosidine crosslinks

- Decreased solubility-neurofibrillary tangles
- Increased resistance to proteases
- Decreased enzyme activity
- Decreased access to coenzymes requiring free amino: B-6, lipoic acid, biotin
- Crosslinks decrease flexibility of structural proteins in collagen and muscles
- Stimulation of autoimmune disease by crosslinked and glycosylated proteins

brain in much the same way that plastic insulating material is wrapped around copper electrical wire. Without an intact myelin cover, the nerve impulses in the brain are short-circuited just like an electrical wire with torn insulation. Most children with autism are not examined by MRI but such an examination on a research basis of children with high urine arabinose values might be helpful to prove a link between high arabinose and demyelination. A summary of the possible adverse effects of pentosidine is given in Table 1.

Arabinose and impaired vitamin function
The epsilon amino group of lysine is a critical functional group of many enzymes to which the vitamins pyridoxal (vitamin B-6), biotin, and lipoic acid are covalently bonded during coenzymatic reactions (26); the blockage of these active lysine sites by pentosidine formation may cause functional vitamin deficiencies(Figure12) even when nutritional intake is adequate. In addition, the epsilon amino groups of lysine may also be important in the active catalytic site of many enzymes.

59

ORGANIC ACID TESTING, BYPRODUCTS OF YEAST AND BACTERIA, AND THEIR RELATIONSHIP TO AUTISM.

Pentosidines, tangled nerves, Alzheimer's disease, and autism

Protein modification caused by pentosidine formation is associated with crosslink formation, decreased protein solubility, and increased protease resistance. The characteristic pathological structures called neurofibrillary tangles associated with Alzheimer disease contain modifications typical of pentosidine formation. Specifically, antibodies against pentosidine react strongly to neurofibrillary tangles and senile plaques in brain tissue from patients with Alzheimer disease(27). In contrast, little or no reaction is observed in apparently healthy neurons of the same brain. Thus, it appears that the neurofibrillary tangles of Alzheimer's disease may be caused by the pentosidines. The modification of protein structure and function caused by arabinose could account for the biochemical and insolubility properties of the lesions of Alzheimer disease through the formation of protein crosslinks. Similar damage to the brains of autistic children might also be due to the pentosidines and neurofibrillary tangles have also been reported in the brain tissue of an individual with autism(28). It has been reported that frequent urinary tract infections are associated with more severe Alzheimer's disease (29). The use of antibiotics to treat urinary tract infections would of course lead to yeast overgrowth. I have found that urine arabinose is elevated in some cases of Alzheimer's disease and have received a report of a favorable response from antifungal therapy to treat Alzheimer's disease from a woman with a child with autism and a father with Alzheimer's disease.

Prevention of pentosidine formation with high doses of vitamin B-6 and other vitamins?

Glutathione has been reported to inhibit pentosidine formation (24). Supplementation with the vitamins biotin, pyridoxal (B-6), and lipoic acid (whose function at protein epsilon amino groups may be blocked by pentosidines derived from arabinose) might also be beneficial. Addition of vitamin B-6 derivatives or vitamin C to proteins helps to

60

prevent pentosidine formation(30). In fact, I suspect that the beneficial effects of vitamin B-6 in autism reported in multiple studies(31) may be mediated by prevention of pentosidine formation. Pamela Scott used the Super-Nuthera which contains high amounts of vitamin B-6 for her child who recovered from autism prior to starting antifungal therapy and I suspect that this reduced somewhat the effects of the yeast die-off reaction. One way to test this idea would be to do a formal study to see if vitamin B-6 supplementation was less effective in treating autistic symptoms after antifungal therapy compared to supplementation before antifungal therapy.

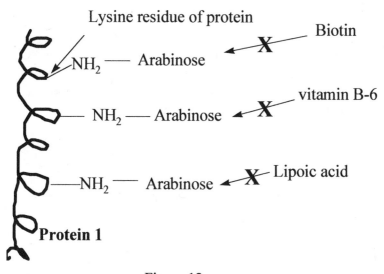

Figure 12

Other compounds called furans that are occasionally elevated in the urine of autistic children are probably derived from fungus such as Aspergillus(32-34) rather than yeast although it is possible they may be produced by yeast as well. The names of these compounds are called 5-hydroxymethyl-2-furoic acid, furan-2,5-carboxylic acid, and furancarbonylglycine. The concentration of furan compounds in the urine also dropped markedly in children with elevated values after nystatin therapy, indicating to me a probable yeast and/or fungal origin of these compounds. Other investigators(35,36) noted that these compounds increased after sugar consumption and assumed that these compounds were sugar products of human metabolism but neglected to take into account the Japanese work and the role of gastrointestinal microorganisms in modification of sugars in the food. My interpretation is that these compounds may be derived from sugar but that they are converted to these furan products by the metabolism of yeast and/or fungi in the intestinal tract.

ORGANIC ACID TESTING, BYPRODUCTS OF YEAST AND BACTERIA, AND THEIR RELATIONSHIP TO AUTISM.

References

1. Scriver C et al. The hyperphenylalaninemias. In: The Metabolic Basis of Inherited Disease. Volume 1.Sixth edition. Scriver C et al, editors. McGraw-Hill, NY pgs495-546,1989.
2. Shaw W, Kassen E, and Chaves E. Increased excretion of analogs of Krebs cycle metabolites and arabinose in two brothers with autistic features. Clin Chem 41:1094-1104, 1995.
3. Gosselin R et al. Clinical toxicology of commercial products, 5th ed. Williams and Wilkins, Baltimore, MD,1984, pg 200.
4. Gold H and Zahm W. A method for the evaluation of laxative agents in constipated human subjects with a study of the comparative laxative potency of fumarates, sodium tartrate, and magnesium acid citrate. J Am Pharm Assoc 32:173-178,1943.
5. Bodansky O et al. The toxicity and laxative action of sodium fumarate. J Am Pharmaceut Assoc 31: 1-8, 1942.
6. Robertson B and Lonneell. Human tartarate nephropathy. Report of a fatal case. Acta Pathol. Microbiol. Scand. 74:305-310,1968.
7. Campbell S and Poddell R. Fibromyalgia Network. April 1997.pg 8.
8. Teitelbaum J. From Fatigued to Fantastic. Avery Publishing Group, Garden City, NY, pgs 8,11,12,41-43,44,50,51,67, 1996.
9. Lewis R. Sr. Food Additives Handbook. Van Nostrand Reinhold, NY,1989. Pg.417.
10. Mahler H and Cordes E. Biological Chemistry. Harper and Row, NY, 1966, pgs 525-553.
11. Holzschlag Molly. CoQ10, malic acid, and magnesium may improve CFIDS/FM symptoms. The CFIDS Chronicle, Summer 1993.
12. Abraham G et al. Management of fibromyalgia: Rationale for the use of magnesium and malic acid. J Nutr Med 3: 49-50,1992.
13. Russell J et al. Treatment of fibromyalgia syndrome with super malic: a randomized, double-blinded, placebo controlled, crossover pilot study. J Rheumatol 22: 953-8,1995.
14. St Amand RP. Exploring the fibromyalgia connection. The Vulvar Pain Newsletter. Fall 1996, 4-6.

15. Kiehn T. et al. Candidiasis: detection by gas-liquid chromatography of D-arabinitol, a fungal metabolite, in human serum. Science 206: 577-580, 1979.

16. Wong B, Brauer K, Clemens J, and Beggs S. Effects of gastrointestinal candidiasis, antibiotics, dietary arabinitol, and cortisone acetate on levels of the Candida metabolite D-arabinitol in rat serum and urine. Infect Immunol 58:283-288,1990.

17. Larsson, Lennart. Determination of microbial chemical markers by gas chromatography-mass spectrometry-potential for diagnosis and studies on metabolism in situ. APMIS 102: 161-169,1994.

18. Roboz J and Katz R. Diagnosis of disseminated candidiasis based on serum D/L arabinitol ratios using negative chemical ionization mass spectrometry. J Chromatog 575: 281-286,1992.

19. Gitzelman R, Steinmann B, and Van der Berghe G. Disorders of fructose metabolism. In: The Metabolic Basis of Inherited Disease. pgs 399-424,1989. 6th edition. Edited by C Scriver. McGraw Hill, NY, NY.

20. Horowitz B, Edelstein S, and Lipman L. Sugar chromatography studies in recurrent vulvovaginitis. J Reproductive Medicine 29:441-443,1984.

21. Varma R and Hoshino A. Serum glycoproteins in schizophrenia. Carbohydrate Research 82:343-351,1980.

22. Varma R, Michos G, Gordon B, Varma RS, and Shirey R. Serum glycoproteins in children with schizophrenia and conduct and adjustment disorders. Biochem Med 30:206-214,1983.

23. Wells-Knecht KJ et al. Mechanism of autoxidative glycosylation: identification of glyoxal and arabinose as intermediates in the autoxidative modification of proteins by glucose. Biochemistry 34: 3702-9, 1995.

24. Nagaraj RH et al. Suppression of pentosidine formation in galactosemic rat lens by an inhibitor of aldose reductase. Diabetes 43: 580-6, 1994.

25. Sell D and Monnier V. Structure elucidation of a senescence cross-link from human extracellular matrix. Implication of pentoses in the aging process. J Biol Chem 264: 21597-21602, 1989.

26. Mahler H and Cordes E. Biological Chemistry. Harper and Row, NY, 1966, pgs 322-375.

ORGANIC ACID TESTING, BYPRODUCTS OF YEAST AND
BACTERIA, AND THEIR RELATIONSHIP TO AUTISM.

27. Smith MA et al. Advanced Maillard reaction end products are associated with Alzheimer disease pathology. Proc Natl Acad Sci USA 91: 5710-5714 , 1994.
28. Hof PR et al. Neuropathological observations in a case of autism presenting with self-injury behavior. Acta Neuropathol (Berl) 82: 321-6, 1991.
29. Soininen H et al. Circulating immune complexes in sera from patients with Alzheimer's disease and subjects with age-associated memory impairment. J Neural Transmission 6:179-188,1993.
30. Khatami M et al. Inhibitory effects of pyridoxal phosphate, ascorbate and aminoguanidine on nonenzymatic glycosylation. Life Sci 43:1725-31, 1988.
31. Rimland B. New hope for safe and effective treatments for autism. Autism Research Review International 8: 3,1994.
32. Sumiki Y. Fermentation products of mold fungi. IV. Aspergillus glaucus.I. J Agr Chem Soc Jap 5 : 10, 1929.
33. Sumuki Y. Fermentation products of molds. J Agr Chem Soc Jap 7: 819,1931.
34. Kawarda A, Takahoshi N, Kitamura H, Seta Y, Takai M, and Tamura S. Biochemical studies on bakanae fungus. Bull Agr Soc Jap 19: 84,1955.
35. Mrochek J and Rainey W. Identification and biochemical significance of substituted furans in human urine. Clin Chem 18: 821-828,1972.
36. Pettersen J and Jellum E. The identification and metabolic origin of 2-furoylglycine and 2,5-furandicarboxylic acid in human urine. Clin ChimActa41:199-207,1972.

Yeasts and fungi. How to control them.

By William Shaw Ph.D.

Since byproducts of yeast and fungi are frequently elevated in urine samples of people with autism, a knowledge of the biology of these organisms and the therapies to control them are essential.

Fungi is a biological group of organisms that include yeasts, molds, and mushrooms. Thus, all yeast are fungi but many fungi are not yeast. One of the most common disease causing species of yeasts is Candida albicans. Other species of Candida include Candida tropicalis, Candida glabrata, Candida pseudotropicalis, Candida guilliermondii, and Candida parapsolis. Probably all of these species can cause disease especially if the immune system is weak (1). Candida albicans can exist in four forms: a yeast or single cell form, a colony of cells or mycelium, a chlamydospore or cyst-like form, and a cell-wall deficient form (2). Both the mycelium type and the chlamydospore are capable of tissue invasion(2). The vitamin biotin is thought to prevent the transformation of Candida from the yeast to the mycelium form and is sometimes included in nonprescription antifungal medications such as Candicyn (3).

The cell-wall deficient Candida may even be able to conceal itself inside of cells and may be the reason that complete elimination of Candida is difficult(2). These cell-wall deficient forms are extremely small—0.15 millionths of a meter. These cell-wall deficient organisms are extremely difficult to identify and would probably not be detected except in advanced research laboratories and not in the vast majority of hospital laboratories. Certain yeast may actually grow faster when antibiotics are included in the growth media(4,5). Aspergillus is a common food-borne mold which is capable of living and reproducing in the gastrointestinal tract (6). The furan compounds, 5-hydroxymethylfuroic and furan-2,5-dicarboxylic which are frequently elevated in urine samples of children with autism(see chapter on organic acids) are known products of Aspergillus species (7-9). The closely related compound   furancarbonylglycine is probably a detoxification product of the other furan compounds which is combined with glycine in the liver. The fact that antifungal drugs decrease the concentration of these products in urine samples of children with autism leads me to suspect that Aspergillus or similar species of mold are producing these compounds in the gastrointestinal tract of many children with autism.

Even ordinary household yeast might cause disease in susceptible individuals. This ordinary yeast is called Saccharomyces cerevisiae. Different strains of this same species are used in both the baking and brewing (alcoholic beverage) industries. Saccharomyces cerevisiae can also exist in the yeast or mycelium form and, like Candida, can cause vaginal yeast infections (10), is being investigated for a role in Crohn's disease(11), an intestinal disorder, and can cause systemic infection in individuals with impaired immune systems(12). The finding of high concentrations of tartaric acid, a product of Saccharomyces cerevisiae, in many urine samples of children with autism, indicates to me a strong possibility that Saccharomyces cerevisiae or a closely related organism may play a role in autism.

Since yeast have the ability to ferment sugar to alcohol, an increase in blood alcohol after intake of sugar can be used as an indicator of yeast overgrowth of the intestine. Dr Eaton and his colleagues(13,14) at The London Medical Centre in England found that blood alcohol concentrations in patients with suspected yeast overgrowth increased one hour after ingestion of glucose.

Furthermore, they found that after dietary restriction of carbohydrates, 42% (27 of 64) of patients were negative on re-test(13). When both dietary restriction and antifungals were used by these patients, 78%(116 of 149) of the patients were negative on re-test, indicating (to me) that this therapy was highly successful in the treatment of the intestinal yeast overgrowth.

Yeast are more complex than bacteria on the evolutionary scale. They are eukaryotic organisms that have cells with defined structures like mitochondria, nuclei, and chromosomes. Many yeast biochemicals are exactly the same as those produced by humans. In many children with autism, there is increased excretion of the compound called 3-hydroxy-3-methylglutaric acid in the urine. Increased 3-hydroxy-3-methylglutaric acid in the urine may be due to a genetic disease called 3-hydroxy-3-methylglutaric acidemia(15). However, the elevated values of urinary 3-hydroxy-3-methylglutaric acid in children with autism are much lower than the values in children with the genetic disease. This chemical compound is used by both humans and yeast to make steroids. I suspect that high values in children with autism are due to yeast overgrowth of the gastrointestinal tract and that it is unlikely (but still possible) that some children with autism have a mild form of the genetic disease 3-hydroxy-3-methylglutaric acidemia.

Diagnosis of yeast disorders.
Why is Candida such a problem to diagnose? The condition that occurs in most children with autism is not technically an infection; it is really an overgrowth of the intestinal tract. Furthermore, the yeasts do not colonize the intestinal tract in an uniform fashion. Instead, they usually form clusters or nests. Sometimes, they settle in the crypts of the intestine, which are small out of the way "side pockets". Therefore, failure to detect these organisms by endoscopy examination(examination with a long tube into the intestinal tract) of the intestinal tract does not rule out their presence(16). There are

several ways of diagnosing such a condition. One of the ways is the stool culture. The problems with stool cultures is that many people have a small number of Candida in them in their stool at any given time(17). Furthermore, if the yeast are in their hyphal or colony form, most of the cells are physically attached to the intestinal lining. Stool culture can only detect the cells that have broken off. If you get a positive test result on a stool culture for yeast, it really doesn't convey much information unless it is a quantitative one. The real question is not whether or not an individual has Candida, but rather how much Candida is there. Even though stool culture is not perfect, I have examined a large number of reports in which the organic acid test and stool testing were done and there is general agreement in the two techniques.

Organic acid test for yeast and bacterial byproducts.
The organic acid test is valuable because it detects byproducts of yeast and fungi produced in the intestinal tract. These byproducts are then absorbed into the blood stream from the intestinal tract and are eventually filtered into the urine. The sample is easy to collect and only a small amount of first morning urine is required. In addition the organic acid test screens for genetic illnesses such as PKU and many other genetic diseases as well as many nutritional deficiencies. In addition, the organic acid test also detects byproducts of bacteria that may also be important in a subgroup of children with autism. This testing is available from :

The Great Plains Laboratory   Phone: 913 341-8949
9335 W 75 Street   FAX: 913 341-6207
Overland Park, KS 66204

E-mail: Williamsha@aol.com
Website: www.greatplainslaboratory.com

YEASTS AND FUNGI. HOW TO CONTROL THEM.

Blood tests for Candida

Severe Candida infection, called systemic Candidiasis is a serious illness with severe symptoms like fever and can even be fatal in individuals with weakened immune systems. Candida infection of the brain called Candida meningitis can be fatal(18). I don't want to alarm anyone since this is a very rare condition that sometimes occurs in HIV-positive individuals or infants with immune deficiency. Finding Candida by blood culture is considered the definitive test for systemic yeast infection. However, in one of the most intensive studies done(18), there was a very high incidence of false negatives using blood cultures for Candida. In children who really did have yeast invasion of their organs including brain, liver, or heart that was confirmed by autopsy, only 17% of the children's blood samples tested positive for yeast even though they had been tested repeatedly (an average of ten times) for Candida.

The reason for the failure of these blood tests may be that the Candida is a fastidious organism and doesn't grow if it doesn't "like" the particular culture of the media in which it is placed or the antibiotics given to the patients may have induced the development of cell-wall deficient forms that could not be detected by ordinary culture methods. Another explanation may be that yeast implanted in the tissues are not shedding very many cells into the blood where they can be detected. Antibodies can be used to detect Candida but such antibodies measure old infections. Even with Candida IgM antibodies that measure recent infections, it is not clear that such an antibody test can pick up the yeast overgrowth of the intestinal tract because most of the time the yeast are not in the blood stream.

However, with a yeast overgrowth in the intestinal tract, fever rarely occurs. Symptoms of yeast overgrowth of the intestinal tract may include behavioral changes such as hyperactivity, psychosis, or depression and non-specific complaints such as fatigue, achy joints and muscles, sleep disturbance, increased allergies and sensitivity to

70

chemicals at home and at work, increased incidence of vaginal yeast infections in women and "jock itch" in males(3,19,20).

There are several places that fungal infections can exist. There can be external or superficial infections which involve the mouth, skin or vagina. Athlete's foot is one of the common kinds of fungal infections. Some people get fungal infections under the nails called onychomycosis. Internal or systemic yeast infection can be life threatening. In this type, the yeast has escaped from the intestinal tract, is inside the body, and can be in the organs. It can invade virtually any organ of the body including the blood, the lungs, bones, kidneys, the liver, the heart, the eyes, and the brain(18).

Interactions of yeast and other bacteria.

Yeast and bacteria live together in the intestinal tract and it is not surprising that sometimes there is synergy or cooperation and competition between the species. For example, a supporting role of Candida albicans in the establishment of Staphylococcus aureus infection with mice has been reported(21). I have also found that treatment of yeast overgrowth with antifungal treatment leads to bacterial overgrowth if beneficial bacteria are not used at the same time as the antifungals. Furthermore, it has been shown that E. coli, a common intestinal bacteria and Saccharomyces can exchange genetic information by exchange of a piece of DNA called a plasmid(22), leading to the possibility that the genetic makeup of common yeast might eventually be contaminated by the genes of intestinal bacteria. An inhibitory effect of Pseudomonas bacteria on Candida growth has been reported(21) and might be evaluated as a potential therapy if a suitable safe species of this bacteria could be developed.

Antifungal Therapies

The major therapies for autism are antifungal products, probiotics to control both yeast and bacteria overgrowth, immune therapies, and nutritional therapies.

YEASTS AND FUNGI. HOW TO CONTROL THEM.

Probiotics

Probiotics(pro=for + biotic=life) are microorganisms that are used therapeutically to control abnormal overgrowth of yeasts, fungi, and bacteria in the intestinal tract. Probiotics were first recommended by the Russian immunologist Metchnikoff who received the Nobel Prize in Medicine for his discovery of the role of the white blood cells in fighting infection. In the early 1900's, Metchnikoff proposed that many human diseases were caused by abnormal overgrowth of harmful bacteria in the intestinal tract. He noted the good health of a European community that included large amounts of yogurt in the diet. Yogurt contains bacteria of the Lactobacillus family and Metchnikoff concluded that the Lactobacillus family was controlling the harmful bacteria that produced harmful "ptomaines". Metchnikoff's observations probably were a major impetus to the development of the health food industry.

There are now over a hundred different brands of beneficial bacteria that are available in mail order supply houses, pharmacies, and health food stores. Some of the common species of bacteria are Lactobacillus acidophilus, Lactobacillus casei, Lactobacillus bulgaricus, Lactobacillus salivarius, Lactobacillus thermophilus, and Lactobacillus plantarum. Other beneficial species include Bifidobacterium bifidum and Streptococcus faecium (not to be confused with Streptococcus faecalis, a pathogen.) In addition to these different species, these bacteria are found in many different formulations as well including suspensions, loose powder, capsules, and flavored chewable tablets. Some of these organisms are grown on dairy products as a source of nutrition while others are dairy-free. Because of the sensitivity of most children with autism to the peptides derived from milk, it may be wise to choose a dairy-free brand.

I do not recommend a particular brand but I generally recommend a dose of 10 billion cells per day for any child over three and half that amount for younger children. These products may help to control both yeast(23)and abnormal bacteria such as Clostridia (24) in the intestinal tract. In addition to probiotics which are bacteria, there is increasing interest in a beneficial yeast called Saccharomyces boulardi (25) to control both yeast and Clostridia overgrowth of the intestinal tract. However, I have very little experience with this yeast and would advise caution until more evaluation has been done especially since a related species Saccharomyces cerevisiae can cause medically significant conditions. **I recommend the simultaneous use of a probiotic product any time an antifungal drug is used. Yeast are part of the intestinal ecosystem and hold other organisms in check. Overgrowth of harmful bacteria may occur unless probiotics are taken simultaneously with prescription or nonprescription antifungal products.**

Nonprescription Antifungal Products.
Antifungal products that are available from a health food store and mail order supply companies without a prescription include garlic or garlic extract, grapefruit seed extract, oregano, caprylic acid and its oil form MCT oil, Tanalbit, goldenseal, aloe vera gel, and lactoferrin. These products are also combined into different formulations. Even though these products do not require a prescription for their use and common experience indicates they are safe, they are best used under the supervision of a health care professional who is familiar with their side effects. All of these products can cause the yeast die-off reaction that is just as severe as the one caused by prescription drugs. One of the difficulties in using these products is that dosing information for children is not usually provided. I have received positive reports from parents of children with autism treated with all of these products. Some of these people undertook therapy on their own because they lived in a remote area where no alternative health professional was available and their family doctor would not prescribe antifungal drugs. Others used these products in the belief that these products were safer than prescription drugs because these

products were "natural". I would like to emphasize that nystatin is a very safe prescription drug and that it is probably just as safe as any of these natural products.

Diet to control yeast overgrowth.

Numerous popular books by William Crook M.D.(18), John Trowbridge M.D.(19), and others have addressed the importance of sugar elimination to control yeast overgrowth of the intestinal tract because of the stimulatory effect of simple sugars on yeast overgrowth. Vargas and his colleagues found that mice given sugar water had 200 times the amount of Candida yeast in the intestine compared to mice given plain water(26). Similar results have also been reported in the treatment of humans for yeast related illnesses(27-29). The rule of thumb for sugar elimination is simple: **If it's sweet, don't eat.** The list of restricted foods includes candy, ice cream, cake, pie, soda pop, Kool-Aid, and even fruit juices. Since your child may be on a dairy-free diet as well, water may become your child's main drink. To ease the transition, you might want to dilute fruit juice ten-fold with water during the transition.

All types of sugar, both "natural" and refined, should be eliminated including honey, syrup, fruit sugar, and refined sugars. You will find some difference of opinion on sugar elimination. Some authorities recommend complete elimination while others allow occasional sugar in the diet. A vitamin C supplement may be needed if your child gets a lot of his daily vitamin C from orange juice. Fruits may have to be eliminated from the diet for a period of about a month to accelerate the yeast elimination. The high-sugar dessert foods may have to be eliminated indefinitely.

What is left to eat since wheat and dairy products may have also been eliminated for the casein and gluten-free diet? Major sources of carbohydrates may include potatoes, corn. rice, yams, and other vegetables such as beans, peas, broccoli, etc. All meat and fish are acceptable although both Pam Scott and Dr Semon are concerned about antibiotic residues and fungal byproducts in commercial meat. Pam Scott went the extra mile to obtain antibiotic-free sources of these meats. I don't know if this is essential but it couldn't hurt and I am not going to argue with success. It is true that complex carbohydrates are broken down to simple sugars in the intestinal tract that can be utilized by the yeast so that diet alone may be insufficient to control a significant yeast overgrowth and will have to be combined with some kind of antifungal therapy. Eaton's data (mentioned earlier in the chapter) indicates that combining diet and antifungals is nearly double the effectiveness of diet alone in eliminating intestinal yeast overgrowth. I always recommend combining the two therapies. No formal assessment of these combined therapies is available but the experience of many physicians who treat for yeast-related illnesses indicates better response when both diet and antifungal products are used simultaneously.

The Yeast die-off or Herxheimer reaction

The Herxheimer reaction is also called the yeast die off reaction(3,19). Usually for about 3 or 4 days after starting antifungal drugs the person may feel a little bit worse during that time. There may be symptoms of extreme tiredness and even fever. The Herxheimer reaction is probably due to the abnormal release of these abnormal organic acids during the yeast die off phase. The yeast are like water balloons filled with toxins. When you give the antifungal drugs, the water balloons burst and the contents of the water balloons are then absorbed into your body and are eventually excreted into the urine. Therefore, the concentration of abnormal urine organic acids rises when antifungals are first given (Figure 1) and then begin to drop as the yeast are all killed and there are no more toxic organic acids to release. This reaction was presumed to be due to the release of toxic compounds by the yeast when they die after exposure to antifungal agents. My research is the first to document a marked increase in certain organic acids for several days

75

after beginning an antifungal drug. The Herxheimer reaction is not limited to yeast. It also occurs when certain of the bacteria overgrowths of the intestinal tract are treated as well.

The Herxheimer or yeast die off reaction lasts 3 to 4 days and sometimes as long as a week if the person has a severe yeast overgrowth. Some of the affects can be lethargy, fever, and an increase in stereotypical behaviors. Symptoms may include bloating, nausea, vomiting, eczema, aching, headache, and stuffiness. In addition, children with autism or PDD may experience an intensification of symptoms during this period including intense craving for sweets, more self-stimulation, more arm flapping, or more hyperactivity. If the child with autism does a lot of hand flapping normally, during the yeast die-off period, there may be an intensification of this behavior. Some of the parents of autistic children who tried nystatin years ago for their children gave up on it because of adverse effects during the die-off reaction.

Four approaches can be taken to reduce the intensity of the yeast die-off reaction:

1. Use nutritional approaches to cut down on yeast burden prior to using an antifungal drug. **Eliminate sugar containing foods** from the diet for two weeks prior to the use of an antifungal drug. Even this dietary change alone may cause a slight to moderate yeast die-off reaction. It doesn't matter whether or not a sugar is natural or artificial. Any simple sugar (glucose, fructose, sucrose, or galactose) will serve as yeast food. Sugared drinks and fruit juices may have more sugar than foods. (You need to give your child vitamin C during this period.) I recommend 500-1000 mg per day.
2. Many of the yeast products are acids and release of the acids which are absorbed into the body may cause a condition called

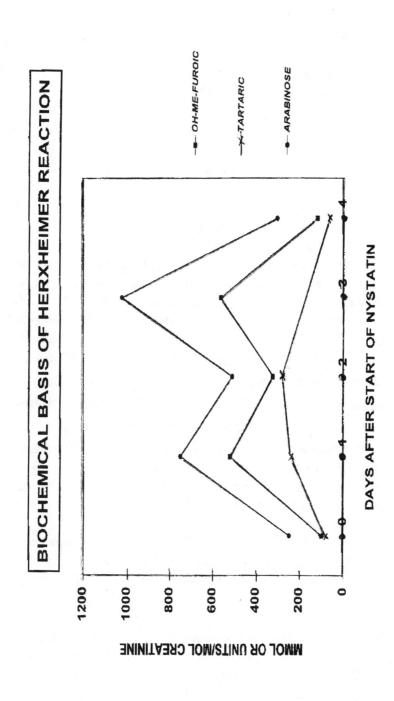

BIOCHEMICAL BASIS OF HERXHEIMER REACTION

- OH-ME-FUROIC
- TARTARIC
- ARABINOSE

MMOL OR UNITS/MOL CREATININE

DAYS AFTER START OF NYSTATIN

metabolic acidosis. An extremely simple therapy used by physicians who treat autism is to supply a mild antidote that neutralizes the excess acids. The most convenient product is a nonprescription drug called AlkaSeltzer Gold. **Do not use any other kind of AlkaSeltzer.** AlkaSeltzer Gold is simply a very safe product called bicarbonate that helps to neutralize excess acids of any kind. The dose for children is on the label. **Do not exceed the number of recommended doses.**

3. If the organic acid test indicates your child has high concentrations of tartaric acid, the tartaric acid may be inhibiting the production of malic acid. Malic acid is essential for the efficient operation of the Krebs cycle and for providing raw material that the body can use to produce its own sugar between meals. The **use of malic acid supplements** will probably help during the yeast die-off reaction and may also be useful until the tartaric acid from the yeast is eliminated by a combination of a low sugar diet and antifungal therapy. **The use of malic acid supplements must be used under the close supervision of a dietitian and/or physician because malic acid supplements frequently contain magnesium.** SuperNuthera has high amounts of magnesium and other supplements may also contain magnesium. It is possible that too much magnesium might be ingested if these different supplements all containing magnesium were combined, leading to magnesium toxicity.
4. Since vitamin B-6 has the ability to prevent the formation of the harmful pentosidines, I would strongly urge the use of Super-Nuthera prior to starting antifungal therapy.

Garlic.
Garlic is a potent antifungal product that also leaves a strong odor on the breath. Fortunately, it has been found that deodorized garlic has essentially the same antifungal activity as fresh garlic. Of course,

fresh garlic is cheap and effective if you don't mind the smell. Allylsulfinyl alanine is a major constituent(3) of garlic that is converted to a compound called allicin when the garlic is crushed or eaten. Allicin and some of its byproducts contain sulfur its characteristic odor. When garlic is allowed to age for an extended time period, the odor dissipates. At lower doses, allicin is fungistatic meaning that it slows the growth of yeast or fungus. At higher doses the allicin actually will kill Candida albicans(30). The recommended dosage of Kyolic brand garlic for antifungal therapy for adults is three capsules per day. A child's dose would be proportionally less on a weight basis. Assume an average adult weight of 150 lb. If your child weighs 50 lb., the garlic dosage would be 50 lb/150 lb. or one-third the adult dosage.

Oregano.
Oregano oil inhibited the growth of Candida albicans in vitro (31) The minimum inhibitory concentration (MIC) was less than 0.1mcg/ml when tested with 3 different strains of Candida; 0.1% survival occurred at a concentration of 45 mg/ml. Carvacrol, a major phenolic constituent of oregano oil, inhibited Candida as effectively as did the oil itself. Parents have indicated to me that oregano was sometimes helpful in their child with autism when nystatin was ineffective in killing the yeast. This killing of yeast by oregano was confirmed by stool yeast evaluation.

Caprylic acid and MCT oil.
Caprylic acid is a fatty acid and is present in a wide variety of foods. Fatty acids have different numbers of carbon atoms ranging from two in acetic acid to twenty-four or more. Caprylic acid has six carbon atoms and thus is considered to be a medium chain length fatty acid. Caprylic acid eventually is just burned up by the body for fuel or may be stored as fat. Caprylic acid was found to have antifungal activity over 40 years ago(32-34). When three molecules of caprylic acid are

combined with one molecule of glycerol, the compound is called a triglyceride. Triglycerides are also called fats or oils. Solid triglycerides are frequently termed fats while liquid triglycerides are termed oils. Triglycerides containing predominantly the medium chain length fatty acids are termed **medium chain triglycerides** or MCT oil.

Caprylic acid is the predominant fatty acid in most commercially available MCT oil. MCT oil is a liquid at room temperature and thus can be administered to a child who cannot or will not take capsules or tablets of caprylic acid. The taste of MCT oil is fairly bland and it tastes very much like corn oil or other vegetable oils. Flavored MCT oil is also available for use as well. When MCT oil reaches the intestine, it is broken down by lipases to form caprylic acid and glycerol. Since children with autism may have defective production of pancreatic enzymes, another property of MCT oil is very important. Medium chain triglycerides are broken down to form caprylic acid at a much more rapid rate than long chain triglycerides (35) so that this compound will be broken down effectively even in children whose pancreas is producing low levels of lipase. Coconut oil is a major natural source of caprylic acid.

Caprylic acid is safe with the following exception. Children with the rare genetic disorder medium chain acyl dehydrogenase (MCAD) deficiency cannot biochemically process caprylic acid(36). Theoretically, caprylic acid could be harmful to these children. The organic acid screen performed in the Great Plains Laboratory checks for MCAD but it is possible that it might not be detected in its dormant form by the organic acid screen. The probability of a child having MCAD is low, probably less than one in six thousand. However, Duran and colleagues(37) reported that no harmful effects were caused by a high MCT oil load in a patient with MCAD at a high dose. MCT oil is found in a variety of foods and in infant formulas and a dose of up to one teaspoon twice a day for children over two years old and half that amount for infants would seem to be completely safe even for a child with MCAD. However, if your child has MCAD or has ever had a lapse into a coma-like state, I would advise against using products containing MCT oil or caprylic acid since other effective antifungal agents are available.

Colloidal silver.

Silver is a metal that is used for jewelry and dinnerware. Solutions of silver have been used as a germicide since the early 1900's. In the Old West, prior to refrigeration. a silver dollar would be put in the milk container to prevent spoilage by microorganisms. Colloidal silver is a suspension of silver that kills almost all intestinal microorganisms including yeast, bacteria, protozoa, viruses, and parasites. My major concerns with this product are: (1)It essentially kills every living thing in the intestine including any beneficial bacteria. (2) Silver is a heavy metal. If the size of the silver particles are too large, the absorbed silver particles may lodge in the body causing a graying of the skin due to the deposited silver, a condition called argyria(38). Most heavy metals that kill microorganisms indiscriminately like mercury and arsenic are also toxic to humans. Although the claim is made that certain products are safe because the particles of silver are too small to be lodged in the capillaries of the skin and organs(38), I would be *extremely* **cautious** about these products and **would not use them** except under close medical **supervision of a physician** who has used these products for a long time and is **certain** of the product's safety.

Lactoferrin.

Lactoferrin is a protein found in many mammals including humans and possesses the ability to bind iron. Studies have shown that both human and cow lactoferrin kills Candida albicans and Candida krusei(39,40). Lactoferrin is only active against Candida when it is

81

free of iron since its mechanism of killing Candida is probably by starving it from iron. Lactoferrin is available as a supplement but because of the iron inactivation and digestion by the body's enzymes, I am unsure as to appropriate dosing. A piece of the lactoferrin molecule called lactoferricin B can also kill Candida. Interestingly, this molecule also possesses potent antiviral activity as well(41). Since this product controls yeast by removing iron, an evaluation of your child's iron intake might be important. If your child has high iron and high iron binding capacity by a blood test, it might be beneficial for yeast control to use vitamins that do not have additional iron.

Combination products.

A large number of different combinations of antifungal products are available. There may be differences in the potency of each of these products as antifungals but there are few large studies with these products since the small profits generated by these products cannot support expensive clinical trials. One product called Candicyn (not an endorsement) contains Pau D'Arco extract, oregano, gentian extract, caprylic acid, grapefruit seed extract, barberry extract, goldenseal extract, ginger, cinnamon, chamomile, and biotin.

Biotin

Biotin is one of the essential vitamins. It was termed vitamin H. Biotin is commonly found in most multivitamin supplements but is usually present in doses well below the recommended daily allowance or RDA even in the most expensive vitamins. In addition, biotin is one of the vitamins that is produced by bacteria in the intestinal tract(42). The use of antibiotics can eliminate this bacterial production of biotin leading to biotin deficiency.

I had a personal experience in my own family with this vitamin. When one of my sons was small, he was on antibiotics for an ear infection. He lost his appetite, began to lose weight, developed a red eczema on the cheeks, became withdrawn, and then his hair began to fall out in large clumps. He began to look like a starved concentration-camp inmate.

Unfortunately, the role of yeast in such cases was unknown at that time. However, I knew that biotin deficiency could cause hair loss probably due to killing off the beneficial germs in the intestine which produce it there. Supplementation with biotin started his hair growing back within a couple of days and he began to look better overall. This episode first brought my attention to the less than miraculous results of the "miracle" antibiotic drugs and stimulated my interest in the role microorganisms play in our human biochemistry.

In addition to its nutritional role in humans, biotin is also needed by most other creatures including yeast. However, when yeast are exposed to biotin, they are stimulated to grow but are less likely to convert to their mycelium form which is the form in which they invade the tissues(19). My recommendation is a supplement of 800-1000 micrograms per day for any person with a yeast-related condition. Biotin is a water-soluble vitamin and is completely safe at this dose. To minimize yeast overgrowth, it might be best to introduce biotin and other vitamins a week after beginning antifungal therapy.

Biotinidase deficiency
Biotinidase deficiency is a genetic inborn error of metabolism that has been found in both autism(43) and another defect of biotin metabolism has been reported in Rett's syndrome(44), a disorder in girls in which many autistic traits are present. Biotinidase deficiency is frequently associated with yeast and fungal infection(42). Biotin from the diet becomes chemically bonded to many of the body's enzymes that require it. Biotin is attached to enzymes by combining specifically with the free amino group of the amino acid lysine(42).

If acetaldehyde or arabinose produced by yeast has previously reacted with these lysine sites as discussed in other chapters, biotin will not be able to attach to these critical sites and can not function properly. When these enzymes are eventually broken down by the body, biotinidase is needed to chemically release biotin from its degraded enzyme.

When biotinidase is deficient, this bound biotin cannot be recycled in the body and, as a consequence, biotin is lost rapidly from the body. The symptoms of biotinidase deficiency are very similar to those in biotin deficiency. The therapy for this disorder is to give large doses of biotin daily: 5000-20,000 micrograms(mcg) per day. Defective regulation of the immune system has been reported in several patients with biotinidase deficiency(42). Some of the patients had Candida dermatitis and some showed defective cellular immunity against Candida. One patient had reduced white blood cell killing against Candida and myeloperoxidase deficiency(see chapter on immune system) that were normalized by biotin supplementation. Developmental delay is also common in biotinidase deficiency(42).

Biotinidase may be especially important in autism because it has been found that the enzyme biotinidase also helps to break down peptides including those with opiate-type activity (45,46). Therefore, patients with a biotinidase deficiency may be over-stimulated by endorphins and other peptides. It is also possible that the conversion of biocytin to free biotin by biotinidase might be inhibited by the high amount of undigested peptides from wheat and milk absorbed by the person with autism so that biotin might not be properly recycled even when biotinidase was present at normal values. Therefore, people with autism who are not on a gluten and casein free diet may need additional amounts of biotin in their diet. This enzyme is zinc dependent so it is possible that this enzyme may not function well if zinc is deficient as is the case in many children with autism.

84

Biotinidase deficiency is tested in only a handful of laboratories in the world and requires a blood test. This test is performed in the laboratory of Dr Barry Wolf at the Genetics Dept at the Medical University of Virginia in Richmond, Virginia. The phone number is 804 828-9632. The easiest way to arrange for this test is to have your doctor request the test and then have a local pediatric hospital skilled in drawing blood from children take the blood sample and ship it to Dr Wolf's lab.

Prescription antifungal products.
Nystatin is one of the oldest and safest antifungal drugs. Its safety is largely due to the fact that it's not absorbed into the blood stream at the doses most commonly prescribed. Your entire intestinal tract is a long tube with your mouth at one end of the tube and your anus at the other end of the tube. Virtually 100% of nystatin is eliminated in the feces. Since nystatin does not get into the blood stream to any appreciable extent, it's very safe and can't cause any serious side effects. Nystatin is so safe that it is available in Germany without a prescription. Nystatin was named after the New York (NY) research laboratory in which it was discovered in the 1940's (*NY*=New York; *stat* = state; *in)*. I know of no serious side effects that have ever been documented with the use of nystatin.

Most children with autism won't take capsules so that the liquid suspensions of nystatin are sometimes the best options. The brand names of nystatin suspensions are Mycostatin made by Squibb and Nilstat made by Lederle. William Crook M.D. advises against the use of these products because they contain both food dyes and sugar(18). However, I feel that most children with autism will not take capsules or plain nystatin powder which is measured out in scoops because of its bitterness. Another option would be to add a natural sweetener like FOS (fructo-oligosaccharides) or Stevia to the dose of plain powder All antifungal drugs cause the Herxheimer reaction or yeast die-off reaction.

I have encountered a significant number of reports of increased aggression of children with autism when doses 4-8 times the recommended dose of nystatin were given. One particular behavior that was reported by several different parents was that the child would pinch women on the breast, even women who were strangers. I suspect that this behavior may have been due to the food dye used in the nystatin.

Amphotericin B, which may be very toxic when given intravenously, is **very safe given orally**. When it is given orally, its safety is comparable to that of nystatin because like nystatin it is poorly absorbed from the GI tract. But to get this in a prescription in the United States that is suitable for oral use, you have to contact one of the special pharmacies that dispense this product including Wellness Health and Pharmaceuticals (1 800 227-2627) or College Pharmacy (1 800 855-9538). This drug is widely available for oral use in European pharmacies.

The other prescription antifungal drugs are different from amphotericin and nystatin in that they are appreciably or completely absorbed from the intestinal tract into the bloodstream. There is a slight incidence of liver toxicity with all of these drugs that is not a factor with oral nystatin or amphotericin B. When these absorbed antifungal drugs are used, it is necessary to do a liver function test to make sure that the liver is not damaged. These absorbed antifungal drugs include **Diflucan (fluconazole), Nizoral (ketoconazole), Sporanox (itraconazole), and Lamisil (terbinafine)**. Even though these drugs can be considered safe for the most part, they are not as safe as nystatin or amphotericin B.

An increase in the activity of liver enzymes due to leakage from a damaged liver is usually an indicator of liver toxicity. However, a moderate increase in the activity of these enzymes **after vitamin B-6** supplementation is **not an indicator of liver toxicity**. Vitamin B-6 increases the activity of certain of the transaminases or liver function enzymes called AST (SGOT) and ALT (SGPT). Vitamin B-6 is an essential cofactor for these enzymes and simply activates these enzymes. You need to be aware of this effect since you might be using these tests to monitor liver function when using systemic antifungal drugs. If B-6 supplementation was started at the same time as the drug, a moderate liver enzyme increase may be due to the B-6 activation of the enzymes rather than the release of these enzymes by a damaged liver.

When these absorbed drugs are used, it is necessary to check other medications that may be processed by similar detoxification mechanisms by the liver. Such drugs include anti-seizure medications, neuroleptics like phenothiazines and haloperidol, and antidepressants like amitriptyline. Other drug metabolism may also be affected and you should check with both your physician and pharmacist before using these drugs for your child. When these drugs are used with the absorbed antifungal drugs, the metabolism of both drugs may be slowed and the amounts of these drugs may increase. Therefore, dosages for both drugs may have to be adjusted downwards. Sporanox has another undesirable side effect in that it inhibits testosterone production at higher doses and might affect a male's sexual development. The reason is that this antifungal drug works by preventing the synthesis of the fungal steroid ergosterol by yeast and fungus. Unfortunately, the human system that produces the human steroid testosterone is also inhibited by this drug. Diflucan does not have this effect at normal doses.

If there are so many concerns with these absorbed antifungals, why use them at all? The simple answer is that some of the yeasts and fungi are resistant to nystatin or oral amphotericin B or the yeast may be inside the deeper layers of the lining of the intestinal tract where nystatin cannot act. Nystatin and oral amphotericin B which act

87

mainly on intestinal yeast may also be ineffective in treating persons with more severe fungal infections of the skin and nails.

How to administer nystatin

I am including more detail about nystatin because it is the most commonly used drug and because it is one of the safest and most effective. The most common suspensions of nystatin are formulated to have 100,000 units per cc or ml. (1 cc equals 1 ml for water-based drugs.) Five cc or five ml is the amount in a teaspoon. Since most people use a regular spoon instead of a measuring spoon to give liquid drugs, I would advise using a precise dropper or other device be used for greater accuracy. There is too much variation in using a plain spoon.

The main consideration in using nystatin is how to avoid the side-effects of the yeast die-off reaction. This can be accomplished by increasing the dosage of nystatin gradually so that the severity of the yeast die-off is minimized. When this approach is used, the yeast are killed over a longer time period instead of during a very short time period. A typical dosing for 2-8 year olds is given in Table 1.

If the symptoms of the die-off reaction are too severe, the dose may be held at the lower level for a day or two before going up to the next dose. If the concentration of yeast metabolites are predominantly in the normal range when re-tested at 30 days, this dosage is continued. If the yeast metabolites are significantly elevated after 30 days of therapy, the dose of nystatin could be increased by 50-100 % or other antifungal drugs might be added. The die-off reaction may occur again when the medication is increased. Doses for children 8- 12 years would be about 50% higher than those in Table 1 and children older than 13 years or adults would be double the above schedule. These doses are my own suggestions. Your

Table 1. Typical dosage of Nystatin to minimize yeast die-off reaction

	Day 1	Day 2	Day 3	Day 4	Day 5	Day 6 on
Total daily dose	50,000	100,000	200,000	300,000	400,000	400,000
Divided daily into	1 dose	2 doses	2 doses	3 doses	4 doses	4 doses

physician may want to prescribe a somewhat different regimen and Dr Semon has a somewhat different dosage schedule in his chapter.

Although there is no reason that the higher doses of nystatin might cause increased aggression, reports to me of such aggression have been fairly common when 4-8 times the dosages recommended above are given. I suspect that nystatin at high doses causes this side-effect although it is possible that the food colors or contaminants in the medication may be responsible. Nystatin is a biological product derived from a mold. A physician who uses nystatin quite frequently in his practice stated to me that he gets better results with the Lederle brand of nystatin (Nilstat). He suspects that other brands of nystatin may be contaminated with other byproducts of the mold that produces nystatin. Furthermore, he attributes some adverse reactions of nystatin to the effects of these contaminants rather than to the yeast die-off reaction.

References

1. Naugle E. Candida & Dysbiosis Foundation Newsletter Vol 2, No 2, p8, 1996.
2. Nolting S et al. Mykosen des Verdauungstraktes, Max Simon KG, Hamburg,Germany,1994.
3. Trowbridge J and Walker M. The Yeast Syndrome. Bantam Books,NY,1986.
4. Kasckin P. Some aspects of the candidosis problem. Mycopathologia et Mycologia applicata 53:173-181,1974.
5. Mattman L. Cell Wall Deficient Forms. Stealth Pathogens. Second Edition. CRC Press. pg 245-246,1993.
6. Ionescu G et al. Zirkulierende immunokomplexe, spezifisches IgE gegen Nahrungsmittel. Immuno Infekt 13:147-155,1985.
7. Sumiki Y. Fermentation products of mold fungi. IV. Aspergillus glaucus. J Agr Chem Soc Jap 5 : 10, 1929.
8. Sumuki Y. Fermentation products of molds. J Agr Chem Soc Jap 7 : 819,1931.
9. Kawarda A, Takahoshi N, Kitamura H, Seta Y, Takai M, and Tamura S. Biochemical studies on bakanae fungus. Bull Agr Soc Jap 19: 84,1955.
10. Sobel J et al. Vaginitis due to Saccharomyces cerevisiae: epidemiology, clinical aspects, and therapy. Clinical Infectious Diseases 16:93-99, 1993.
11. McKensie H et al. Antigenic heterogeneity of strains of Saccharomyces cerevisiae and Candida albicans recognized by serum antibodies from patient's with Crohn's disease. FEMS Microbio. Immunol 89: 219-224,1992.
12. Sternberg S. The emerging fungal threat. Science 266:1832-1834,1994.
13. Eaton K et al. Abnormal gut fermentation: Laboratory studies reveal deficiency of B vitamins, zinc, and magnesium. J Nutr Biochem 4: 49-52,1993.
14. Humnisett A et al. Gut fermentation(or the autobrewery syndrome): a clinical test with initial observations and discussions. J Nutr Med 1:33-38,1990.

15. Sweetman L. Branched chain organic acidurias. In : The Metabolic Basis of Inherited Disease. Sixth Edition. Volume 1. C. Scriver et al, editors. McGraw-Hill, New York, pgs 791-819,1989.

16. Hauss R. Gastrointestinal mycoses: Insights and clinical pearls from the German experience. Proceedings of the American Academy of Environmental Medicine in Boston MA. pgs 281-285,1996.

17. Conway P. Microbial ecology of the human large intestine. In: Human Colonic Bacteria. Role in Nutrition, Physiology, and Pathology. CRC Press. Ann Arbor. Gibson and MacFarlane, editors. pgs 1-24.

18. Hughes, WT. Candidiasis. In: Textbook of Pediatric Infectious Diseases. Third edition. Volume II.W.B. Saunders Co., Philadelphia, pgs.1907-1915,1991.

19. Crook,W. The Yeast Connection Handbook. Professional Books, Jackson,TN,1996.

20. Yeast-related mental disturbances. Psychiatric symptoms elicited through biological (physical) mechanisms. An interview with Richard G Jaeckle M.D.. Mastering Food Allergies. 10(1): 1-4, 1995.

21. Ruchel R et al. Bacteria accompanying clinical Candida isolates from respiratory secretions and the genitourinary tract. Mycoses 34: 235-238, 1991.

22. Heinemann J and Sprague G. Bacterial conjugative plasmids mobilize DNA transfer between bacteria and yeast. Nature 340: 205-209,1989.

23. Crook W. The Yeast Connection and the Woman. Professional Books. Jackson, TN, pgs. 442-445.

24. Gorbach S et al. Successful treatment of relapsing Clostridium difficile colitis with Lactobacillus GG. Lancet ii: 1519,1987.

25. Bergogne-Berezin E. Ecologic impact of antibiotherapy. Role of substitution microorganisms in the control of antibiotic-related diarrhea and colitis. Presse Med 24:145-148, 151-152, 155-156,1995.

26. Vargas S et al. Modulating effect of dietary carbohydrate supplementation on Candida albicans, colonization and invasion in a neutropenic mouse model. Infection and Immunity 61: 619-626, 1993.

27. Miles M et al. Recurrent vaginal Candidiasis: importance of an intestinal reservoir. JAMA 238:1836-1837,1977.

28. Reed B et al. The association between dietary intake and history of vulvovaginitis. J Family Practice 29:509-515,1989.

29. Horowitz B, Edelstein S, and Lipman L. Sugar chromatography studies in recurrent vulvovaginitis. J Reproductive Medicine 29:441-443,1984.

30. Appleton J and Tansey M. Inhibition of growth of zoopathogenic fungi by garlic extract. Mycologia 67: 882-885,1975.

31. Stiles JC, et al. The inhibition of Candida albicans by oregano. J Appl Nutr 1995; 47 (4):96-102.)

32. Keeney EL. Sodium caprylate: a new and effective treatment of moniliasis of the skin and mucous membranes. Bull John Hopkins Hosp 78:333-339,1946.

33. Neuhauser I and Gustus EL: Successful treatment of intestinal moniliasis with fatty acid resin complex. Arch Int Med 93: 53-60,1954.

34. Rotmistrov M et al. Study of the antifungal properties of ammonium caprylate. Mikrobiol Zh 32: 780-787,1970.

35. Bartley J. Lipid metabolism and its disorders. In: Clinical Biochemistry of Domestic Animals. Third Edition. J Kaneko, editor. Academic Press, NY, pgs 53-96,1980.

36. Roe C and Coates P. Acyl CoA dehydrogenase deficiencies. In: The Metabolic Basis of Inherited Disease. Volume I. Sixth edition. C. Scriver et al, eds. McGraw Hill, NY, pgs 889-914,1989.

37. Duran M et al. Cis-4-decenoic acid in plasma: a characteristic metabolite in medium chain acyl-CoA dehydrogenase deficiency. Clin Chem 34:548-551,1988.

38. Carlsen G. The Candida Yeast Answer. pg 17, 1997. The Candida Wellness Center, Provo, Utah.

39. Nikawa H et al. The fungicidal effect of human lactoferrin on Candida albicans and Candida krusei. Archives of Oral Biology 38:1057-1063,1993.

40. Bellamy W et al. Killing of Candida albicans by lactoferricin B, a potent antimicrobial peptide derived from the N-terminal region of bovine lactoferrin. Med Microbiol and Immun 182:97-105,1993.

41. Hasegawa K et al. Inhibition with lactoferrin of in vitro infection with human herpes virus. Jap J of Med Sci and Biol 47:73-85,1994.

42. Wolf B and Heard G. Disorders of biotin metabolism. In: The Metabolic Basis of Inherited Disease. Volume II. Sixth edition. C. Scriver et al, eds. McGraw Hill, NY, pgs 2093-2103 ,1989.

43. Personal communications with both parents and physicians of children with autism, which included examination of medical records.
44. Bachmann C et al. Rett syndrome revisited: a patient with biotin dependency. Eur J Pediat 144: 563-566,1986.
45. Oizumi J. Hayakawa K. Enkephalin hydrolysis by human serum biotinidase. Biochimica et Biophysica Acta. 1074: 433-8, 1991.
46. De Felice C, Hayakawa K, Nihei K, Higuchi S, Tanaka T, and Watanabe T. Changes in cerebrospinal fluid biotinidase activity in Staphylococcus aureus meningitis. Brain & Development 16: 156-8, 1994.

Immune deficiency, immunizations, and yeast suppression of the immune system

by William Shaw Ph.D.

Overview of the immune system.

The critically important job of fighting off infections falls to our immune system. As you might expect, this is a complex system; it must be, because the invasions faced by the human body include diverse infectious agents including bacteria, viruses, fungi, etc.

Recent research by several scientists has shown that children with autism have serious abnormalities in this all-important system. In order to understand these abnormalities, and to show what effect they might have for the child with autism, it is essential to have a basic understanding of the immune system.

The immune system is made up of several different parts.
- B-cells produce antibodies or immunoglobulins.
- T-cells (so named because they are derived from the organ called the thymus) are the cells involved in what is called cellular immunity. The functions of the T-cells are to kill foreign tissue or tissues infected with virus, to produce lymphokines, which are large proteins that regulate other cells of the immune system and to help to enhance the immune response.
- The complement system is a group of proteins involved as a nonspecific helper to the immune system.
- The phagocytic cells include cells called macrophages and neutrophils that engulf bacteria and yeast and digest them.

A large part of the immune system is located in or near the intestinal tract and helps to prevent germs from the intestine from entering into the rest of the body. Defects in the immune system may therefore lead to overgrowth of the intestinal tract with organisms like yeast.

IMMUNE DEFICIENCY, IMMUNIZATIONS, AND YEAST SUPPRESSION OF THE IMMUNE SYSTEM

A defect in any of these systems may lead to increased incidence of infection. Defects in all parts of the immune system have been documented in children with autism. Studies done by Reed Warren Ph.D. at Utah State University, Sudhir Gupta M.D. Ph.D., a clinical immunologist at the University of California at Irvine Medical School, and others indicate that most children with autism have a substantial immune abnormality of some type (1-20). This probably explains why frequent infections are a common feature of the autistic child's medical history. In our society, frequent infections leads to frequent use of antibiotics. Some parents of children with autism have reported to me over 50 consecutive ear infections in their children. The antibiotics prescribed for ear infections also kill many of the normal organisms in the intestinal tract, and allows abnormal organisms such as yeast and bacteria such as Clostridia to proliferate in the intestinal tract.

Antibodies or immunoglobulins.

The B-lymphocyte cells of the immune system produce antibodies called immunoglobulins. These antibodies are designed to react against specific antigens—foreign molecules introduced into the system by germs of various types. Antibodies react against viruses, yeast, and bacteria and allow them to be killed by the white blood cells. Composed mostly of amino acids, antibodies are proteins that can be divided into five major antibody classes called IgA, IgG, IgM, IgD, and IgE. Each has a unique chemical structure and a specific function. IgG stands for immunoglobulin G or antibody G and so forth.

- **IgM** is usually the first antibody produced by the immune system when a new germ is encountered and is the body's early defense system. The presence of high amounts of specific IgM antibodies indicates a recent infection. Thus high levels of IgM antibodies against Candida would indicate a recent Candida infection of the bloodstream. IgM antibodies diminish a few months after infection.

- **IgG** antibodies are produced by the B-lymphocytes when a germ attacks in a subsequent invasion and may also be involved in causing food allergies.
- **IgE** is the antibody most widely known for its involvement in allergies of all kinds and may also be involved in protection of the body from parasites. Elevated IgE in blood is associated with a history of excessive allergies.
- **IgA** is the antibody that is involved with protection of the lining of the nasal passages and intestinal lining from germs. Secretory IgA or sIgA is a special form of the IgA antibody that is secreted to protect the mucosa, which is the lining of the intestinal tract. Secretory IgA is apparently secreted by the gall bladder and then trickles down the bile ducts into the small intestine. Some children with autism have very low or even completely absent levels of IgA (1,2); in such cases there is probably also a deficiency of a secretory IgA since secretory IgA is derived from IgA.
- **IgD** is an antibody that is usually present in very small amounts in the bloodstream and is probably involved as a receptor antibody on certain of the white blood cells and may help to regulate antibody production.

One of the factors that leads to recurrent otitis media or other recurrent infections is called immunodeficiency, meaning the presence of a weak or deficient immune system. Immunodeficiency can be caused by a deficiency of antibodies such as IgG, IgA, and IgM. Children with autism have a high frequency of abnormalities of these different kinds of antibodies (20). Deficiencies of any of the total antibodies indicates a probable immunodeficiency. In addition, the total amount of a particular antibody could be normal but the amount of a specific antibody might be deficient. For example, I

97

suspect that many children with autism and PDD may be deficient in producing antibodies against yeast.

Cellular immunity.

The T-cells (so named because they are derived from the organ called the thymus) are the cells involved in what is called cellular immunity. T-cells kill foreign tissue or tissues infected with virus, and produce lymphokines. Lymphokines are large proteins that regulate other cells of the immune system, and help to enhance the immune response. Some of these proteins are called interleukins (IL). Eighteen different interleukins have been identified. Other proteins produced by the white blood cells include interferon, granulocyte-macrophage colony stimulating factor(GC-CSF), and tumor necrosis factor. Concentrations of IL-12 and interferon gamma are much higher in the blood of children with autism than in normal children, indicating an immune activation, possibly due to adverse vaccine reactions. In addition to T-cells, another type of lymphocyte(a white blood cell type) called natural killer (NK) cells are also important in the immune system. The data from Warren and Gupta indicates that 38-45% of children with autism have low NK cell numbers as well as significant T-cell abnormalities. The decrease in children with autism of CD4 cells, a T-cell subtype, may be another cause of increased colonization with Candida albicans.

Types of immune deficiency that occur in autism.

Myeloperoxidase deficiency.

Myeloperoxidase is an enzyme present in the white blood cells (neutrophils) that combines hydrogen peroxide and chloride ions to form hypochlorite ion, the same active ingredient present in household bleach (21). The hypochlorite ion kills yeast just like household bleach does. If this enzyme is deficient, the white blood cells cannot produce sufficient hypochlorite to kill the yeast and the affected person cannot fight off yeast infection satisfactorily.

98

This disorder can be detected by the use of automated flow cytochemistry instruments that detect an absence of peroxidase in the neutrophils and monocytes, and should be tested in autistic children. Because the disorder is quite rare, most physicians will not be aware of this test; you should be assertive and ensure that the right type of blood test is used. Because these cells look completely normal under the microscope, a routine blood examination is not a satisfactory test for this disorder. Most patients with this disorder have frequent yeast and fungal infections and often have fungal infections of the nails or even systemic yeast infections. Myeloperoxidase deficiency can be genetic or acquired. The genetic type is due to a mutation on chromosome pair 17 or to biotinidase deficiency (21,22). Acquired causes include lead poisoning, folic acid or vitamin B-12 deficiency, severe infection, and leukemias(21).

• A child with autism whose parents have consulted me has had severe external manifestations of yeast from a very early age. The child had fungal infection of the skin and nails and had been on antifungal drugs for years. The child was ultimately diagnosed with myeloperoxidase deficiency, and she responded well to intravenous gamma globulin therapy which is described later in the chapter. Every child with external manifestations of yeast or fungal infections should be tested for possible myeloperoxidase deficiency.

Severe combined immunodeficiency disease (SCID).
Severe combined immunodeficiency disease is a defect in both the T and B-lymphocytes so that both antibody production and cellular immunity are impaired(23,24). This disease can be due to a genetic deficiency on the X chromosome or on one of the other chromosomes. Genetic deficiencies of the enzymes purine nucleoside phosphorylase or adenosine deaminase also cause SCID. Candida infection as well as other infections are common in this disorder. (Although not published in the medical literature, I have had personal

99

communication with parents of autistic children with this SCID disorder.)

Selective IgA deficiency.

This extremely common immunodeficiency occurs in 1 in 600-1000 persons of European ancestry(23). The causes of IgA deficiency are not completely known. There are some cases in which the deficiency runs in families while in other cases it does not. It has been reported in association with abnormalities of chromosome 18, but most individuals with IgA deficiency have no detectable chromosomal abnormalities. IgA deficiency may also be caused by drugs or viral infection. Patients with IgA deficiency are usually deficient in both subtypes of IgA, IgA1 and IgA2.

A number of patients with IgA deficiency are also sensitive to gluten. In Gupta's study (20), 20% of the children with autism had a deficiency of IgA and 8% lacked it completely. Reed Warren and his colleagues (2) also found that 20% of individuals with autism had low serum IgA compared with none of the normal controls. Thus, IgA deficiency in autism is somewhere between 100 and 200 times higher in the autism population compared to a normal Caucasian population.

IgA replacement therapy cannot be used currently because the short half-life of IgA would make it an extremely expensive therapy.[1] IgG therapy can be used with patients with low IgA values. If the IgA values are so low that they cannot even be detected, however, giving IgG therapy is too risky. It is possible that the immunodeficient person's body would produce antibodies against IgA, causing potentially fatal anaphylatic shock.

---

[1] A half-life is the length of time required for half of a substance to disappear from the bloodstream. When a medicine or chemical has an extremely short half life, it must be administered very frequently.

IMMUNE DEFICIENCY, IMMUNIZATIONS, AND YEAST SUPPRESSION OF THE IMMUNE SYSTEM

IgG subclass deficiency.

Sometimes the total IgG in the blood may be normal but the concentration of one or more subtypes of IgG may be low. There are four subtypes of IgG: IgG1, IgG2, IgG3,and IgG4. Antibodies against proteins are mainly of the IgG1 and IgG3 subtypes while antibodies against carbohydrates(sugars) are of the IgG2 subtype (23). In Gupta's study (20), 20% of the children with autism had an IgG subclass deficiency(Table 1). There are hundreds of different kinds of antibodies within each antibody type so that there could be an IgG antibody against rubella, another against smallpox, and another against whooping cough and so on. When all the different types of IgG are measured simultaneously, the total IgG is measured.

Complement deficiency.

The complement system is a complex group of 20 proteins that assist or "complement" the work of the immune system by destroying invading yeast, viruses, and bacteria. The complement system can disintegrate the cell membranes of many species of bacteria, and complement byproducts attract scavenger white blood cells to the site of the bacteria destruction. These scavengers then clean up the dead bacteria debris.

Some of the complement components also coat the bacteria which allows the bacteria to be more easily digested by the scavenger white blood cells. Reed Warren and his colleagues found that the average concentration of one of the proteins in the complement system termed C4b was significantly lower than normal in individuals with autism(15). Complement C4b deficiency is also increased in schizophrenia(25). Individuals with low amounts of this protein are more susceptible to infection from yeast and bacteria such as Streptococcus pneumoniae and Haemophilus influenza, two of the bacteria most commonly responsible for ear infections(15).

101

IMMUNE DEFICIENCY, IMMUNIZATIONS, AND YEAST SUPPRESSION OF THE IMMUNE SYSTEM

Table 1

Kinds of immune abnormalities in Dr. Gupta's study of 20 children with autism

Disorder	Number of cases*
Common variable immunodeficiency	2
IgG1 deficiency	1
IgG2 deficiency	4
IgG4 deficiency	2
IgG3 and myeloperoxidase deficiency	1
Low IgG	1
Increased IgE	7
Increased antibodies to myelin basic protein	6
Specific antibody deficiency with normal IgG and IgG subclasses	1
IgA deficiency	4

*The number of types of immune deficiency are greater than 20 because some children had more than one immune abnormality.

IMMUNE DEFICIENCY, IMMUNIZATIONS, AND YEAST SUPPRESSION OF THE IMMUNE SYSTEM

Immunodeficiency testing for IgG, IgG subclasses, IgA, IgM, IgG, and zinc can be performed at:
The Great Plains Laboratory, Inc.
9335 W. 75th Street
Overland Park, KS 66204
(913) 341-8949 or fax: (913) 341-6207
www.greatplainslaboratory.com   Email: GPL4U@aol.com

Role of immunizations in causing immune deficiencies.
Gupta found high amounts of antibodies to rubella (German measles) in mothers of children with autism (20). Gupta states that these high amounts of antibodies would be transferred across the placenta and may also persist for a prolonged period in the child. If the infant receives the rubella immunization while antibodies are still present (which is now more likely because of earlier immunization schedules), the antibodies may react with the rubella virus in the vaccine forming immune complexes that "confuse" the immune system (20). Dr. Hugh Fudenberg (26), a clinical immunologist reported that some patients with autism "developed symptoms (of autism) within a week after immunization with the measles, mumps, and rubella (MMR) vaccine." Dr. Fudenberg also found that some of these children also had extremely high fever or seizures within one day of the vaccine. Reed Warren and his colleagues (15) think that children with this immune deficiency "may not be able to clear certain viruses completely or before the viruses affect the central nervous system."

One mother whose child reacted unfavorably after the MMR writes (27): "Nicholas has severe mental impairment after having the MMR injection. He has no speech, no understanding of language at all, no concentration, bizarre behavioral problems, and rarely acknowledges anyone. He has become very strong and aggressive. He is having constant tantrums, screaming and flinging himself to the ground and biting anyone who tries to restrain him. He is very

103

child with autism who complains of gastrointestinal pain or who reacted adversely to the MMR should receive an endoscopic examination of the intestinal tract to detect damage to the intestinal lining. Increased mortality in children in developing nations receiving measles vaccine has been reported to occur six to twelve months after immunization probably due to immune suppression (J Inf Dis 173:1320-6,1996; Lancet 348: 1257-8,1996). The vaccine damage fund in the United States that compensates families for harm caused by vaccines does not award compensation for autism caused by vaccination. The legislation establishing the compensation fund should be amended to include vaccine damage causing autism and other severe diseases. The amendment of this legislation should be a top political priority of the Autism Society of America.

Thus, it is possible that a viral infection (derived from a live vaccine) of the intestine has caused certain of the intestinal cells to malfunction in the production of secretin or peptidases needed to prevent the toxic effects of wheat or milk peptides. Based on many similar case reports, parents who already have a child with autism who reacted adversely to an immunization might wish to consider delaying immunizations for subsequent children to two years or later or ask that the vaccines be given separately rather than in the combined form like the MMR. The diseases prevented by these immunizations might also increase the risk of harm to a growing child but this risk is decreased when most other children in the community are immunized.

Gliotoxins and other immunotoxins produced by yeast and fungi
Another cause of the recurrent infections associated with yeast overgrowth are chemical compounds called gliotoxins. Gliotoxins are immunotoxic, meaning they are toxic to the immune system. They are compounds that are produced by both yeast(28,29) and fungi such as Aspergillus(30). (Gliotoxins have no relationship to the

child but this risk is decreased when most other children in the community are immunized.

Gliotoxins and other immunotoxins produced by yeast and fungi
Another cause of the recurrent infections associated with yeast overgrowth are chemical compounds called gliotoxins. Gliotoxins are immunotoxic, meaning they are toxic to the immune system. They are compounds that are produced by both yeast (28,29) and fungi such as Aspergillus(30). (Gliotoxins have no relationship to the glial cells of the brain and were named after the species of fungus Gliocladium in which they were first discovered.) Most strains of Candida that were isolated from humans have the ability to produce gliotoxins (28). Gliotoxins are important because they selectively fragment the DNA of white blood cells called T-lymphocytes and macrophages so that they are ineffective in fighting off infections (31,32). This is probably why the gliotoxins are so important and why Candida often causes recurrent infections. I suspect that exposure to gliotoxins may be a major cause of the frequent immune deficiencies in autism.

A second toxic effect of gliotoxins is probably due to their action on the sulfhydryl group of proteins, which they inactivate. These sulfhydryl groups are necessary for the functioning of a wide variety of enzymes (33). Supplements of glutathione, N-acetyl cysteine, and lipoic acid might be useful to prevent this toxic action of gliotoxins since they help to regenerate free sulfhydryl groups.

A third way that gliotoxins may be causing their damage is by the generation of compounds called free radicals (33). Free radicals are highly reactive chemicals that can cause many harmful effects to the body such as damaging our genetic material DNA. Many of these harmful reactions can be counteracted by compounds called antioxidants such as vitamin C, vitamin E, lipoic acid, glutathione, or N-acetyl cysteine. Several physicians who treat large numbers of children with autism have indicated to me significant improvement

105

of symptoms in some children with autism after treatment with the nutritional supplements glutathione or N-acetylcysteine. It seems likely that prevention of free-radical damage induced by gliotoxins may be one of the reasons these supplements are effective.

Mannan is another yeast product that comes from both Candida and Saccharomyces cerevisiae(35). Other compounds produced by yeast also have a significant immunosuppressant effect on the immune system (36-39).The fact that Saccharomyces cerevisiae (baking yeast) produces immune suppressants is one of the reasons that I recommend a yeast-free diet in addition to sugar restriction to control a yeast overgrowth of the intestinal tract. Even if the yeast cells are completely killed by baking (and some people think they may survive in the center of baked goods where the temperature may be lower), these immunosuppressant mannan compounds may not be destroyed by heating.

Other toxic byproducts of Candida.
According to Orion Truss M.D., the pioneer in the treatment of yeast-related illnesses, acetaldehyde is one of the most important toxic yeast byproducts (40). Vitamin B-6 is an aldehyde that must react with amino groups on many different enzymes throughout the body in order for them to function. If these amino groups have been used up by reacting with acetaldehyde, then other biochemical reactions mediated by vitamin B-6 cannot take place. The vitamin is subjected to an increased rate of elimination, resulting in low blood and tissue levels of this vitamin even though there may be an average intake of this vitamin (41). I suspect that high doses of vitamin B-6 may overcome the competition with acetaldehyde caused by the yeast and may be one of the main reasons that this vitamin is effective for the treatment of autism. I also suspect that high doses of vitamin B-6 may not be needed if the yeast are controlled; (see chapters on organic acids and vitamin therapy). A controlled study needs to be done to prove this idea.

106

Acetaldehyde may also react with neurotransmitters such as dopamine and serotonin to form opiate-like compounds called tetrahydroisoquinolines (42), which have been isolated from the urine of alcoholics. This is another way that an intestinal yeast overgrowth may affect brain function. Acetaldehyde also decreases the flexibility of the red blood cells(43) so that they are less able to deliver oxygen to the tissues. In addition, acetaldehyde decreases the ability of the protein tubulin to assemble into microtubules, which may interfere with transfer of essential biochemicals into the dendrites, the fibers that are used for nerve cell communication in the brain (44). In a study on rats given lethal doses of acetaldehyde (34), administration of lipoic acid or N-acetyl cysteine was able to prevent the death of any of the rats. This animal study indicates that humans exposed to this same byproduct due to yeast overgrowth might also benefit from increased intake of these same nutritional products.

Autoimmunity, molecular mimicry, and Candida. The wheat and yeast connection.

Singh has found that a high percentage of children with autism possess antibodies against their own tissues called autoantibodies (18). One of these autoantibodies is directed against myelin a fatty sheath that insulates the axons of nerve cells like the plastic insulator on electrical wire. Why is the body producing antibodies against its own tissue? Sometimes the body mounts an attack against an invading germ and produces antibodies against it. If one of the germs possesses proteins on its surface that resemble human tissue, then the antibodies may be "fooled" to react against the human tissue. The best known example of this molecular mimicry is rheumatic fever in which antibodies produced against a Streptococcal or "Strep" infection later react against the heart valve tissue (45,46). The autoimmune reaction from untreated Strep throat is the main reason that this condition is treated as a serious medical condition.

107

Vojdani has found that individuals with Candida infections often produce **antibodies against Candida that also react against various tissues of the human body** including brain, kidney, pancreas, spleen, thymus, and liver (46). Furthermore, these same anti-yeast antibodies also reacted against wheat protein which may explain why so many children with autism have high titers of wheat antibodies and are sensitive to wheat. A portion of one of the major wheat proteins called alpha-gliadin is very similar to a portion of one of the yeast proteins that is involved in yeast reproduction (47). **Antibodies produced against yeast may be "tricked" into reacting against wheat because of the great similarity of portions of the two different proteins. This protein could be an important link between wheat and yeast sensitivity in autism.**

If Orion Truss's acetaldehyde hypothesis is correct, the high reactivity of acetaldehyde may also provide an explanation for the high percentage of children with autoantibodies as well as the severe reactions some children experience after vaccination. Acetaldehyde reacts with virtually any free amino group on both proteins and amino acids. The amino acid lysine is one of the 20 amino acids found in most proteins. It is unusual in that it possesses two amino groups instead of one. This extra amino group on lysine is the target for acetaldehyde when it reacts with proteins. (This amino group is also the site at which arabinose reacts; see chapter on organic acids.)

It has been found that alcoholics who form greater than usual amounts of acetaldehyde possess antibodies against acetaldehyde-altered proteins (48). Furthermore, it has been found antibodies against acetaldehyde-altered proteins may cross react against formaldehyde-altered proteins (49). The toxins from diphtheria and tetanus bacteria are treated with formaldehyde to prepare the DPT vaccine (50). It is possible that if a child possesses antibodies against acetaldehyde-modified proteins due to yeast overgrowth, the vaccine may stimulate a marked increase in the autoimmune reaction, perhaps leading to a severe adverse immune reaction.

According to Ellen Bolte of Cure Autism Now, her child's autism began a few days after her child was vaccinated with the DPT injection. He was on antibiotics for ear infection at the time of the immunization and it is possible that a yeast overgrowth may have predisposed him to the adverse immune reaction.

I think that a possible role of human antibodies to Candida in reacting against myelin and other brain structures should be thoroughly investigated. In the future, it may be possible to deactivate or remove auto-antibodies that are causing harm to the body's own tissues. It appears to me that existing technology could be adapted for this purpose. As a matter of fact, Gupta's success in treating autism with gamma globulin might be working by removal of such autoantibodies (20).

Therapies

Gamma globulin therapy.
Dr. Gupta has used intravenous immunoglobulin (IVIG) successfully to treat a small number of autistic children (20). IVIG therapy is also called gamma globulin therapy. This product of human plasma has been used to treat immunodeficiency since 1952. Gamma globulin is purified from human blood components and then treated to remove harmful germs such as the HIV virus. Varying degrees of improvement after this therapy reported by Gupta included improved eye contact, calmer and improved social behavior, reduced echolalia, and improved speech in terms of better articulation and improved vocabulary. Speech improvement took the longest time to improve. Several patients regressed when the infusions stopped and then improved again when they were restarted. One child had a nearly complete reversal of the autism after about a year of therapy.

What is the mechanism of this improvement? No one knows for sure. I suspect that the immune system has a better ability to fight yeast and that the reduction of yeast byproducts allows the brain and the body to function better. It may have the effect of suppressing the production of antibodies against myelin, the covering of the nerve fibers in the brain. Elevated levels of this antibody have been reported in this illness. It may be that a specific component of the gamma globulin is responsible for the effects.

Intravenous IgG is usually given once a month due to the 28 day half-life of IgG. After administration of IgG, a child with low IgG values may have values in the normal range. An intravenous infusion takes about 2 hours. A sedative may be given the child to keep the child from being frightened during the procedure.

There are occasional mild and self-limiting reactions to IVIG including fever, muscle aches and pains, headache, nausea and vomiting, dizziness, and tachycardia that occur in less than 5% of all cases. The gamma globulin is derived from human blood so there is also a risk that unknown viruses might be present in the gamma globulin. The gamma globulin is checked for any known viruses such as HIV and hepatitis.   Rarely, there are severe allergic reactions (less than 0.1%). This is a very expensive therapy that may cost as much as $1500-$2500 per month.

Insurance coverage for immune therapies.
Because immunological therapy for the treatment of autism is considered experimental, most insurance companies and HMO's will not cover these (substantial) medical expenses. Since virtually every company *will* cover expenses due to immune deficiencies, it is essential that the physician document the fact that the child has a significant immune deficiency. Because some insurance companies may not even cover the laboratory tests for the diagnosis of immunodeficiency, the wisest course is to contact a clinical immunologist.

110

IMMUNE DEFICIENCY, IMMUNIZATIONS, AND YEAST SUPPRESSION OF THE IMMUNE SYSTEM

Clinical immunologists are often physicians who are working part-time in the treatment of patients and part-time in research activities as well in a large medical center or medical school. These physicians may be of assistance in getting insurance coverage for therapies, which are based on an immune deficiency diagnosis—such therapies might not be covered with an autism or PDD diagnosis.

When medical plans and HMOs are reluctant to provide even testing, it may be necessary to begin a letter writing campaign, which includes scientific books (such as this one) and articles (referenced herein). If education does not help, it is sometimes necessary to bring in letters from an attorney, to show that you are very serious about pursuing testing and treatment. You may want to consider contacting the news media about your dilemma.

Cimetidine.
Cimetidine (Tagamet) is a drug that is primarily used to treat ulcers and is now available as an over the counter (nonprescription) drug. In a review article on candidiasis, Dupont (51) states that this drug is relatively safe and well-tolerated and recommends that this drug should be used more frequently to treat patients with Candidiasis who do not respond adequately to antifungal drugs. Cimetidine has been used at a dose of 30 mg/kg body weight/day to stimulate in the immune system in patients with chronic mucocutaneous Candidiasis (52,53). This drug stimulates the white blood cells to kill the Candida. Cimetidine may reduce the rate of metabolism of many other drugs such as the antifungal drugs that are absorbed into the bloodstream as well as antidepressant drugs and antiseizure drugs. Combining zinc supplementation with cimetidine has proven to be very successful in the treatment of recurrent infections in patients with immune deficiency (Int J Clin Lab Research 27:79-80,1997.) **Check with your physician and pharmacist before using this drug about an appropriate pediatric dose and about any drug interactions that might be associated with the use of this drug.**

111

Transfer factor therapy.

Transfer factors are molecules that may contain both protein and nucleic acids (54) produced by the white blood cells. These molecules can transfer immunity from a healthy donor to a recipient who has impaired immune function. Dr. Masi found that severe Candidiasis could be effectively treated by Candida-specific transfer factor (55). Recent studies show that transfer factor can be given orally; this was a surprising result, since many proteins are destroyed by digestive enzymes when taken orally (56). Dr. Hugh Fudenberg, a clinical immunologist from the Neuroimmuno-Therapeutics Foundation, found that 21 of 22 autistic children treated with transfer factor from parental cells responded favorably to transfer factor therapy. Ten improved enough to be mainstreamed into regular school classrooms. (26). Dr. Fudenberg believes that a live virus from one of the vaccines or an adverse reaction between the antibodies obtained from the mother and the vaccine are responsible for the impairment of the immune system in autism. (Dr. Fudenberg can be reached at the Neuroimmuno-Therapeutics Foundation, 1092 Boiling Springs Rd, Spartanburg, SC 29303.)

Pentoxifylline.

Pentoxifylline is a drug that is a purine derivative and is an inhibitor of an enzyme called phosphodiesterase. Purines are one of the components of DNA, the genetic material for most living creatures. Pentoxifylline was given to a child with autism in Japan to treat suspected brain damage from an accident (57,58). After this treatment, the boy showed marked improvement of his autistic symptoms. When 23 children with autism were treated with pentoxifylline (150-600 mg/day), the drug was reported to be remarkably effective in 10 of the children with some of the group no longer considered to be autistic. The drug was also very effective in treating seizures. Side effects included nausea, vomiting, low blood pressure, and headache. Since the primary use of this drug is to improve blood circulation, you may find it difficult for a physician to prescribe it to treat autism.

IL-2

Interleukin-2(IL-2) is a protein called a cytokine that stimulates the proliferation and activation of T cells, B cells, granular lymphocytes, and macrophages. When T-helper cells are stimulated by antigens from the Candida, white blood cells called T-helper cells produce IL-2 and activate other resting T-cells. IL-2 also stimulates natural killer cells to produce gamma interferon, granulocyte macrophage stimulating factor and other factors that help to fight Candida. Gupta's work shows that natural killer cells are deficient in children with autism. Although IL-2 is toxic at high doses, low doses of IL-2 are relatively safe. The use of low doses for several weeks would result in selective expansion of natural killer cells that will kill yeast(51). IL-2 is available as a pharmaceutical agent prepared using recombinant DNA. Most family doctors or pediatricians will probably be reluctant to use this product but a clinical immunologist might be willing to discuss the possible use of low dose IL-2 therapy.

Allergic phenomena, food sensitivity, and altered behavior

A number of reports and books have documented the fact that **allergies** to foods, molds, and other allergens or direct toxic effects of certain foods **can markedly alter behavior** and that removal of such foods or desensitization can restore normal behavior (59-71). Doris Rapp M.D. has written several books including *Is This Your Child* (59) in which she documents behavioral disorders in children caused by allergic reactions. She also has several videotapes available that dramatically demonstrate bizarre behavior after the introduction of an extract of an allergenic substance. This book or *Solving the Puzzle of Your Hard-To-Raise Child.* by William Crook M.D. (72) give many details on how to identify and eliminate food allergies and sensitivities. Dr. Jaeckle, a physician trained as both a psychiatrist and allergist in Austin, Texas has recorded on videotape severe psychotic reactions following mold exposure (73) and indicates that many cases of schizophrenia may have a significant yeast involvement. The Feingold Association, started by the late

113

allergist Ben Feingold M.D., can provide a list of foods that commonly cause hyperactivity, which is a common problem in autism and PDD.

Tests of allergies.
There are numerous allergy tests that are available including those that introduce the allergenic substance into the skin (prick test) as well as many other tests that are done on blood. Many laboratories perform the blood tests for IgE antibodies against specific allergens and IgG antibodies against specific allergens. **These tests should not be confused with tests of total IgG and total IgE that were done to assess a possible immune deficiency; they are completely different tests and give completely different information.** Thus, an individual could be deficient in total IgG and yet still have high levels of IgG against a specific food.

Another kind of test called the ELISA-ACT test assesses food allergies by measuring the toxic effects of both antigen-antibody reactions and cell-mediated toxic reactions. This latter test is somewhat more comprehensive and may also be able to assess sensitivity to heavy metals, environmental chemicals, and food additives, which may be important but are not involved directly with the immune system. The Serammune test can evaluate over 300 different foods and chemicals but the cost is over $1000. The allergy tests offered by The Great Plains laboratory are only a fraction of this amount.

The laboratories that offer these tests are listed below:

IgG food allergy test.
The Great Plains Laboratory, Inc.
9335 W. 75th Street
Overland Park, KS 66204
(913) 341-8949 or fax: (913) 341-6207
www.greatplainslaboratory.com   Email: GPL4U@aol.com

ELISA ACT TEST.
Serammune Physicians Lab,
1890 Preston White Drive, Second Floor,
Preston, VA 22091
(703)758-0610 or (800) 553-5472

IgE allergy test.
The Great Plains Laboratory also performs the IgE allergy test. I recommend **IgE allergy testing for inhalants** like dust, mold, mildew, and pollen, and the **IgG allergy test for foods**. I have noticed that many people with autism may have completely normal results for foods in the IgE allergy tests but very abnormal results for foods in the IgG allergy tests. **These tests should not be confused with tests of total IgG and total IgE that were done to assess a possible immune deficiency; they are completely different tests and give completely different information.** The Great Plains Laboratory can provide testing to anyone in the world.

Immunotherapy with enzyme-potentiated desensitization (EPD)
In autism and PDD, allergies to foods, molds, pollen and other materials may lead to behavioral disturbances in addition to the usual allergic phenomena such as sneezing, asthma, and skin rashes.

EPD is a method of immunotherapy developed by Dr. Leonard McEwen (74-78). The method involves desensitization with a combination of very low dose mixed allergens with the enzyme, beta-glucuronidase. The beta-glucuronidase increases the immunizing effects of the allergens and acts directly on T-suppressor cells, apparently inducing a longer lasting desensitization than does any type of previously known immunotherapy, and necessitates injections only be given every 2 to 3 months at first, and then decreasing over time. The frequency of injections varies with the condition being treated and patient response, but once maintenance is reached, average patients seem to require treatment 2 to 3 times yearly. Furthermore, it has been the experience of

115

McEwen that at least 50% of patients can discontinue EPD after between 8 and 20 injections. Patients have remained in remission without immunotherapy for over 20 years. EPD also appears useful in the treatment of a large variety of conditions not previously considered responsive to immunotherapy of any kind (78).

Numerous parents of children with autism and other behavioral disorders (see chapter by Pamela Scott) have reported beneficial results with this therapy. They also report that their children often don't do as well when the effects of the EPD begin to wear off just before the next series of EPD injections. As with every therapy, some children respond much more dramatically than others.

Homeopathy.
Homeopathy is a technique employed by both physicians and non-physicians called homeopaths. The theoretical basis of this technique is unknown but those who use this technique prepare dilutions of substances to which a person is sensitive and the person takes these dilutions by mouth and becomes desensitized in a way that is not completely understood. It appears that the small amount of a harmful substance is able to mobilize the body's own defenses against the substance. Although not generally approved of by mainstream medicine in this country, many alternative medicine physicians may use this technique in their medical practices. This technique is also recognized as valid by the World Health Organization and is part of mainstream medicine in France. When trying any new therapy, the best approach is to talk to the physician and with other people who have employed a particular therapy and find out how helpful the particular medical practitioner was. One physician who employs homeopathy reported that homeopathic dilutions of arabinose, the sugar derived from Candida, favorably improved behavior of children with autism but that the response only lasted a few days. Homeopathic treatment also appears to be more effective than antibiotic therapy (79) for the treatment of earaches (otitis media).

116

IMMUNE DEFICIENCY, IMMUNIZATIONS, AND YEAST SUPPRESSION OF THE IMMUNE SYSTEM

References

1. Warren R. et al. Immunoglobulin A deficiency in a subset of autistic subjects. J. Autism Develop Dis. 27:187-192,1997.
2. Warren R. Immune abnormalities in patients with autism. J. Autism Develop Dis. 16, 189-197, 1986.
3. Warren R et al Possible association of the extended MHC haplotvpe B44-SC30-DR4 with autism. Immunogenetics 36: 203-207, 1992.
4. Warren R et al. Association with decreased plasma levels of the complement C4B protein. Neuropsychobiology 39: 53-57, 1995.
5. Singh, V, Warren, RP, Odell, JD, and Cole, P. Changes in soluble interleukin-2, interleukin-2 receptor, T8 antigen, and interleukin-I in the serum of autistic children. Clin. Immunol. Immunopath. 61: 448-455, 1991.
6. Yonk LJ, Warren RP, Burger RA, Cole P, Odell JD, Warren WL, White E, Singh VK: D4+ per T cell depression in autism. Immunol Lett 25: 341-346, 1990.
7. Abramason RK, Self S, Genco P, Smith N, Pendleton A, Valentine J, Wright HH, Cuccaro M, Powell D: The relationship between lymphocyte cell surface markers and serotonin in autistic probands (abstract). Am J Hum Genet 47(3):A45, 1990.
8. Wood Frei B, Dennv D, Gaffney GR, O'DonneU T: Lymphocyte subsets and the interleukin-2 system in autistic children (abstract). Sci Proc Annu Meet Am Acad Child Adolesc Psychiatry 7: 53, 1991.
9. Plioplys AV, Greaves A, Kazemi K, Silverman Lymphocyte function in autism and Rett syndrome. Neuropsychobiology 7: 12-16, 1994.
10. Stubbs EG, Crawford ML, Burger DR, Vanderbark AA: Depressed lymphocyte responsiveness in autistic children. J Autism Child Schizophr 7:49-55, 1977.
11. Warren RP, Margaretten NC, Pace NC, Foster A: Immune abnormalities in patients with autism. J Autism Dev Disord 16:189-197, 1986.
12. Singh VK, Fudenberg HH, Emerson D, Coleman M: Immunodiagnosis and immunotherapy in autistic children. Ann NY Acad Sci 540:602-604, 1988.

117

13. Ferrari P et al. Immune status in infantile autism: Correlation between the immune status, autistic symptoms and levels of serotonin. Encephale 14: 339-344, 1988.
14. Warren RP, Foster A, Margaretten NC: Reduced natural killer cell activity in autism. J Am Acad Child Psychol 26: 333-335, 1987.
15. Warren PP, Singh VK, Cole P, Odell JD, Pingree CB, Warren WL, White E: Increased frequency of the null allele at the complement C4B locus in autism. Clin Exp Immunol 83: 438-440, 1991.
16. Warren R et al. DR-positive T cells in autism: association with decreased plasma levels of the complement C4B protein. Biological Psychiatry 31: 53-57,1995.
17. Weizman A, Weizman R, Szekely GA, Wijsenbeek H, Livini E: Abnormal immune response to brain tissue antigen in the syndrome of autism. Am J Psychiatry 139:1462-1465,1982.
18. Singh VK, Warren RP, Odell JD, Warren WL, Cole P: Antibodies to myelin basic protein in children with autistic behavior. Brain Behav Immunity 7: 97-103,1993.
19. Plioplys AV, Greaves A, Kazemi K, Silverman Immunoglobulin reactivity in autism and Rett's syndrome. Dev Brain Dysfunct 7: 12-16, 1994.
20. Gupta S., Aggarwal and Heads C. Dysregulated immune system in children with autism. Beneficial effects of intravenous immune globulin on autistic characteristics. Autism Develop Dis 26:439-452, 1996.
21. Forehand J, Nauseef W, and Johnston R. Inherited disorders of phagocyte killing. In The Metabolic Basis of Inherited Disease. Sixth Edition. Volume II. Edited by C. Scriver et al. Pgs 2779-2801,1989, McGraw Hill, NY
22. Wolf B and Heard G. Disorders of biotin metabolism. In "The Metabolic Basis of Inherited Disease. Volume II. Sixth edition. C. Scriver et al, eds. McGraw Hill, NY,1989, pgs 2093-2103.
23. Butler J and Cooper M. Antibody deficiency diseases. In The Metabolic Basis of Inherited Disease. Sixth Edition. Volume II. Edited by C. Scriver et al. Pgs 2683-2696,1989, McGraw Hill, NY
24. Blaese M. Genetic immunodeficiency syndromes with defects in both T- and B-lymphocyte functions. The Metabolic Basis of Inherited

Disease. Sixth Edition. Volume II. Edited by C. Scriver et al. Pgs 2697-2709,1989, McGraw Hill, NY

25. Rudduck C, Beckman L, Franzen G, Jacobsson L, Lindstrom L: Complement factor C4 in schizophrenia. Hum Hered 35:223-226,1985.

26. Fudenberg H. Dialyzable lymphocyte extract in infantile onset autism: a pilot study. Biotherapy 9:144,1996.

27. Dawbarns Solicitors Fact Sheet. Mumps, measles, and rubella MMR) vaccines and measles rubella (MR) vaccines. Dawbarns Solicitors. Bank House. King's Staithe Square. King's Lynn, Norfolk, Great Britain PE30 1RD

28. Shah D and Larsen B. Identity of a Candida albicans toxin and its production in vaginal secretions. Med Sci Res 20:353-355,1992.

29. Shah D and Larsen B. Clinical isolates of yeast produce a gliotoxin-like substance. Mycopathologia 116:203-208,1991.

30. Mullbacher A et al. Identification of an agent in cultures of Aspergillus fumigatus displaying anti-phagocytic and immunomodulating activity in vitro. J Gen Microbiol 131:1251-1258,1985.

31. Kobayashi M. Gliotoxin treatment selectively spares M-CSF- plus IL-3-responsive multipotent haemopoietic progenitor cells in bone marrow. Eur J of Haematol 46:205-211,1991.

32. Sutton P et al. Evidence that gliotoxin enhances lymphocyte activation and induces apoptosis by effects on cyclic AMP levels. Biochem Pharmacol 50:2009-2014,1995.

33. Waring P et al. Gliotoxin inactivates alcohol dehydrogenase by either covalent modification or free radical damage by redox cycling. Biochem Pharmacol 49:1195-1201,1995.

34. Sprince H et al. Protective action of ascorbic acid and sulfur compounds against acetaldehyde toxicity: implications in alcoholism and smoking. Agents and Actions 5:164-173,1975.

35. Podzorski R et al. Pathogenesis of candidiasis. Immunosuppression by cell wall mannan metabolites. Arch Surgery 124: 1290-1294,1989.

36. Witkin, S. Defective immune responses in patients with recurrent candidiasis. Infections in Medicine. May / June pg 129-132,1985.

37. Iwata K and Ichita K. Cellular immunity in experimental fungal infections in mice. Mykosen Supplement 1:72-81,1978.

38. Fischer A, Ballet J, and Griscelli C. Specific inhibition of in vitro Candida-induced lymphocyte proliferation by polysaccharide antigens present in the serum of patients with chronic mucocutaneous candidiasis. J Clin Invest. 62: 1005-1013,1978.
39. Carrow E and Domer J. Immunoregulation in experimental murine Candidiasis: specific suppression induced by Candida albicans cell wall glycoprotein. Infection and Immunity 49:172-181,1985.
40. Truss O. Metabolic abnormalities in patients with chronic candidiasis: the acetaldehyde hypothesis. J Orthomolecular Psychiatry 13:66-93, 1984.
41. Lumeng L. The role of acetaldehyde in mediating the deleterious effect of ethanol on pyridoxal-5-phosphate metabolism. J Clin Invest 62:286-293,1978.
42. Blum K and Payne J. Alcohol and the addictive brain. The Free Press. NY,NY, pgs 99-216,1991.
43. Tsuboi K et al. Acetaldehyde-dependent changes in hemoglobin and oxygen affinity of human erythrocytes. Hemoglobin 5: 241-250,1981.
44. Tuma D et al. The interaction of acetaldehyde with tubulin. Ann NY Acad Sci 492:277-286,1987.
45. Oldstone M. Molecular mimicry: Immunologic cross reactivity between dissimilar proteins (microbial and self) that share common epitopes can lead to autoimmunity. Cell 50: 819-820,1987.
46. Vojdani A et al. Immunological cross reactivity between Candida albicans and human tissue. J Clin Lab Immunol 48: 1-15, 1996.
47. Camonis J et al. Characterization, cloning, and sequence analysis of the CDC25 gene which controls the cyclic AMP level of Saccharomyces cerevisiae. EMBO J 5:375-380,1986.
48. Worrall S et al Relationship between alcohol intake and immunoglobulin A immunoreactivity with acetaldehyde-modified bovine serum albumin. Alcohol Clin Exp Res 20: 836-40,1996.
49. Pietrzak E et al . Antibodies made against a formaldehyde-protein adduct cross react with an acetaldehyde-protein adduct. Implications for the origin of antibodies in human serum which recognize acetaldehyde-protein adducts. Alcohol 30:373-8, 1995.
50. Corey L and Petersdorf R. Prevention of Infection: Immunization and antimicrobial prophylaxis. In: Principles of Internal Medicine. Tenth

edition. R Petersdorf et al, editors. McGraw Hill, New York, pgs 908-917,1982.

51. Dupont P. Candida albicans, the opportunist, a cellular and molecular perspective. J Amer Podiatr ,Med Assoc 85:104-115,1995.

52. Gill F and Portnoy J. An unusual combination of immunologic abnormalities in a patient with chronic mucocutaneous candidiasis. Annals of Allergy 63:147-148,1989.

53. Jorizzo J. Cimetidine as an immunomodulator: chronic mucocutaneous candidiasis as a model. Ann Intern Med 92: 192-195,1980.

54. Fudenberg H and Wilson G. Dialyzable transfer factor: clinical uses and studies on purification of the activity. In Clinical Immunochemistry. The American Association of Clinical Chemistry Press, Washington, DC pgs 228-250, 1978.

55. Masi M et al. Transfer factor in chronic mucocutaneous candidiasis. Biotherapy 9: 97-103,1996.

56. Kirkpatrick C. Activities and characteristics of transfer factor. Biotherapy 9: 13-16,1996.

57. Gupta S., Rimland B. and Shilling P. (1995). Pentoxifylline: A review and a rationale for its possible use in the treatment of autism. J. Child Neurol 11:501-504,1996.

58. Shimoide M. (1981) Effect of pentoxifylline (Trental) on infantile autism. Clin. Exp. Med. 58: 285-288.

59. Rapp D. Is This Your Child? 1991.

60. Eggar, J., Stolla, A., McEwen, L.M. Controlled trial of hyposensitization in children with food-induced hyperkinetic syndrome. Lancet 339:1150-3,1992.

61. Rowe K. S., Synthetic food coloring and hyperactivity: A double-blind crossover study. Aust. Paediatr. J. 24: 143-47,1988.

62. Rowe K, S., Rose K. J. Synthetic food coloring and behavior: A dose response effect in a double-blind, placebo-controlled, repeated-measures study Journal of Pediatrics 12: 691-698,1994.

63. .Mayron L. Allergy, learning, and behavior problems. Journal of Learning Disabilities 12: 41-51, 1979.

64. Rapp D. Does Diet Affect Hyperactivity? J. of Learning Disabilities, 11: 56-62, 1978.

65. Kaplan, B. J., McNicol J., Conte, R., Moghadam, H. K. Dietary Replacement in Preschool Aged Hyperactive Boys. 83: 7-17,1989.
66. Hunter J. 0. Food allergy-or enterometabolic disorder The Lancet 338: 495-6, 1991.
67. Egger J., Carter C. M., Wilson J., Turner M. W., Soothill J. F. Is migraine food allergy? A double-blind controlled trial of oligoantigenic diet treatment. Lancet ii : 865-69, 1983.
68. Egger J., Carter C.M., Graham P.J., Gumby D., Soothill J.F. Controlled trial of oligoantigenic treatment in the hyperkinetic syndrome, Lancet i: 540-45,1985.
69. Crook W. G., Can What a Child Eats Make Him Dull, Stupid, or Hyperactive? Journal of Learning Disabilities, 13: 53-58,1980.
70. Clarke, T. The relation of allergy to character problems in children. A survey. Annals of Allergy March-April, 1950, pp. 175-87.
71. Boris M., Mandel F. Food and additives are common causes of the attention deficit hyperactive disorder in children. Annals of Allergy 72: 462-68,1994.
72. Crook W and Steven L. Solving the Puzzle of Your Hard-To-Raise Child. Professional Books.Jackson,TN,1987.
73. Yeast-related mental disturbances. Psychiatric symptoms elicited through biological (physical) mechanisms. An interview with Richard G Jaeckle M.D.. Mastering Food Allergies. 10(1): 1-4,1995.
74. McEwen, L.M., Starr, M.S. Enzyme potentiated hyposensitization I, The effect of pre-treatment with beta-glucuronidase, hyaluronidase, and antigen on anaphylactic sensitivity of guinea pigs and mice. Int Arch Allerg42: 152-8, 1972.
75. McEwen, L.M. Enzyme potentiated hyposensitization II, Effect of glucose, glucosamine, N-acetylamino-sugars and gelatin on the ability of beta-glucuronidase to block the anamnestic response to antigen in mice. Ann Allerg 31:79-83,1973.
76. McEwen, L.M., Nicholoson, M., Kitchen, I. and White, S. Enzyme potentiated hyposensitization III, Control by sugars and diols of the immunological effect of beta-glucuronidase in mice and patients with hay fever. Ann Allerg 31:543-9,1973.
77. McEwen, L.M., Nicholoson, M., Kitchen, I., O'Gorman, J., White, S. Enzyme potentiated hyposensitization IV, Effect of protamine on the

immunological behavior of beta-glucuronidase in mice and patients with hay fever. Ann Allerg 34:290-5,1975.

78. McEwen, L.M. Enzyme potentiated hyposensitization V, Five case reports of patients with acute food allergy. Ann Allerg 35:98-103,1975.

79. Friese KH et al. Otitis media in children: A comparison of conventional and homeopathic drugs. Head and Neck Otorhinolaryngology 44:462-466,1996.

Abnormalities of the digestive system.

by William Shaw Ph.D.

Gluten and casein sensitivity

Numerous studies by Dohan, Reichelt, Shattock, Cade and others have established elevated urinary excretion of peptides derived from certain proteins in milk and wheat in children with autism and in adults with schizophrenia(1-18). Restriction of these proteins from the diet or dialysis to remove the peptides causes improvement in the symptoms of these diseases. The major protein in milk is called casein while the major protein in wheat is called gluten. Each of these proteins is made of a combination of amino acids. There are 20 amino acids that are commonly found in proteins. A protein can be thought of as analogous to a string of pearls. The pearls may have 20 different colors. The amino acids would be individual pearls on the string. The DNA or genetic code selects which particular amino acid(which of the 20 different colored pearls) is present in each protein (string of pearls). When proteins are eaten, they are broken down by enzymes in the gastrointestinal tract to smaller pieces called peptides and then the smaller pieces are broken down into individual amino acids. The individual amino acids are then absorbed through the intestinal lining into the bloodstream.

Historical perspective

Both cow's milk and are fairly new on the evolutionary scale to human beings and were probably first used as foods by many our ancestors in the Mideast approximately 10,000 years ago; at this time the first sickles used to harvest cereals were used in Turkey (19). Up until this time our ancestors ate a very varied diet of wild plants, fish, animals, and insects. Civilization from the Mideast spread throughout Europe as these new farmers moved into lands just vacated by retreating glaciers that covered northern Europe, Asia, and North America. The milk cow and domesticated grain seeds moved with these invaders. Many of the native people in Europe were not biochemically adapted to eating these foods, did not do well on such diets, and many died. Children who ate these foods did not do as well either and many died. As a result, the genes associated with gluten sensitivity from the population became reduced in the population. In countries such as Ireland which were invaded most recently by people subsisting on a diet high in wheat and milk, the incidence of sensitivity to wheat is higher than in any other country because the toxic wheat and milk products have not had very long to kill off the sensitive individuals in the population. Western Ireland has the highest incidence of schizophrenia in the world (20) probably because it also has the highest incidence of wheat-sensitive people. Dohan found that schizophrenia was essentially absent from primitive people in the East Indies until they adopted a Westernized diet with increased grains(2).

Effects of gluten sensitivity
What are the effects of gluten sensitivity? In the medical disorder called celiac disease, there is a reduced ability to digest wheat and there is often a direct toxic effect of gluten on the lining of the intestine called the intestinal mucosa. Symptoms may include diarrhea, failure to thrive, short stature, discolored dental enamel, depression, premature degeneration of the nervous system, seizures, arthritis, nutritional deficiencies due to malabsorption, and abdominal distension (21-24). Long eyelashes, premature balding, and clubbing of the fingers are also commonly reported in this disease. In celiac disease, there is also an increase in the blood of antibodies to wheat. It is thought that the immune system produces antibodies against the undigested wheat proteins. In celiac disease, there is an increased incidence of certain antigens on the white blood cells called HLA(human leukocyte antigen). These HLA types are most commonly used to determine suitability for tissue transplants and for paternity testing.) Patients with celiac disease have increased frequency of the HLA-B8 and HLA-Dw3 types compared to the population as a whole (25). The HLA-B8 antigen is present on the

125

white blood cells of about 85-90% of celiac patients compared to only 20% of the general population.

Differences between wheat sensitivity in autism and celiac disease

In celiac disease the cells of the mucosa(the lining of the intestinal tract) lose their characteristic features, do not function as well, and may have impaired ability to produce hormones like secretin that stimulate the pancreas to function properly. As a consequence, the absorption of food from the intestine is impaired and there may be severe diarrhea due to this malabsorption. Severe nutritional deficiencies may also occur due to this defective absorption of nutrients. In individuals with autism and schizophrenia, the intestinal cells do not appear to be as badly damaged as in celiac disease and if a small piece of the intestinal lining is removed in a biopsy, the microscopic pattern of the tissue is not usually the same as in celiac disease.

Autism is also different from celiac disease in that patients with autism frequently have elevated antibodies against both wheat and milk. The major difficulty in both autism and schizophrenia appears to be the absorption of the incompletely digested pieces of the gluten and casein proteins called peptides. One of the reasons for the incomplete digestion may be a deficiency of enzymes that break down these small peptides. I have talked with numerous parents who had the biopsy done to test for celiac disease and none of the tests indicated the microscopic pattern of classic celiac disease even though the child improved on a gluten-restricted diet. The anti-endomysial antibody test which is positive in most people (around 95%) with celiac disease is negative in all but a small percentage of people(less than 5%) with autism.

These peptides from gluten and casein are important because they react with opiate receptors in the brain, thus mimicking the effects of opiate drugs like heroin and morphine. The peptide from wheat is called gluteomorphin (gluten + morphine) and the peptide from milk

126

is called caseomorphin (casein + morphine). These compounds have been shown to react with areas of the brain such as the temporal lobes which are involved in speech and auditory integration. Furthermore, the administration of drugs like naltrexone(see chapter by Bruce Semon M.D. Ph.D.) that block the effects of opiate drugs lessen the symptoms of autism (26). Children with autism frequently improve overall after restriction of these foods. Slip-ups can be catastrophic. One mother reported to me that her teenage son with autism who was doing very well on a gluten-restricted diet severely damaged her house in a rage after eating a few wheat crackers. I have personally been informed of so many cases of improvement after gluten and casein restriction that there is no doubt in my mind that this dietary restriction should be considered for every child with autism. Conversely, I would be very cautious in changing the diet if it has been successful. Because the milk and wheat peptides function as opiates, a withdrawal reaction similar to that of a drug addict may occur when these foods are removed from the diet.

The withdrawal reaction from gluten and casein can sometimes be severe. Sidney Baker M.D. describes the reaction of one child with autism to the removal of gluten and casein in his book *Detoxification and Healing* (27). The child refused to eat, lost 15 pounds, was extremely hyperactive, barely slept, increased biting and hitting behaviors, and had to have liquids forced on him to prevent dehydration. Repeated doses of Alka-Seltzer Gold provided temporary relief from the symptoms. At the end of the six weeks, the withdrawal ended and the child was significantly improved. Alka-Seltzer Gold is bicarbonate that helps to neutralize stomach acid. **Warning! Other types of Alka-Seltzer are not the same as Alka-Seltzer Gold and could cause serious side effects if given excessively.**

Restriction of gluten and casein from the diet.
Lisa Lewis, Pamela Scott, and Karyn Seroussi, and Bruce Semon deal extensively with dietary therapies and I will not cover them here.

127

Alpha-1-antitrypsin deficiency

Alpha-1-antitrypsin is a protein produced by the liver. Deficiency of this protein is associated with chronic obstructive lung disease or emphysema, cirrhosis of the liver, and respiratory distress of the newborn. Alpha-1-antitrypsin is an inhibitor of enzymes that break down proteins (proteases). It inhibits the action of a number of naturally occurring proteases including trypsin, chymotrypsin, collagenase, white blood cell proteases, and plasmin and thrombin, which are released in inflammatory reactions of the lung. In the absence of sufficient alpha-1-antitrypsin, plasmin and thrombin may begin to digest the lung itself. Elevated values for this protein are found in patients who are genetically heterozygous deficient for alpha-1-antitrypsin, during infection, during pregnancy, in bacteria infection, following estrogen or steroid therapy, and in rheumatoid arthritis. In the gastroenterology department of a children's hospital in Australia, it was discovered(28) that 8 of 15 children with autism had abnormally low values of alpha-1-antitrypsin. In children with celiac disease, there was also an increased incidence of low values of alpha-1-antitrypsin.The authors think that the low level of alpha-1-antitrypsin might predispose children to wheat sensitivity.

Pancreatic atrophy, hypoglycemia, and antibiotics

I reviewed the results of a very interesting case which illustrates the possible damage of yeast byproducts. (I encountered many similar cases but this child was tested over an extended time period and was extensively evaluated by many different medical specialists so that the child's biochemistry had been analyzed exhaustively.) At about 10 months of age, this normal child whom I'll call Ralph developed a Strep throat and began to be given antibiotics. The Strep throat cleared up but the conscientious parents were advised to be sure to finish giving the entire 14 day supply of antibiotics. When Ralph's mom went to check on him, she found that he was having convulsive seizures. She rushed Ralph to the emergency room at the hospital where his blood glucose (blood sugar) was near zero. Ralph would have been dead if his mother had brought him in any later. Ralph was given an infusion of glucose into his vein and began to recover.

Because of Ralph's extremely low blood sugar, the attending physician sent a urine sample to my organic acid laboratory to see if Ralph had one of the genetic disorders that caused low blood sugar. When I examined Ralph's urine organic acid profile, he had none of the abnormalities associated with any of the genetic diseases that cause hypoglycemia(low blood glucose) such as fatty acid oxidation disorders. What Ralph did have was very high levels of the sugar arabinose, indicating (to me) a severe yeast overgrowth resulting from his antibiotic treatment for Strep. I reported my findings. A new physician at the hospital was sure Ralph had one of the genetic disorders and ordered a retest. Again, the only significant abnormality was the elevation of the same yeast-related compounds that I had found in children with autism.

When Ralph returned home, his parents became concerned because he began to stagger at certain times of the day. When tested repeatedly, his blood glucose was low again, testing between 30-50 mg per dl. Normal is about 100 mg per dl. Many other endocrine tests revealed no cause for Ralph's hypoglycemia. Ralph was referred to another specialist who suspected that Ralph might have a tumor of the pancreas that was oversecreting insulin which lowers blood sugar. However, repeated testing revealed only a slight increase in insulin at most, not a value high enough to indicate a tumor.

His parents were taught how to perform a blood sugar test and tested Ralph's blood sugar several times a day. The child's pancreas where the insulin-secreting cells are found was examined by an imaging technique called an MRI and it was found that there was a severe atrophy of the pancreas. In addition, the tail of the pancreas was completely missing. But a tumor secreting insulin was not found. Additional organic acid tests at later times revealed the same elevation of yeast byproducts. Several times I recommended the use of an antifungal drug but my suggestions were ignored.

Instead, the parents of the child were instructed to give the child multiple doses a day of a food called cornstarch which is broken down into sugar in the intestine. The idea was that sugar derived from cornstarch would increase the child's blood sugar. However, the child's blood glucose continued to be abnormal and the parents were reprimanded for not being diligent enough in giving enough cornstarch throughout the day. More than likely, the excessive cornstarch was feeding Ralph's untreated yeast overgrowth and just made his hypoglycemia worse. Low blood sugar is prevalent in fibromyalgia(29), a disorder in which yeast overgrowth is common (30,31). Finally, at about the age of two and a half years, I learned that Ralph was being referred to a developmental pediatrics department with the diagnosis of a probable autistic-spectrum disorder. At this time, a trial of nystatin was introduced. Ralph's blood sugar returned to normal in about a week and his organic acids were normal for the first time since he had started antibiotics as an infant. There is no doubt in my mind that I had witnessed and documented over a span of about two years the transformation of a normal infant into a child with autism.

I have lost contact with the child's parents and do not know what happened to him later on. Ralph's story indicated to me that yeast overgrowth could cause severe hypoglycemia and that it might also severely damage the pancreas. The hypoglycemia could be due to the yeast byproducts. I suspect that the damage to the pancreas was due to antibodies against the yeast that cross-reacted with the pancreas in an autoimmune reaction. (See the chapter on the immune system.) It is possible that protein crosslinks of pentosidines caused by abnormally high arabinose might also be responsible for some of the damage. (See the chapter on organic acids.) The pancreatic damage probably resulted in deficient production of digestive enzymes by the severely damaged pancreas. This deficiency of digestive enzymes would also result in the incomplete digestion of wheat and milk proteins which would then be absorbed and cause their opiate effects on the brain.

Secretin.

Secretin is a small protein called a polypeptide produced by the cells of the small intestine and is made up of 27 amino acids (32). The function of secretin is to cause the pancreas to release bicarbonate after a meal. After a meal, the stomach secretes acid. The food passing through the stomach is very acidic. The pancreas secretes digestive enzymes to digest the food arriving into the small intestine from the stomach. These enzymes will not function properly to digest food if the acid from the stomach is not neutralized by bicarbonate from the pancreas. Thus, if secretin secretion is deficient, no bicarbonate will be formed and foods will not be digested properly. Secretin is produced by certain cells in the intestine and is stimulated by the presence of stomach acid. Secretin is available as a drug from pig intestine that is used to assess the function of the pancreas. Human and pig secretin are very similar and differ in only 2 of the 27 amino acids in the molecule(33). In order to assess pancreatic function, secretin in injected into the vein and is transported by the bloodstream to the pancreas. If the pancreas is functioning properly, then bicarbonate will be produced by the pancreas. The production of bicarbonate can be monitored through a tube down the esophagus and stomach while the patient is sedated.

At an eastern United States medical school, a child with autism was being tested for pancreatic function at the insistence of a parent (Confidential Personal Communication) who noticed a lot of undigested food in her child's stool. When the secretin was administered to her child, the physician noticed that not only was bicarbonate being produced, the pancreatic secretion was literally **gushing out**. More importantly, **the development of her child began to gush as well.** Before the secretin infusion, the child spoke only two words, did not make eye contact, and was zoned out most of the time. Within three weeks of the infusion, he made eye contact most of the time, spoke in short sentences, and could say hundreds of words. Similar responses have now been found in other children with autism but some children have had only slight improvement (Confidential Personal Communications).

Why are these children reacting to these infusions so dramatically? (1) Children with autism are not producing secretin in sufficient amounts and their digestive process is impaired as a result. The gush of bicarbonate after secretin might be due to the fact that the pancreas has not been stimulated adequately with the body's own secretin and therefore it overacted to the external secretin administered intravenously. This explanation is the most likely explanation. Reduced secretin production may be related to gluten sensitivity or viral damage to the intestinal mucosa caused by the live virus vaccines such as the MMR. In celiac disease, the gluten damages the intestinal cells that produce secretin(32). Presumably, the same mechanism is operating in autism. (2) Children with autism are producing a defective type of secretin that is not capable of stimulating the pancreas. It is also possible that secretin has some direct beneficial effect on brain functioning. It is also possible that autoantibodies against the pancreas induced by Candida may be preventing the pancreas from responding to the normal amount of secretin produced by the child's own body.

Tests of pancreatic function
A common way to evaluate pancreatic function is to measure the concentration of pancreatic enzymes in the stool or blood. Trypsin is one of the enzymes most commonly measured and can be done by most of the large reference labs.

If the function of the pancreas is inadequate, then secretin production or digestive enzyme production might be impaired. Another simple way to assess the secretin production of the intestinal lining is to measure the acidity of the stool. If insufficient bicarbonate is being produced, then the stool will be more acidic or have what is called a low pH. A pH value less than 6 may indicate insufficient bicarbonate due to defective secretin production. The pH can be measured with simple paper called pH indicator paper which changes to different colors at different acid concentrations or pH levels. You can get pH paper from lab supply companies and do this at home or get a nearby lab to do it for you if you don't prefer to play in poop. You'll need a physician request for the lab to do the test.

Digestive enzyme supplements.
Numerous parents have reported improved functioning of their children with autism following supplementation with digestive enzymes. This improvement may be because: (1) The children are not producing enough secretin. The decreased secretin causes reduced bicarbonate. The digestive enzymes are secreted in enough quantity but function at a reduced rate because the food passing from the stomach is too acidic. (2) The pancreas is not producing enough enzymes on its own. (3) Both of the above factors are involved.

What kind of digestive enzyme supplements might be helpful? Since undigested peptides appear to be a problem, the use of peptidase supplements that would help to digest peptides would seem appropriate. A drug store in Dallas, Texas called the Apothecary supplies a product called "peptidase" that is a mixture of carboxypeptidase and aminopeptidase. The phone number of the Apothecary is 800 969-6601; a physician's prescription is required to obtain this material. These enzymes break down peptides starting at different ends of the molecule. It seems possible to me that the supplementation of sufficient peptidases might be able to resolve the problem of gluten and casein sensitivity. If these peptides were sufficiently digested to individual amino acids, these products would not be toxic. However, other digestive enzymes in addition to peptidases might also be deficient and supplementation with a variety of digestive enzymes might be better in such a case. The function of different digestive enzymes is listed in Table 1. Many other digestive enzymes from a number of plant sources are also available generally as capsules. Since animal sources of enzymes may be more subject to contamination with bacteria or viruses, it may be safer to use plant enzymes as supplements. Many children may not be able to swallow capsules.

133

Could children who can't swallow capsules be given these digestive enzymes in a loose form? Probably. Meat tenderizer is really just a plant digestive enzyme that breaks down meat protein fibers. People have used this product for years and I am aware of no significant health problems associated with this product. Some of these enzymes may be denatured in the very low pH of the stomach. **Do not administer these products as loose powder unless you review such therapy with the supplier and your physician.**

Behavior, food dyes ,and inactivation of digestive enzymes
Several studies have documented adverse effects of food colors on behavior (34-36). One possible mechanism for the negative effects of food dyes may be an inhibition of digestive enzymes by the food colors. In a study done in Germany (37), it was found that the biochemical function of the digestive enzymes amylase and trypsin were significantly inhibited by many common food colors. Thus, one of the best things you might due for your child is to remove food dyes from his diet. Children who may have pancreatic damage due to autoantibodies or intestinal damage due to toxic peptides do not need the additional burden of food colors to inhibit any functional enzymes that remain active.

Table 1. Human Digestive Enzymes

Amylase-converts starches to sugar

Sucrase-converts sucrose to simple sugars

Lactase-converts milk sugar(lactose) to glucose and galactose

Nucleases-convert nucleic acids(DNA and RNA) to nucleotides

Lipase-converts fats(triglycerides) to fatty acids and glycerol

Phospholipase-converts phospholipids to fatty acids and
glycerophosphate

Trypsin-converts proteins to peptides

Chymotrypsin-converts proteins to peptides

Carboxypeptidase-converts peptides to amino acids

Aminopeptidase-converts peptides to amino acids

Cholesterol esterase-converts cholesterol esters to free cholesterol

Nucleosidase-converts nucleosides to nucleic acid bases

Phosphatase-converts organic phosphates to free phosphates

References

1. Dohan FC. Cereals and schizophrenia - data and hypothesis. Acta Psychiatr Scand.42:125,1966.
2. Dohan FC. Schizophrenia: possible relationship to cereal grains and celiac disease, In: S Sankar, editor. Schizophrenia: Current Concepts and Research. P.J.D Publications, Hicksville, NY pg 539, 1969.
3. Dohan FC The possible pathogenic effect of cereal grains in schizophrenia - Celiac disease as a model. Acta Neurol.31:195, 1976.
4. Dohan FC et al. Relapsed schizophrenics. More rapid improvement on a milk and cereal-free diet. Br. J. Psychiatry 115:595, 1969.
5. Kinivsberg, A et al. Dietary Intervention in Autistic Syndromes. Brain Dysfunction 3: 315-327,1990.
6. Reichelt K et al. Gluten, milk proteins and autism: dietary intervention effects on behavior and peptide secretion. Journal of Applied Nutrition 42: 1-11, 1990.
7. Reichelt K et al. Biologically active peptide-containing fractions in schizophrenia and childhood autism, Adv Biochem Psychopharmacol 28: 627-43, 1981.
8. Reichelt K et al. Probable etiology and possible treatment of childhood autism. Brain Dysfunction 4: 308-19, 1991.
9. Reichelt K et al. Nature and consequences of hyperpeptiduria and bovine casomorphins found in autistic syndromes. Developmental Brain Dysfunction 7: 71-85, 1994.
10. Reichelt K et al. Child autism: a complex disorder. Biological Psychiatry 21: 1279-90, 1986.
11. Reichelt K et al. The effect of gluten-free diet on urinary peptide excretion and clinical state in schizophrenia. Journal of Orthomolecular Medicine 5: 1223-39, 1990.
12. Shattock Pet al. Role of neuropeptides in autism and their relationships with classical neurotransmitters. Brain Dysfunction 3: 328-345,1990..
13. Shattock P., Lowdon G. Proteins, Peptides and Autism.- Part 2-. Implications for the Education and Care of People with Autism 4: 323-334, 1991.
14. Cade et al. The effect of dialysis and diet on schizophrenia. In: Psychiatry: A World Perspective. Volume 3.Stefanis et al ,editors. Elsevier Science Publishers. Pgs 494-500,1990.

15. Reicheit KI et al. Gluten, milk proteins and autism: Results of dietary intervention on behavior and urinary peptide secretion. J. Applied Nutrition 42: 1-11, 1990.
16. Reichelt KI et al Nature and consequences of hyperpeptiduria and bovine casomorphins found in autistic syndromes. Develop Brain Dysfunct 7: 71-85, 1994.
17. Reichelt KI et al Probable etiology and possible treatment of childhood autism. Brain Dysfunct 4: 308-319, 1991.
18. Shattock P et al Role of neuropeptides in autism and their relationships with classical neurotransmitters. Brain Dysfunct 3: 328-346, 1990.
19. Greco L. From the neolithic revolution to gluten intolerance: benefits and problems associated to the cultivation of wheat. Posted on an internet celiac disease discussion group by Luigi Greco M.D., Dept of Pediatrics, University of Naples, Naples, Italy. June 30,1995.
20. Torrey EF et al. .Endemic psychosis in western Ireland. Am J Psychiatry 141: 966-970, 1984.
21. Schmitz J. Coeliac disease in childhood. In Coeliac Disease. M Marsh, editor. Blackwell Scientific Publications. Oxford, England. pgs 19-22,1992
22. Hallert C et al Psychic disturbance in adult coeliac disease III. Reduced central monoamine metabolism and signs of depression. Scand J Gastroenterol 17:25-28,1982.
23. Gobbi G et al Coeliac disease, epilepsy and cerebral calcifications. The Lancet 340:439-443,1992.
24. Kinney HC et al. Degeneration of the central nervous system associated with coeliac disease. J Neurol Sci 5: 9-22, 1982.
25. Kagnoff M. Genetic basis of coeliac disease: role of HLA genes. In Coeliac Disease. .M Marsh, editor. Blackwell Scientific Publications. Oxford, England. Pgs 215-238, 1992.
26. Bovard, et al. Low-dose naltrexone effects on plasma chemistries and clinical symptoms in autism: a double-blind-placebo controlled study. Psychiatry Research 58: 191-20,1995.
27. Baker S. Detoxification and Healing. Keats Publishing, Inc., New Canaan, CT .pgs.85-92,1997.
28. Walker-Smith J and Andrews J..Alpha-1-antitrypsin, autism, and coeliac disease. The Lancet II: 883-884, 1972.
29. St Amand RP. Exploring the fibromyalgia connection. The Vulvar Pain Newsletter. Fall 1996, 4-6.

30. Teitelbaum J. From Fatigued to Fantastic. Avery Publishing Group, Garden City, NY, pgs 8,11,12,41-43,44,50,51,67, 1996.
31. Poddell R and Campbell S. Alternative therapies. Fibromyalgia Network.pg.8, 37th edition. April 1997.
32. William R. Gastrointestinal hormones. In: Textbook of Endocrinology. Sixth edition. WB Saunders Co, Philadelphia. R Williams, editor. pgs 697-698,1981.
33. Carlquist M et al. IRCS Med Science 13:217,1985.
34. Rowe K. S., Synthetic food coloring and hyperactivity: A double-blind crossover study. Aust Paediatr. J. 24: 143-47,1988.
35. Rowe K, S., Rose K. J. Synthetic food coloring and behavior: A dose response effect in a double-blind, placebo-controlled, repeated-measures study. Journal of Pediatrics 12: 691-698,1994.
36. Boris M., Mandel F. Food and additives are common causes of the attention deficit hyperactive disorder in children. Annals of Allergy 72: 462-68,1994.
37. Kroyer G. Artificial food colours as food additives. Effect of artificial food colours on the enzyme activity of alpha-amylase, pepsin, and trypsin. Nutrition (Ernahrung) 10: 465-467, 1986.

Frequently Asked Questions
by William Shaw Ph.D.

Do I have to get a physician's approval to get the urine sample tested for the organic acid test? Yes. A medical practitioner who is licensed to order urine testing in your state must approve the test order. Regulations vary from state to state so an approved medical practitioner could be a medical doctor(M.D.), osteopath(D.O.), nurse practitioner, chiropractor(D.C.), or naturopath (N.D.).

How often should I get my child re-tested? As a general rule, every three months may be satisfactory. However, I recommend retesting be done sooner if there is the child does not respond favorably by the end of one month of antifungal therapy since the yeast or bacteria might be resistant to the drugs used for treatment.

My physician says everyone has some yeast in their intestine. Why isn't everyone sick? The most important question is not whether yeast are present or not. The critical factors are the **quantity** of yeast and the **kinds** and **amounts of toxic products** they produce. Everyone in this society has carbon monoxide in their blood from auto exhaust and secondhand cigarette smoke and can tolerate a **low** value. When the amount of carbon monoxide increases, some individuals feel depressed, some have headaches, some develop muscle weakness, some feel tightness in the chest or angina, some experience nausea and vomiting, some become dizzy, some develop dimming of vision. As values further increase, symptoms may include convulsions, coma, respiratory failure, and death. Some individuals who recover from severe carbon monoxide poisoning may suffer residual neurological damage. Different people will respond with different symptoms to the same concentration of carbon monoxide.

Why is it surprising that exposure to a wide range of toxic yeast products at different times and at different ages might produce different symptoms? If I suggested that there were a carbon monoxide connection with all of the diverse symptoms associated with carbon monoxide exposure, no one would challenge me. The reason that the carbon monoxide connection is accepted is because carbon monoxide can be easily measured in blood. The toxic yeast byproducts were only recently discovered. As knowledge of them increases, acceptance of the yeast-related illnesses will increase.

My child is currently taking antibiotics now. Should I wait until after the antibiotics until I get tested? An assumption is frequently made that if the child has a significant yeast overgrowth of the intestine while on antibiotics that the yeast overgrowth will disappear when the antibiotics are stopped. However, this is not necessarily the case and the yeast overgrowth may even become worse especially if the person is on a high sugar, high carbohydrate diet. There is no evidence that the yeast overgrowth will spontaneously disappear on its own. Furthermore, the yeast overgrowth may be suppressing the immune system, preventing your child from recovering from the infection. The sooner the yeast problem is controlled, the sooner the vicious cycle of antibiotics and frequent infections may be broken.

Why should I get the organic acid test? Why don't I just start the nystatin? Some children with autism don't have the yeast problem but may have an overgrowth of the Clostridia bacteria. Treating these children with an antifungal could make the bacteria problem even worse. Also, if your child has the yeast problem, he will likely require major changes in his diet (and that of your family) and drug therapy for six months or longer. I think that it will be very difficult to make a commitment to the diet and drug therapy if you are nor even sure if your child has the yeast problem. Your child could have a yeast overgrowth with a drug-resistant yeast and if you don't do the testing beforehand, it would be difficult to know what is happening. Also, if the problem is severe, the yeast die-off reaction may be more severe and you may want to take additional steps to control the yeast before using antifungals. And it may be very difficult to get your doctor's cooperation for the prescriptions and insurance reimbursement if there is no evidence that the yeast problem even exists.

Where can I get the organic acid test done?
The organic acid test is available from:
The Great Plains Laboratory
9335 W 75 St
Overland Park, KS 66204
Phone: 913 341-8949   E-mail: GPL4U@aol.com

What other information will I get from the organic acid test?
The test evaluates all of the well-defined inborn errors of metabolism that can be detected with this technology called GC/MS such as PKU, maple-syrup urine disease, and many others. In addition, the organic acid test checks for many other abnormalities such as vitamin deficiencies and abnormal metabolism of catecholamines, dopamine, and serotonin. We currently quantitate 62 substances but also evaluate other substances that are not quantitated. Some of the other biochemical abnormalities common in autism include elevated uracil and elevated glutaric acid.

I already had the urine organic acid test done earlier by another lab. Can't I get the information from the earlier test? No. No other laboratory routinely analyzes the same compounds as this laboratory. Most test for the inborn errors of metabolism and that's all.

I have an HMO and they have to send the test to a certain lab. Is that OK? No. No other laboratory routinely analyzes the same compounds as this laboratory including Labcorp, SmithKline, or Mayo Medical laboratories. If you do not specify our laboratory, your child's urine will be sent to one of the large reference labs, which cannot accurately evaluate your child's condition. Most test for some of the inborn errors of metabolism and that's all.

FREQUENTLY ASKED QUESTIONS.

Do most insurance companies reimburse for your test? Yes, but we cannot guarantee how much (if any) reimbursement will be given. Most HMO's will pay but you may need some additional documentation to get payment. Use the information in this book to indicate to your HMO why no other labs are acceptable.

What about reimbursement for Medicaid and Medicare? We now are set up for Medicare but we do not yet have Medicaid authorization. Medicaid reimbursement has different regulations in each state which makes the paperwork to get established very difficult and time-consuming.

Can I test my infant who is having frequent ear infections or other frequent infections and who now seems "spacey" to see if they are developing the abnormal yeast byproducts? Yes. We provide tape-on bags to collect the urine from infants or children who are not potty trained.

My child has a large number of food allergies. Could this be related to the yeast problem? When should I get food allergies tested? Yeast can exist in two forms: a floating single cell form or a colony form. When yeast form colonies, they secrete enzymes such as phospholipase and proteases that break down the lining of the intestinal tract in order to attach the yeast colony to the intestinal wall. The holes made by the yeast produce a condition called leaky gut syndrome in which large undigested food molecules are absorbed into the bloodstream and elicit food allergies. Once the underlying yeast problem is controlled, the holes in the intestine will heal. Then less undigested food gets into the blood and the number of food allergies will decrease. I recommend that the allergy testing be done three months after the yeast problem is controlled so that you will have fewer allergies to deal with and therefore fewer foods to restrict from the diet. The yeast control diets are already complicated enough without further dietary restrictions and/or allergy desensitization shots.

142

Where can I get the food allergy test done?
The food allergy test, which is a blood test, is available from:
The Great Plains Laboratory
9335 W 75 St
Overland Park, KS 66204
Phone: 913 341-8949
Fax: 913 341-6207
Website:www.greatplainslaboratory.com
E-mail: GPL4U@aol.com

Do the food allergy tests at The Great Plains Laboratory check for wheat and dairy sensitivity?
Yes, both the basic and comprehensive food allergy tests check for wheat and dairy sensitivity. The basic food allergy test includes: gluten, casein, wheat, milk, oats, barley, rye, corn, cheddar cheese, and baker's yeast. The Comprehensive Food Allergy Panel identifies 92 foods (including wheat and dairy), allowing for recognition of virtually any food, which stimulates an immune response. Both of these test require a blood sample. We have found that children with autism have increased amounts of IgG antibodies to both wheat and dairy.

Do I need to do both food allergy tests on blood as well as the urine peptide test? Most children with autism have both elevated IgG antibodies to gluten and casein as well as elevated peptides in the urine. If the allergy test is positive, it is not essential to do the peptide test also. However, if the allergy tests for wheat and dairy were negative, it would be a good idea to do the peptide test.

How does the gluten/casein sensitivity common in autism and other diseases relate to the yeast problem or are they separate issues? There does appear to be some relationship between the two medical problems. Gluten and casein are proteins. Gluten is one of the major proteins in wheat. Casein is the major protein in milk and cheese but is an additive in a wide variety of other foods such as soup and TV dinners. If these proteins are absorbed before being

143

completely digested, the undigested pieces of protein enter the brain and attach to opiate receptors in the areas of the brain controlling language and other areas of the brain and impair the brain function. These pieces of protein called peptides are eventually eliminated in the urine where they are measured. The test is called the urinary peptide test.

Where can I get the urinary peptide test done?
    The Great Plains Laboratory
    9335 W 75 St
    Overland Park, KS 66204
    Phone: 913 341-8949
    Fax: 913 341-6207
    Website:www.greatplainslaboratory.com
    E-mail: GPL4U@aol.com

Where can I get SuperNuthera (a combination of vitamin B-6, magnesium, and other vitamins)?
This product is available from Kirkman Sales Co, PO Box 1009, Wilsonville, OR 97070. The phone no is 888-KIRKMAN or 503 694-1600. E-mail is kirkman@portweb.com. The company provides a sheet indicating the recommended dosage and ways to give it in the food.

Where can I get dimethylglycine? This product is available from the Kirkman Company. Their toll-free phone number is 888-KIRKMAN. From outside the U.S., the number is 503-694-1600.

Will drugs or any of these nutritional supplements interfere in the organic acid test? No, there is no interference from any known drug or supplement since the technology of mass spectrometry is the most accurate technology available. If your child takes vitamin supplements like vitamin C, then high concentrations of vitamin C will be detected in the urine. However, if antifungal supplements or drugs are taken before the test, you will probably get a lower value for the yeast byproducts. I advise you to get the test first so that you will know what the starting point is.

Will the use of nystatin interact adversely with other medications the patient is taking? Nystatin is not absorbed from the intestinal tract in any appreciable quantity unless **extremely** large doses are used. Therefore, there are no adverse reactions with drugs such as antiseizure medications, antidepressants such as Prozac or Elavil, or any other medications. If you use antifungals that are absorbed from the intestinal tract such as Lamisil, Sporanox, Diflucan, and Nizoral, then drug interactions must always be considered. Other drugs used simultaneously may be more potent or make the antifungal more potent when these latter drugs are used.

What about starting all of these therapies at the same time? I recommend that the antifungal therapy precede the allergy and gluten/casein testing since the yeast may be making the situation worse. As far as the supplements such as SuperNuthera and DMG, I recommend that they be tried out before or after the antifungal therapy so that you can know which therapies have been most beneficial to your child. If you do everything simultaneously, you won't be able to say which therapy is most beneficial.

Could there be adverse reactions to the food colors and flavors in the nystatin? Yes, that is a possibility. If that is the case, then you may have to use the pure nystatin powder and disguise it in food. One way to disguise it might be to combine it with fructo-oligosaccharides (FOS), an unusual sugar that cannot be utilized by the yeast, or with the herbal sweetener Stevia. FOS and Stevia are available in most large health food stores.

My child has a yeast infection in the genital or anal area. Does this indicate a yeast overgrowth of the intestinal tract? Yes, but it is impossible to know for sure without testing to confirm it.

If my child has no external signs of yeast such as thrush, or anal or genital rashes, could he still have the yeast problem? Yes, in many cases the **behavioral** abnormality is the only clue to the underlying yeast overgrowth of the intestinal tract.

Could intermittent low-grade fever be a symptom of yeast infection? Fever often accompanies yeast infection of the blood stream, which is termed systemic yeast infection. To test for yeast in the blood, you need to have a yeast culture and/or yeast antibody tests on blood. Remember that these tests may give a high percentage of false negative results. Your child may also have an intestinal yeast overgrowth as well.

My insurance company won't reimburse for any lab test dealing with autism. What can I do?
Many different diagnoses that accurately describe the medical condition of your child can be used for insurance reimbursement and many times reimbursement can be obtained when an appropriate diagnosis is used.

I don't have insurance and can't afford the price. Can you help me? We would be happy to work out an installment plan for you.

My child has a white coating of the mouth. Could this be a yeast problem? Yes. One of the most common yeasts in the intestine is Candida albicans. Albicans is a Latin word for white and a white coating of the tongue may very well be Candida.

What foods have Lactobacillus acidophilus in them? Yogurt is high in Lactobacillus acidophilus. The unflavored kind or plain is more highly recommended than the flavored because yeast may grow in the kind with fruit on the bottom. Some milk now also has acidophilus added. Just read the labels. However, most children with autism are sensitive to casein so the use of these sources may not be wise.

What kind of changes might I expect with the antifungal drug therapy? Results are highly variable but the most usual improvement noted is increased focus and concentration. Other

146

improvements may include increased and clearer vocalization, less stimming, decrease in aggressive or self-abusive behavior like head-banging, better sleep pattern, increased socialization, and more eye contact. Antifungal therapy may help individuals with normal or marginally elevated yeast metabolites but the percentage of those benefiting is lower than in individuals with high concentrations of these metabolites. Antifungal therapy is not usually a cure for autism by itself but may significantly improve the life of the child and his family. Antifungal therapy combined with other measures such as gluten and casein restriction, elimination of food allergies, and behavioral therapies have been successful in reversing autism in two cases in which these therapies were started at a very young age. Their accounts are included later in this book. Both of these successful families adopted very similar therapies completely independently of one another and started treatment about two years of age. Only large long-term studies will determine if these successes can be translated into successful therapies for the majority of children with autism.

What side-effects may be associated with the use of Flagyl or oral Vancomycin to control the overgrowth of Clostridia in the intestinal tract?
I have found that a new strain of Lactobacillus acidophilus called Culturelle is nearly as effective as drug treatment for the control of Clostridia and has minimal side effects. This strain is available at some drug stores and health food stores and can be purchased by phone from two nutritional companies in the United States:

Vitamin Research Products
800 877-2447 (Toll free)
775 884-1300

Klaire Laboratories
800 533-7255 (Toll free)
208 665-1882

The main side effects of drug therapy are probably due to the release of bacterial toxins as the Clostridia and other bacteria die. Side effects may be very severe and usually last from 2-10 days. *The child should be under close medical supervision while on this drug.* Side effects may include severe diarrhea, heart palpitations, extreme lethargy, and fever with drenching sweats. Talk to your physician about the use of adsorbent materials such as Bentonite and/or charcoal (available in pharmacies and health food stores and by phone from Vitamin Research Products) to adsorb the toxins since they may decrease the die-off reaction. The child should not start both the Flagyl/Vancomycin and antifungal therapy simultaneously because the combined die-off reaction may be too severe. Both Flagyl and Vancomycin will kill the friendly bacteria and it is very important to start Lactobacillus acidophilus as soon as the Flagyl/Vancomycin therapy stops or there may be a recurrence of the Clostridia or a yeast overgrowth. It is OK to continue nystatin during Flagyl/Vancomycin therapy. Just don't start the antifungal and antibacterial therapies simultaneously. Antifungal therapy and Culturelle can and should be started together.

My child has urinary tract infections or a vaginal yeast infection. Could the microorganisms in the urinary tract affect the test results? Microorganisms might contaminate the sample and lead to erroneous results if the urine stands too long at room temperature. We suggest that you freeze the sample right away to minimize any effects of such contamination since no new metabolites will form while frozen.

My child only eats bread, dairy products, cereal or pasta. How can I change his diet without starving my child? Parents have reported to me that their children may refuse the altered diet for three or four days and then give in and eat the new foods. I think that it would be wise to consult your physician and/or a dietitian before starting the diet. I do not think a **short** time without eating is harmful to most children but might be significant if your child has special medical problems like diabetes. Some children have not adjusted well to the gluten/casein free diet and may have to go back

148

to gluten or casein containing foods because of substantial weight loss on the restricted diets.

How long will my child need to be on the antifungal therapy? This is a difficult question that will only be answered by future research. I have personal knowledge that many children helped by antifungal therapy regress following the discontinuation of therapy even after six months to two years of antifungal treatment. This regression is virtually always accompanied by an increase in abnormal yeast metabolites. Discovering a way to overcome this resistance should be a national priority for future research. Call and write your congressmen in the House and Senate to inform them about this problem.

Which geographic areas does The Great Plains Laboratory serve? Testing can be done for people in any state, nation, or continent. None of the testing requires the person being tested to travel to the laboratory. Samples are transported by overnight delivery services.

What other testing is available from The Great Plains Laboratory?

- Immune deficiency profile
- Vitamin analysis
- Metals testing
- Essential fatty acids test
- Amino acids
- Antibodies to transglutaminase for celiac disease
- Stool testing for yeast and bacteria

TREATING YEAST IN CHILDREN WITH AUTISM:TYPICAL RESULTS OF ANTI-YEAST THERAPY

by Bruce Semon M.D. Ph.D.

Introduction

I am a child psychiatrist and nutritionist who has been treating children with autism using anti-yeast therapy for the past six years. What follows are some representative cases based on my clinical experience. The cases I have selected involve children ranging in age from 20 months old to eight years old, all of whom showed significant improvement in the first few weeks and months following anti-yeast therapy. Their names have been changed to protect their identities. As you will see, these cases (except in the case of the 20 month old) are not "cures," but they do show the possibility for improvement in autistic children. Nor is the anti-yeast therapy intended to be the only therapy that a child receives. I firmly believe, however, that use of the diet and nystatin treatment vastly improves the child's baseline physical functioning, eliminating headaches, stomach and gut pain, and for some children, pain in hands and feet. By using the anti-yeast therapy, these children have the potential to achieve more in their lives and profit more from the other therapies and education that their parents offer to them.

Case histories

JON

Jon is a 6 year old boy who had been diagnosed as autistic at age 3. He presented for aggressive behavior toward teachers and parents. Mother stated (on a follow-up visit) that he was hitting her so much that she was black and blue. He also hit his teachers regularly. He was kicking, biting and head butting, more so when tired or at transitions. He had lost language at age 18 months but some language had come back and he could use about 50 words. Jon had a history of head banging but this symptom had improved after a second set of ear tubes were placed.

Jon had had ear infections since age 1 with four sets of ear tubes being placed. He had chronic loose stools, eczema on his back and he was not toilet trained.

He had been placed on Mellaril before coming to see me due to violence against teachers. The Mellaril did little at low doses (10 mg). Higher doses were too sedating. He was off all dairy.

At the initial visit, Jon did not answer any questions and made little eye contact.

Jon was started on the anti-yeast diet and nystatin. Jon returned six weeks later. His mother reported that his language had blossomed and his aggression had diminished from being constant to being only at transition times and at these times, the aggression was less. His sleep was improved and mother had stopped his Mellaril.

Jon returned three and a half months later. He was continuing to improve. He was now toilet trained for urine during the day. He was not hitting anyone in the family and he was interacting with his brother.

Jon has been treated for about nine months now and he has continued to improve. At each visit he has more speech and language. He also benefited from the addition of a low dose of naltrexone (explained below) daily.

ANDREW

Andrew is a 2 and a half year old boy who presented with autism. He had stopped responding to his name at 15 months and had stopped playing with toys. His hearing was tested at 18 months and was fine. At 20 months he was referred by a child development

151

specialist to a "birth to three program" for occupational and speech therapies. He was over active. He also had rashes, eczema and loose stools. At the first visit, he ran throughout the room and did not speak. Parents stated that he could vocalize at the 12 month level. Andrew was started on the anti-yeast diet and nystatin.

He returned four weeks later and his mother reported he was "more with it". School people told mother that Andrew was sitting longer with better attention. His bowel movements had firmed up. On exam, Andrew was vocalizing more and he sat in one spot on the floor with a pen and paper. He was no longer overactive.

JOSHUA
Joshua is a 20 month old boy who presented for being "crazy" the last few months, ripping things apart and being destructive. He was up four times per night screaming and yelling. His mother noted that he had a high tolerance for pain. He had had frequent antibiotics for ear infections which had sometimes caused diarrhea and he was plagued by frequent hives. His mother reported that he could understand speech but his expressive speech was behind and that he had lost some words. He had been an easy infant. On exam he was unhappy and unsmiling.

Joshua was started on diet and nystatin (but continued on milk). Two weeks later, his mother noted a huge improvement in how he felt. He no longer screamed at night. His activity level was lower. I noted that in my office he was smiling and playing with toys. A month later his mother reported that his speech had improved, that more words were coming and he was putting two words together.

BARBARA
Barbara is a three year old girl who presented for speech delay. She had seemed normal until about 18 months when she had a severe vaginal yeast infection. This infection continued for six months. At that time her speech stopped developing. At the interview her parents reported she could say a few words. I could not discern any

intelligible speech. She was unhappy and screamed occasionally and ran around.

She was started on diet and nystatin. She came back three weeks later. Her parents reported that she was attending better at school and could sit for longer periods of time. She was having fewer temper tantrums and was saying 4 to 5 words per day. In my office she said "mama" and smiled. She played with a toy and was not hyperactive.

STEVEN

Steven is a three year old boy who was reported to be normal until age 2. At 25 months he began screaming and arching his back. Speech was noted to be delayed. Before his third birthday, he was diagnosed as autistic. He had constant loose stools. He had skin rashes until his parents took milk away a few weeks before the interview. He had a history of milk intolerance with vomiting and diarrhea.

At his first appointment, Steven had no meaningful speech and he would not sit down. He moved all over the room.

He was started on the anti-yeast diet and nystatin. He returned four weeks later and his parents reported that he was more verbal and was showing some control. He was having normal bowel movements. I observed Steven walk around the room, rather than run. He was responsive to his parents and he smiled and talked appropriately several times with his parents.

ANN

Ann is a two and a half year old girl who had not developed much speech. She was making little eye contact and was screaming regularly. She had already been diagnosed as autistic by the time she was first seen. At the time of the first interview, she had no meaningful speech, although she occasionally said single words spontaneously.

153

She was started on the anti-yeast diet. Her mother noticed an improvement in speech after only four days on the diet. She asked for juice, using the word. She was put on nystatin at this time. Within a few days, she was putting two words together meaningfully. By six weeks she appeared at my office naming body parts and saying "I want ..." on a regular basis. She had been involved in intensive in-home applied behavior analysis therapy for several months preceding the anti-yeast therapy. Her therapists expressed amazement at her progress once she started the diet and nystatin.

DAVID
David is an eight year old boy who had not developed language by age 3. He received a diagnosis of autism at age 6. He had been in an applied behavioral analysis discrete trial program for a year when first seen. He had made some progress in the behavioral program but his speech was unclear and he would only occasionally speak spontaneously. At the time he was seen, he responded to "What is your name?" in a whisper, which I could not understand. He otherwise was non-responsive and made little eye contact.

He was seen six weeks later after being put on diet and nystatin and his mother reported that there was more spontaneous speech. He could name things more completely. Before, if a request was made to touch his father, he would touch anyone. Now he would respond by touching his father. At this visit, he talked with his mother about going to eat. His mother told me that he had been taught such phrases in behavioral therapy. What struck me was that I could understand this time what he was saying. His speech was much more intelligible.

Diet and antifungal treatment.
I use a combination of a special diet and the anti-yeast drug nystatin to treat children with autism. Dr. Shaw describes nystatin elsewhere in the book, but I will review it briefly. Nystatin is a non-absorbed chemical compound which kills the yeast Candida albicans. There

154

are no toxic side effects from nystatin and nystatin can be taken for long periods of time. Although nystatin is a potent anti-fungal medication, it only reaches its maximum effectiveness when combined with a special diet. Before describing the specific treatment, including the steps to achieving the diet and directions for using nystatin, I will describe how I arrived at the diet.

Origin of the treatment

I began treating autistic children in 1991. My first patient was my son. He had developed normally until age two and a half and from age two and a half to age four his development slowed. From age four to four and a half, he lost most of the function he had. He lost most of his speech and he lost his fine motor skills. He also began screaming much of the day and he was awake for three to five hours every night. No doctor had helped us. We had taken him to some of the best in the Washington, D.C. area.

But, on this early morning day in January 1991, there was to be an insight. My wife was sitting up with our son, as she had been each night for the previous month, during his waking hours of two to seven AM. He was staring at something, saying "the lights, the lights." All of a sudden, it hit her: our son was experiencing a migraine. He had had a peanut butter sandwich for bedtime snack, a food known to cause migraines, and this was it.

I grew up with a strong family history of migraines, and my wife Lori suffered from them occasionally. Both of us experience what is called an "aura" before the pounding pain of the headache: flashing lights, dizzying patterns dancing before their eyes. My father had had several migraines a week when he was in college, until he read an article in a magazine, stating that if one avoided certain foods, the migraines would decrease in frequency. My father avoided these foods and his migraines diminished considerably. The list included such foods as chocolate, pickles, salad dressing, bacon, alcoholic beverages, nuts, and aged cheese. I have since seen from other

155

headache clinics similar lists of foods to avoid. We decided to take away from our son a small list of foods known to cause migraines.

We took away chocolate, peanut butter, orange juice, aged cheeses, and some other foods. The improvement was immediate. Our son looked and acted as if a weight had been lifted from his head. Two years later , at the age of six, his headaches completely disappeared unless, by mistake, he ate something we knew was bad for him. His tactile defensiveness completely disappeared, too. At the beginning, however, we did not know how far we had to go.

After taking away several foods, we began to see the onset of separate headaches, when we would make a mistake and give him foods we should not have, or when he would eat something that we learned later caused problems. We saw the headaches set in about three times a week instead of being chronic. This change only took a few days to see.

Our son's symptoms of what we now know to be autism also began to diminish. He no longer screamed all the time. His behavior improved. He seemed more with us, more engagable. If he accidentally got into the wrong foods, the screaming began again.

In the first few weeks, we noted that not all the screaming went away. We tried to determine what foods were still causing problems. At the time, I was a research fellow at the National Cancer Institute, in a laboratory concerned with nutrition and cancer. Using the vast resources of the National Institutes of Health, I began researching what might be causing our son's problems. Based on my research, we decided to eliminate vinegar, a staple of our lives. Our son was a kid who ate ketchup (a significant source of vinegar) on everything, including popcorn, and loved Asian food, sprinkled with rice vinegar. Again, we saw immediate improvement, but knew that we were still missing something. I had no idea what the relationship was among the foods on the original list. Around this time, we also found that something in children's pain relievers were causing the headaches to last longer than necessary. We do not know exactly what that substance is, suspecting many of the additives, including aspartame (NutraSweet) but we do know that switching to pure acetaminophen, and later to pure ibuprofen, considerably shortened the life of the headaches. Life for our son improved considerably, but he still suffered considerable pain and still continued to lose his speech. We heard his last real word for five years in March, 1991.

We got our next break about eight weeks later with the Jewish holiday of Passover. For this holiday, all food containing yeast, leavening and fermented foods are eliminated. This holiday lasts eight days. By about three days into Passover, our son was clearly improving again. He appeared much more comfortable. By this time his speech was gone, so we were dependent on how he looked and behaved. His behavior had improved to the point that he was accepted into a special education speech and language summer program.

After those eight days, though, our son deteriorated. The screaming intensified. We had no idea what had happened. What was in the food that we were now giving again? We had many snack foods from the health food store, all supposedly healthy. I read the labels and the one ingredient that I did not recognize was "barley malt." What was barley malt?"

Barley malt is a byproduct of beer manufacturing. Yeast is mixed with barley to split the barley. Anytime that yeast is allowed to degrade a food, the process is called fermentation. The liquid part of this fermentation mixture goes off to be made into beer and the solid part is a nice sweet mash, which is then called barley malt or malt extract or simply malt. Malt is a fermented product.

What was the relationship among items on the list? Vinegar is literally spoiled wine, so it comes from fermentation. Barley malt is clearly a product of fermentation. But what was chocolate and what about nuts? I went back to my research to find out. I knew about

157

certain cancer causing chemicals in food. One is called aflatoxin, a potent cancer causing chemical found in small amounts in peanuts. Aflatoxin comes from a fungus, called Aspergillus, which contaminates the peanut plant. Chocolate beans are dried with a fungus. Now the relationship among the items on the migraine headache list became clear. They are all products of yeast fermentation or of fungus contamination. Yeast and fungus contain many similar biochemical pathways, although in general, fungus produce poisons much more potent than yeast can produce.

Something produced by yeast and fungus was wreaking havoc on our son. We needed to know what it was. My lab happened to be at the same site where the US Army has its germ warfare labs and there are several people there who work in specialized fermentation. One research group was right down the hall. They got me started. The first chemical I found that I thought might be causing a problem is called acetol. Acetol is a skin irritant and an eye irritant (probably known from research to see if it could be used in cosmetics). Acetol is in vinegar. Acetol is also found in maple syrup and in cheese. I thought I was making progress. I had found something toxic in vinegar which may be causing problems. The identification of what foods could cause problems for our son was becoming easier. As I identified what foods contain which chemicals and we took these foods away, our son improved, albeit slowly.

Once we eliminated barley malt, vinegar, and yeast, the improvement was dramatic. We began to see the light at the end of the tunnel, but little did we know how long that tunnel was. At the time, simply decreasing his headaches to once a week or once every two weeks, and seeing his behavior improve and his autistic symptoms decrease were major victories. We had turned the tide before we lost our son Avi altogether. He was coming back to us, very, very slowly.

We found, though, that foods were not the only key to our son's puzzle. We were introduced to a book called The Yeast Connection by Dr. William Crook, about people who have problems with something called Candida albicans. We found a similar list of foods recommended for avoidance. Could it be that our son had a yeast problem? Certainly no professional had ever mentioned this, but certainly no professional had been able to help us to this point. We decided to try treating him with a non-toxic medication called nystatin. Nobody would prescribe it for us, but fortunately, I have a medical license.

Within a few days of starting on the nystatin, our son made a year's growth in playground development. He got off the swings and climbed jungle gyms, went down slides, and began to look like a four year old kid again. He still did not get his speech back, but he was better able to function.

Over the next few years, we were able to refine the diet, gradually eliminating all fermented foods, and, in addition, eliminating casein, gluten and eggs. He has remained on nystatin. He is a completely different child than he was in 1991, when he sat for hours screaming or spinning on a swing, making emotional contact with virtually nobody. He is a happy, healthy child, has been able to tolerate a regular classroom at school since first grade, and began to talk again with the help of significant intensive applied behavioral analysis therapy at home. Any deviations from the diet bring back autistic symptoms to some extent; some foods are worse than others. Screaming, aggression, including scratching, kicking, and biting; non-cooperation; lack of progress in school--all of these remind us what life would be like with untreated autism.

I have since treated several other children, only some of whose cases I noted above, with excellent results. My son, and these children, responded well to being treated with a combination of diet changes and the taking of nystatin. Why did this regimen help, and what is this regimen?

Although it seemed at first that the diet recommended in The Yeast Connection could have saved us a lot of work, and perhaps could have saved our son's speech had we discovered the book sooner, we found that it did not answer the questions that our son posed to us. Had we followed that diet, which at the time was the standard for anti-yeast diets, our son still would have been eating many of the foods that we know cause him, and many others, tremendous problems.

The main difference is that in diets based on The Yeast Connection recommend eating a great deal of meat and eliminating most carbohydrates. The reason for this is that Dr. Orion Truss, who first published the idea that Candida albicans can cause health problems in The Missing Diagnosis, observed that yeast grow well in carbohydrate and not particularly well in protein. Therefore, he reasoned, one should remove carbohydrate from the diet so the yeast doesn't grow as well. Subsequently, the standard anti-yeast diet recommends eliminating all sugar and yeast from bread and substitute more meat and fish. However, in my practice, I have found that this diet is not optimal. The human body is not as simple as a test tube nor is the human diet as simple as culture media for yeast in a Petri plate.

In my practice I have seen many frustrated patients with many symptoms, ranging from autism to chronic fatigue syndrome to arthritis and fibromyalgia to multiple sclerosis, who had followed these recommendations, eliminating sugar and bread from their diets, probably increased meat and fish, and enjoying few results. The reason for their lack of results is not their lack of effort, but the fact that the main dietary yeast offenders (vinegar and barley malt) had been left in their diets. In fact, most of the anti-yeast and allergy related cookbooks have vinegar as a staple food and recommend a diet high in animal protein, which is problematic, and nuts, which are thoroughly mold contaminated. Our experience with our son and with my other patients is that this recommendation of using meat and eliminating almost all carbohydrate is wrong.

160

When yeast spoils meat, the toxic chemicals formed are worse than those formed by yeast in carbohydrate. In addition, chicken and pigs are fed cottonseed meal which is contaminated with a fungus called Aspergillus. I speculate that the animals store in their fat the Aspergillus poisons. This technique is a common way for animals to handle poisons. It is possible that storing the fungus poisons is one reason why yeast sensitive patients should not eat large amounts of meat. Meat from the right sources and in small quantities is acceptable on the anti-yeast diet, however. We have found that the easiest meat to eat is veal. Cattle receive less or no cottonseed meal (other feeds are cheaper) and there is little time for any poisons to accumulate in the calf prior to slaughter. We found with our son and again with many patients since that a diet of complex carbohydrate is the best for yeast problems.

I left the National Cancer Institute in August of 1991. A month later I began treating patients for Candida albicans using the dietary principles I developed while working with our son and using the non-toxic anti-yeast drug nystatin. I found that I could treat supposedly untreatable conditions such as autism, psoriasis, eczema, chronic fatigue syndrome, multiple sclerosis, chronic vaginal yeast infections, attention deficit disorder and refractory depression. These conditions all respond to treatment of Candida albicans.

I also found that other children with autism responded well to the same treatment as I had given my son. I have never had a child not respond to the treatment for yeast, when the parents make an effort to follow the treatment. In fact, the improvement seen with this treatment regimen is often dramatic. The best explanation for the results for the children described above is that Candida produces compounds which affect the brain and reduction of Candida by diet and nystatin leads to fewer of these chemicals reaching the brain which leads to a reduction in autistic symptoms.

TYPICAL RESULTS OF ANTI-YEAST THERAPY

The medical regimen: diet plus nystatin
An overview of the schedule for treatment is helpful to understand that this treatment is a long term process, and a long term treatment. The first three to four months are spent adjusting to the appropriate diet and level of nystatin. After that, other medications may be introduced, if appropriate.

Schedule for treatment:

Preceding treatment, you may wish to have urine testing done using Dr. Shaw's testing. If so, first see the doctor; order testing, then at return visit, assuming yeast problem, start the following:

Week 1: Doctor's Appointment
Start diet, Stage I, for 3 days, on 4th day: start nystatin

Week 2: Continue diet Stage I; continue nystatin up to the prescribed maximum dose.

Week 3: Doctor's Appointment to help with questions, assess progress. Continue diet Stage I. Continue on nystatin.

Weeks 4, 5: Continue diet Stage I; continue nystatin. By week 5 patient should be at full dose.

Week 6: Doctor's appointment. Start diet Stage II if appropriate.

Week 7-9: Continue diet Stage II; continue nystatin.

Week 10: Doctor's appointment; assess progress to determine whether to go to Stage III. Continue diet and nystatin.

Weeks 11, 12, 13: Continue following doctor's instructions.

Week 14:   Doctor's appointment to assess progress; at this point, patient may consider retesting urine, and/or   doing allergy testing for food allergies.

After this point, patient should return to the doctor to evaluate any testing results.   Other medications such as naltrexone may be considered.   Patient should continue on the prescribed treatment plan, returning in 4 weeks, then 6 weeks, then 8 weeks, then every 3 months for the first year.

THE DIET

Changing diet is extremely difficult for everyone, including our family.   As my wife often says, if she didn't live with the doctor, she would have a much harder time sticking with the program.   Food has social and emotional contexts as well as nutritional value.   To change diet, you need to have a good reason.   A chance to allow someone with autism to live a "normal" life, to me, is the best reason. Autism is a lifelong condition that can cause tremendous suffering, not only to the person who has autism, but to the person's entire family.   Recognizing these problems, I have tried to make dietary change simpler and more gradual by dividing it into stages.   Some children respond so well to the first stage of the diet that further adjustments are unnecessary.   Other children need more intervention.

STAGE I: Eliminate:

- **barley malt**-a by-product of beer making found in many cereals, crackers, breads and bagels and in many health food snacks. **Substitute: similar foods that do not contain barley malt.** For example, many breakfast cereals contain barley malt, but others do not   (most General Mills cereals, such as Cheerios and Kix, do not contain barley malt).   Similarly, some brands of pretzels, graham crackers, etc., contain barley malt, but others do not.   When shopping read labels carefully and **avoid** anything with **malt** in it.
- **vinegar-** is literally spoiled wine and is very concentrated in toxic yeast products.   Vinegar is found in virtually all condiments,

including ketchup and mustard, sauces and salad dressings. **Substitute: freshly squeezed lemon juice; tomato paste for ketchup**

- **chocolate** - Chocolate has two problems. Chocolate is dried with a fungus. Chocolate also contains a chemical compound which is similar to one of the yeast products. Unfortunately, there is no substitute for chocolate.
- **pickles and pickled foods such as herring, tomatoes, and pickled peppers (yes, there are such things)**
- **alcoholic beverages and non-alcoholic beer**
- **aged cheese**
- **soy sauce (substitute: sea salt)**
- **Worcestershire sauce**
- **anything containing cottonseed oil** (The cottonseed plant is often mold contaminated and the products of the mold end up in the cottonseed oil.)
- **nuts and peanuts**
- **apples and apple products**
- **grapes and grape products**
- **coffee**
- **Hot dogs, salami, and other processed meats containing nitrates and/or nitrites. "Natural" hot dogs can still be eaten at this point.**

These foods must be eliminated for 3-4 days prior to starting nystatin according to the schedule listed below. Continue the diet and nystatin for 4-6 weeks, then consult the doctor to consider whether going to Stage II.

These foods are the most concentrated in toxic yeast and fungal chemicals. Without eliminating these foods, nystatin will not work well and children will not get much better, even if they are given nystatin. Apples and grapes contain yeast byproducts that Dr. Shaw has isolated, and in my clinical experience, wreak havoc in a child sensitive to yeast.

TYPICAL RESULTS OF ANTI-YEAST THERAPY

STAGE II:

Eliminate all of the above, plus:

- **Baked goods containing yeast, including bread. Substitute: non-yeast bread (Dr. Semon's recipe for Delicious and Nutritious Whole Wheat Bread), but not sourdough bread (this too is highly fermented)**
- **corn and rye** - corn and rye are both highly contaminated with mold
- **vanilla extract** - highly fermented; contains alcohol
- **Dried fruits and raisins**
- **Concentrated fruit juice**
- **monosodium glutamate (MSG) and aspartame (NutraSweet)**
- **Maple syrup**
- **Bananas**
- **Cut back on all meat and fish except veal**
- **Spices such as cinnamon, dried mustard, curry powder, chili powder, cayenne pepper. (All green herbs, fresh or dried, are acceptable.)**
- **Mushrooms**
- **Soda drinks**
- **Cooking oils except safflower oil, soy oil, and olive oil. Canola oil is acceptable unless a child reacts badly to it.**
- **Sugar, including both white and brown. Substitute: unprocessed honey**
- **Margarine** - margarine has a host of problems. The human body does not metabolize it. Butter, a natural product, is much better for the body, even though it contains cholesterol. **Substitute: butter**
- **Buttermilk**

Patients should follow Stage II for a period of four to six weeks, continuing with the nystatin. After consultation with the doctor, they should consider moving on to Stage III, eliminating gluten and casein (dairy and all grains containing gluten, including wheat, barley, oats,

165

rye, and others.) Note that there is little information on what is in eggs. However, they do seem to stimulate food allergies. Any child with a chronic skin problem should have eggs removed to see if this helps with the skin problem.

STAGE III: eliminating gluten and casein

ELIMINATE all of the above, plus:

- **All foods containing milk protein--butter is acceptable.** Butter in small amounts is acceptable because butter is a fat which does not contain the milk protein casein.
- **All foods containing gluten, including wheat, oats, barley, rye**

The transition to a casein/gluten free diet is described elsewhere in this book by Lisa Lewis Ph.D. The difference between her description and my description is that the diet I recommend also eliminates yeast products and fermented products, so some gluten-free grains, such as corn, which are acceptable on a gluten-free diet, are not acceptable on a yeast free diet.

Patients should follow Stage III for four to six weeks, continuing with the nystatin, then consult the doctor. At this time, they might move on to Stage IV. In my experience, only the most severe cases of sensitivity need to continue to Stage IV. At this point, patients might consider retesting urine by Dr. Shaw, and at this point, they could consider testing for food sensitivity using immunological testing.

STAGE IV. ELIMINATE all of the above, plus:

- **Melons**
- **Grapefruit and oranges**
- **All meat except veal**
- **Yellow onions (leeks are acceptable)**

166

- **Fruits except very fresh fruit in season, such as berries**
- **canned goods** - canned goods often contain mold contaminated food, because the canning process does not allow for discrimination
- **fish**

ALLOWABLE FOODS on Stage IV: WHAT <u>CAN</u> WE EAT?

In my practice, I have found that the basic diet, and the best foods to eat, which should form the staple part of your diet unless you have documented food allergies or sensitivities to them, are the following:

- **Beans (kidney, black, garbanzo, Navy, etc.)**
- **Brown rice (long grain, short grain)**
- **Tomatoes**
- **Potatoes**
- **Herbs (marjoram, dill, basil, oregano, etc.), including seeds from herbs (dill seed, celery seed, etc.)**
- **Butter**
- **Safflower oil**
- **Green Vegetables (zucchini, broccoli, celery, spinach, kale, lettuce, etc.)**
- **Roots, such as parsnips**
- **Fresh fruit in season, especially berries (you can freeze berries in season for use later in the year)**
- **Unprocessed honey**

Some people choose to stick with only these foods, rather than eliminating everything else slowly, but I do not advise this. Most children will not end up at Stage IV. You may be able to continue eating a variety of foods not on this list. You don't want to lose that opportunity!

Even if this restrictive list is where you ultimately will end up, and this is where we have ended up after several years, I do not recommend starting with it, because the change is too drastic for most families, including my own. You will end up failing your child because you simply cannot enforce the diet. It is much better to implement the diet over the course of several months in a way that enables you to stick with it. After all, you are the gatekeeper for your child's health and the role model for your children.

Is this treatment worth the family's aggravation for the sake of my child?
This diet is inconvenient. Remember, though, how inconvenient untreated autism is that led you to seek medical help: all of the nights of screaming, the extreme sensitivities to touch and chemical substances, and the behavioral issues, all of which I have seen improve more rapidly using the anti-yeast treatment than on any non-biological therapy. Changing diet is relatively easy compared with a life in agony. To my knowledge, I repeat, all children I have treated with the above diet (that is excluding foods containing toxic yeast chemicals) and nystatin have improved. I have never had a parent come back to me saying they followed the diet and the nystatin, and the child failed to respond. This response is totally different from the response to many of the medications I have prescribed for autistic children in my psychiatric practice.

The tragedy in waiting to decide about whether you are ready to tackle this diet is that autistic children respond best the earlier and sooner the intervention. The longer you wait, the more function the children lose. All children I have treated who still have some speech left, gain more speech with this treatment. Once children have lost their speech entirely, there is less hope that speech can come back.

Using nystatin
I have heard often from people that they gave nystatin and it was not helpful. I have found nystatin to be of little benefit without the diet, so these stories do not surprise me. However, the dose of nystatin is also important.

Dr. Shaw writes elsewhere in this book about the problem of "die-off". That is when nystatin kills the yeast, it is similar to bursting a water balloon with a pin. The yeast are like the balloons: once pricked, they release all of their contents at once, which are these same toxic chemicals that make the patient feel bad to begin with. The person can feel worse temporarily. Nystatin can cause some temporary nausea when it is first started but this nausea is not "die-off". This nausea will go away. To avoid "die-off", Dr. Shaw suggests starting the nystatin dose very low and increasing the dose over a week. His final dose is much lower than I recommend to patients.

I also recommend starting with a small dose of nystatin, increasing gradually. Using this strategy combined with the diet, I have never seen this "die-off" with autistic children. When the diet is combined with nystatin, I believe that the yeast do not grow back. This problem of "die-off" and whether "die-off" can be prevented with the diet described here needs to be tested further.

Another possibility can be seen from some of Dr. Shaw's test results. He has shown that giving nystatin alone can result in an increase in bacterial byproducts found in the urine. He suggests that clearing out the yeast may leave room for bacteria to grow and make toxic byproducts. He suggests treatment for the bacteria also.

I suspect that my suggested nystatin dosages combined with my suggested diet may prevent the overgrowth of these harmful bacteria but further testing will be needed to confirm this idea.

I prescribe the nystatin powder, which is the most effective form of nystatin. I recommend mixing the powder with a small amount of unprocessed honey, enough to dissolve the nystatin (about 1/2 teaspoon). For convenience, you can mix one day's worth of doses at once in well washed film canisters, and store them in the refrigerator. These are hermetically sealed. You can send these premixed doses with your child to school. Use a chopstick to mix, and a baby spoon to scoop out the nystatin from the film canister.

The important thing is to get the nystatin down to your child's digestive tract, not have it all over their faces, shirts, and your floor. Especially for the first few days, use anything possible that is acceptable on Stage I of the diet to mix your nystatin, including ice-cream, orange juice, syrup, butter: that is, anything. Once your child begins to associate taking nystatin with feeling better, giving it will be easier for you, and you can switch to honey.

For those who cannot in any manner get a child to take the nystatin, it does come premixed in a sugar syrup. This is not optimal, as it is much more dilute than the powdered nystatin and is full of sugar.

The truly tough (adults) can put the powder on their tongue and wash it down. Nystatin powder can be pushed into capsules. Nystatin also comes in pill form.

Dosing schedule:

Notes: An eighth teaspoon of nystatin is about 500,000 units. When "twice in the day" is recommended, that means spaced evenly--e.g., take one at breakfast and one at dinner. Three times a day might be breakfast, lunch and dinner. I recommend taking nystatin after you have eaten something, to avoid possible nausea.

****Week 1

Day 1   1/16 teaspoon once in the day
Day 2   1/16 teaspoon twice in the day
Day 3   1/16 teaspoon three times in the day
Day 4   1/16 teaspoon four times in the day
Days 5, 6 and 7   1/16 teaspoon four times in the day

****Week 2

Day 1 1/8 teaspoon once in the day, 1/16 three times
Day 2 1/8 teaspoon twice in the day, 1/16 two times
Day 3 1/8 teaspoon three times in the day, 1/16 1 time
Day 4 1/8 teaspoon four times in the day
Days 5, 6 and 7: 1/8 teaspoon four times in the day

***Week 3 (First alternative)-

Day 1 1/4 teaspoon once in the day, 1/8 three times
Day 2 1/4 teaspoon twice in the day, 1/8 two times
Day 3 1/4 teaspoon three times in the day, 1/8 one time
Day 4 1/4 teaspoon four times in the day
Days 5, 6 and 7 1/4 teaspoon four times in the day

****Week 3 (Second alternative)-

Day 1 1/8 tsp. 5 times per day
Day 2 1/8 tsp. 6 times per day
Day 3 1/8 tsp. 7 times per day
Day 4 1/8 tsp. 8 times per day
Days 5,6,7, continue at 1/8 tsp. 8 times per day

****Two alternatives are listed for week 3 because many people have a hard time taking 1/4 tsp. at a time. Smaller amounts are easier to take.

Other anti-fungal medications
There are both over-the-counter remedies and herbs and other prescription medications that kill yeast. Dr. Shaw has written about them in this book. In my experience, nystatin is the most effective and least toxic means to fight yeast. The problem with the other medicines is that they are absorbed and have toxic side effects. Both Diflucan and Nizoral can affect the liver. Thus they can only be

given for a short period of time. Once they are stopped the yeast can grow back.

Nystatin is a totally natural substance that pharmaceutical companies have harnessed and made a prescription medication. Nystatin has been available longer than 35 years. According to all of the literature on it, including the standard PDR (Physicians Desk Reference) nystatin has no known toxic side effects. Apart from some possible nausea during the first few days, there really are no side effects from nystatin. It can be taken indefinitely because it is not absorbed into the blood stream. Nystatin acts only in the intestinal tract. Autistic children must be treated for a long time to allow their brains to recover and develop as much as possible. Treatment for a few weeks is not sufficient. The only drug which can be used for long periods of time is nystatin. My son, for example, has been on nystatin for more than six years, with no ill effects.

How long does treatment last?
Parents are accustomed to treating problems for a few days or weeks, then stopping treatment. Usually other people, including some doctors, encourage them to cease treatment to see what happens. This is unfortunate, because many people never resume treatment, even when they see their child's behavior deteriorate. They assume that the treatment did not work.

When treatment is stopped, so do the gains made while on the treatment, and, if you are unlucky, your child may lose all of the gains over time. Dr. Shaw has tested children for whom nystatin doses are simply reduced and he has shown that toxic yeast chemicals in the urine increase when the nystatin dose is reduced. Unfortunately, the yeast come back when nystatin is stopped.

Anti-yeast treatment is a long-term treatment, and it is effective in combating autism.

How does the anti-yeast treatment compare with standard psychiatric medication for children with autism?
I am a child psychiatrist and have prescribed many medications for children with autism, including Clonidine, Ritalin and others. **Not one of the children on any of these medications has done as well as any of the children on the anti-yeast diet and nystatin.**

One medication to consider adding to the diet and nystatin treatment is naltrexone. This is most effective when combined with the Stage III diet (anti-yeast and free of casein and gluten). Naltrexone blocks opioids in the brain. I said above, the opioids from milk and wheat may slow the brain down. At low doses, naltrexone may help clear the brain of opioids which have already gotten into the brain. Unfortunately, the doses of naltrexone which have been used in academic studies have been too high, and the studies show that sometimes naltrexone has the opposite effect of what is intended. These studies also have not combined use of naltrexone with elimination of dairy products and wheat. In my clinical experience, the best results are obtained from naltrexone if dietary opioids are also eliminated (that is, dairy and wheat), and using a very low dose of 3 to 6 milligrams per day (the pills are 50 milligrams each). The doses used in studies have been 25 to 50 milligrams per day, and in my experience, those high doses can cause children to have increased pain and headaches.

Are Vitamins Necessary?
I do not recommend any vitamins until the Stage III diet, or the last stage prescribed for your child, has been in effect for several months. The recommended diet contains all of the vitamins a child needs. Many picky eaters become good eaters after eliminating the foods they were eating that were causing stomach and other problems. Eliminating toxic yeast chemicals from the diet, eliminating casein and gluten, and treating intestinal yeast are the first priorities. After six months of continuous treatment, parents may wish to experiment with vitamin mixtures, described elsewhere in this book.

173

Are there any other natural substances to treat autism?
First, remember that although nystatin is a prescription medication, it is a totally natural substance.

There are many other possible substances advanced to treat autism. Again, I do not recommend trying any until the Stage III diet, or the most restrictive diet prescribed for your child, has been in place for at least six months, and with the consultation of your supervising doctor. Eliminating toxic yeast chemicals from the diet, eliminating casein and gluten, and treating intestinal yeast are the first priorities. After six months of continuous treatment, parents may wish to experiment with substances.

One herb I have found helpful is called ginkgo biloba. This herb opens up blood vessels. There is evidence that blood flow is reduced in the brains of autistic children. Ginkgo may help reverse this lack of flow. I think ginkgo may be most helpful when combined with anti-yeast treatment. The brain may be closing down the blood flow to protect itself from toxic yeast chemicals. When these are removed, ginkgo may do more good.

Conclusion.
I would advise any parent of an autistic child to try treating their child with diet and nystatin. The presence of yeast chemicals in the urine can be verified using Dr. Shaw's test. Symptoms such as skin problems, diarrhea, constipation, and behavioral problems following antibiotic use also strongly suggest an overgrowth of the intestine with the yeast Candida albicans. Following Stage I of the diet and using nystatin for two to four weeks will tell you if the treatment is beneficial to your child, with no adverse effects or risk to your child.

I have treated many children with autism who showed significant gains by following the diet prescribed along with the nystatin. I have designed the dietary regiment to allow for a gradual transition to the yeast-free level of least intervention necessary for your child. The nystatin dosing schedule is similarly graduated to provide for the least die-off effect. Combining the two will yield gratifying results, for you, your child, and your family.

The Use of Vitamin B6, Magnesium, and DMG in the Treatment of Autistic Children and Adults.

by Bernard Rimland, Ph.D.

The following information is condensed from articles appearing in the Autism Research Review International, the newsletter of the Autism Research Institute. The original articles, including summaries of and literature references to the 18 studies of vitamin B6 in autism, as well as to other studies referred to below, are available on request from the **Autism Research Institute, 4182 Adams Avenue, San Diego, CA 92116.**

Vitamin B6 (and magnesium) in the treatment of autism.
From the Autism Research Review International, Volume 1, No. 4

All 18 studies known to me in which vitamin B6 has been evaluated as a treatment for autism have provided positive results, and no significant adverse effects have been reported in any of the studies. This is a rather remarkable record of efficacy and safety, since the many drugs that have been evaluated as treatments for autism have produced very inconsistent results; and all drugs pose a risk of serious side effects. If a drug shows positive results in about half of the evaluation studies, it is considered a success and the drug is then advocated for use with autistic patients. However, despite the remarkably consistent findings in the research on the use of vitamin B6 in the treatment of autism, and despite its being immeasurably safer than any of the drugs used for autistic children, there are at present few practitioners who use it or advocate its use in the treatment of autism. The reasons are obvious: most physicians know little about vitamins and have no economic incentive to recommend a substance that does not require a physician's prescription.

Research on the use of vitamin B6 with autistic children began in the 1960s. In 1966 two British neurologists, A. F. Heeley and G. E. Roberts, reported that 11 of 19 autistic children excreted abnormal metabolites in their urine when given a tryptophan load test. Giving these children a single 30 mg tablet of vitamin B6 normalized their urine; however, no behavioral studies were done. A German investigator, V. E. Bonisch, reported in 1968 that 12 of 16 autistic children had shown considerable behavioral improvement when given high dosage levels (100 mg to 600 mg per day) of vitamin B6. Three of Bonisch's patients spoke for the first time after the vitamin B6 was administered in this open clinical trial.

After my book Infantile Autism was published in 1964, I began receiving hundreds of letters from parents of autistic children throughout the United States, including a number who had tried the then-new idea of "megavitamin therapy" on their autistic children. Most had begun experimenting with various vitamins on their autistic children as a result of reading books by popular nutrition writers. I initially was quite skeptical about the remarkable improvement being reported by some of these parents, but as the evidence accumulated, my interest was aroused. A questionnaire sent to the 1,000 parents then on my mailing list revealed that 57 had experimented with large doses of vitamins. Many of these had seen positive results in their children. Intensive study of the medical literature convinced me the vitamins were safe. As a result, I undertook a large-scale study, on over 200 autistic children, of megadose quantities of vitamin B6, niacinamide, pantothenic acid, and vitamin C, along with a multiple-vitamin tablet especially designed for the study. The children were living with their parents throughout the U.S. and Canada. We required that each child be medically supervised by the family's own physician. (Over 600 parents had volunteered for the study, but most could not overcome their physicians' skepticism.)

At the end of the four-month trial it was clear that vitamin B6 was the most important of the four vitamins we had investigated, and that in some cases it brought about remarkable improvement. Between 30% and 40% of the children showed significant improvement when the vitamin B6 was given to them. A few of the children showed minor side effects (irritability, sound sensitivity and bed-wetting), but these quickly cleared up when additional magnesium was supplied.

The magnesium not only eliminated the side effects, it often brought about even more improvement in speech and behavior.

Two years later two colleagues and I initiated a second experimental study of the use of megavitamin therapy on autistic children, this time concentrating on vitamin B6 and magnesium. My co-investigators were Professors Enoch Callaway of the University of California Medical Center at San Francisco and Pierre Dreyfus of the University of California Medical Center at Davis. The double-blind placebo-controlled crossover experiment utilized 16 autistic children, and again produced statistically significant results. For most children dosage levels of B6 ranged between 300 mg and 500 mg per day. Several hundred mg/day of magnesium and a multiple-B tablet were also given, to guard against the possibility of B6-induced deficiencies of these other nutrients.

In both studies the children showed a remarkably wide range of benefits from the vitamin B6. There was better eye contact, less self-stimulatory behavior, more interest in the world around them, fewer tantrums, more speech, and in general the children became more normal, although they were not completely cured.

People vary enormously in their need for B6. The children who showed improvement under B6 improved because they needed extra B6. Autism is thus in many cases a vitamin B6 dependency syndrome.

After completing his participation in our study, Professor Callaway visited France, where he persuaded Professor Gilbert LeLord and his colleagues to undertake additional B6/magnesium research on autistic children. The French researchers, although skeptical that anything as innocuous as a vitamin could influence a disorder as profound as autism, became believers after their first, reluctantly undertaken, experiment on 44 hospitalized children. They have since published a number of additional studies evaluating the use of vitamin B6, with and without additional magnesium, on autistic children and adults. Their studies typically used as much as a gram a day of vitamin B6 and half a gram of magnesium.

LeLord and his colleagues measured not only the behavior of the autistic children, but also their excretion of homovanillic acid (HVA) and other metabolites in the urine. Additionally, they have done several studies in which the effects of the vitamin B6 and/or the magnesium on the brain electrical activity of the patients was analyzed. All of these studies have produced positive results.

LeLord et al. recently summarized their results on 91 patients: 14% improved markedly, 33% improved, 42% showed no improvement, and 11% worsened. They noted that "in all our studies, no side effects were observed." Presumably, no physical side effects were seen.

Several studies by two groups of U.S. investigators, Thomas Gualtieri et al., at the University of North Carolina, and George Ellman et al., at Sonoma State Hospital in California, have also shown positive results on autistic patients.

While no patient has been cured with the vitamin B6 and magnesium treatment, there have been many instances where remarkable improvement has been achieved. In one such case an 18-year-old autistic patient was about to be evicted from the third mental hospital in his city. Even massive amounts of drugs had no effect on him, and he was considered too violent and assaultative to be kept in the hospital. The psychiatrist tried the B6/magnesium approach as a last resort. The young man calmed down very quickly. The psychiatrist reported at a meeting that she had recently visited the family and had found the young man to now be a pleasant and easy-going young autistic person who sang and played his guitar for her.

Another example: a frantic mother phoned me to ask for information on sheltered workshops in her city, since her 25-year-old autistic son was about to be expelled for unmanageable behavior. I knew of no alternate placements for the son, but I suggested that the mother try Super Nu-Thera, a supplement containing B6, magnesium and other nutrients. Within a few weeks she called again to tell me excitedly that her son was doing very well now and his piecework pay had risen dramatically from the minimum pay of $1.50 per week to $25 per week.

In view of the consistent findings showing the safety and efficacy of the nutrients B6 and magnesium in treating autistic individuals, and in view of the inevitability of short and/or long-term side effects of drug use, it certainly seems that this safe and rational approach should be tried before drugs are employed.

****

Vitamin B6 in autism: the safety issue
From the Autism Research Review International, Volume 10, No. 3

There is no biological treatment for autism which is more strongly supported in the scientific literature than the use of high dosage vitamin B6 (preferably given along with normal supplements of magnesium). Eighteen studies have been published since 1965, showing conclusively that high dose vitamin B6 confers many benefits to about half of all the autistic children and adults on whom it has been tried. While B6/magnesium is not a cure, it has often made a big, worthwhile difference.

Included among the 18 studies are 11 double-blind, placebo-crossover experiments, 8 experiments in which abnormal substances appearing in the urine of autistic children have been normalized by the B6, other studies in which brain waves have been normalized, and a wide range of other improvements: 18 consecutive studies showing megadose B6 to be effective and no studies failing to show that megadose B6 is effective. No drug even comes close.

None of the studies of B6 in autism have reported any significant adverse effects, nor would any significant adverse effects be expected. I conducted an intensive analysis of the literature on B6 safety before embarking on my first study of B6 in the late 1960s. A review published in 1966 by the American Academy of Pediatrics confirmed my own conclusion: "To date there has been no report of deleterious effects associated with daily oral ingestion of large doses of vitamin B6 (0.2 to 1.0 grams per day)."

Tens of thousand of people, including thousands of autistic children and adults, took large doses throughout the '60s, '70s, and beginning '80s with no reported signs of any adverse effects. However, in 1983, a paper by Schaumburg et al. reported significant, though not permanent nor life-threatening side effects in 7 patients who had been taking 2,000 mg to 6,000 mg per day of B6. The side effects, peripheral neuropathy, were numbness and tingling in the hands and feet-the sensation one gets when one's hand or foot "falls asleep." The foot numbness in some cases interfered with walking. These patients were not taking magnesium, the other B vitamins, nor any of the other nutrients that should be taken if one is taking large amounts of B6. It is at least possible that the adverse reactions were due not to B6 "toxicity" but to deficiencies of magnesium and the other B vitamins induced by taking large amounts of B6. It is also possible that the problem was caused by a contaminant in the B6, rather than by the B6 itself.

It should be noted that the Schaumburg study covered only 7 patients and had 7 authors from several major medical centers throughout the United States. It would seem that a national search had been done to locate these patients, once the first case had been identified.

In the ensuing years, a few other patients have been reported in the literature who showed similar symptoms of peripheral neuropathy.

In my own experience, covering almost 30 years, and many thousands of autistic children and adults, I have, to the best of my knowledge, encountered only four cases of peripheral neuropathy. In these cases the numbness in the hands and feet was noticed by the parents, who reported that the child would: a) shake the hands as though to try to get the circulation back, b) have difficulty in picking up objects, such as bits of food, or c) have difficulty walking, because of numbness in the soles of the feet. When the B6 was discontinued, or the dosage was markedly reduced, these symptoms went away very quickly and completely.

Some individuals may be exceedingly sensitive to larger than normal amounts of B6. These cases are very few and far between, and discontinuing the B6 seems in all cases thus far to resolve the problem.

If you contrast these findings with the findings reported on a daily basis on the drugs that are used for autism, it becomes instantly clear that the B6 is immeasurably safer. There has never been a death or serious illness associated with ingestion of even very large amounts of B6. Deaths and permanent disability from prescription drugs are commonplace.

My own son, now 40, has been taking about 1 gram per day of B6 (along with 400 mg of magnesium, and other nutrients) for some 30 years. If there is a healthier person in North America, I would be surprised. Mark's only physical problem to date occurred in his early 20s, when a dentist found one small cavity in one tooth.

Despite the extraordinary safety of B6, I have been told, over the years, by thousands of parents, that their physicians have warned them against giving their children high doses of B6, because of the supposed risks involved. It is unfortunately very typical of most of the medical establishment (which of course makes its money by prescribing drugs) to denigrate and exaggerate the dangers of taking nutritional supplements.

A case in point: recently the national news media gave heavy coverage to a paper from the University of Michigan which warned the public against the dangers of taking vitamin B6. This report was given national television coverage, and we received a number of alarmed inquiries in our office from parents who were frightened by the warning, "B6 is toxic!"

When I read the study, I was truly appalled. The authors, from the University of Michigan Medical School, were supposedly investigating the value of vitamin B6 in the treatment of carpal tunnel syndrome (a painful malady of the wrists, which has become very common in recent years, and is usually considered a repetitive motion injury). The conventional treatment is surgery, which is often ineffective, as well as being disfiguring, expensive, and painful. There are a number of well-documented reports that high doses of vitamin B6 successfully treat carpal tunnel syndrome, in the majority of cases, so that over a six-week period people who were scheduled for surgery no longer need such drastic treatment.

The Michigan researchers had not given even one milligram of B6 to even one of their subjects (not patients)! Their warning was based primarily on the 1983 Schaumburg report. Further, they had not included even a single subject who actually had carpal tunnel syndrome! They did blood and nerve conduction studies on people who were "potentially" at risk for carpal tunnel syndrome, but did not in fact have carpal tunnel syndrome. The anti-vitamin B6 bias in the report is very evident when you read, in their review of research, that "several" studies have reported B6 to be effective in treating carpal tunnel syndrome, while "numerous" reports have failed to confirm the finding. If you look at the actual references in their study, you will see that there are 12 favorable reports, and only 7 negative reports. So, to them, "several" equals 12 and "numerous" equals 7!

The University of Michigan study, with its highly publicized and totally irrelevant conclusions, is certainly one of the worst and most appalling studies I have ever read. Alan Gaby, M.D., author of The Doctor's Guide to Vitamin B6, referred to it as a "disgusting" display of bias, and I certainly agree with that assessment.

Nothing is perfectly safe, but B6 is exceptionally safe, particularly when compared to the alternative, drugs, which are infinitely more likely to cause severe illness, injury, and even death. An autistic person will improve on high dosage B6 only if that person's body requires extra B6. The benefits of B6 often start within a few days. If no benefits are seen in three to four weeks (in about 50 percent of cases), or if any signs of peripheral neuropathy appear (very rare), stop giving the B6.

A 1995 paper by Ellis and McCully reported that elderly patients who had been taking 100-300 mg per day of B6 for some years experienced only 27% the risk of heart disease, and among those who died of a heart attack, the average age at death was 84.5- eight years longer life than control group patients from the local area. In a 1993 study of epileptic newborns, Pietz found 300 mg of B6/kg/day-18 times the dosage used in autism-to be superior to seizure drugs. And B6, in amounts as high as 50 grams per day, is used as an antidote for victims of certain poisons. Is vitamin B6 toxic? Hardly!

****

Frequently Asked Questions about vitamin B6

Does vitamin B6 and magnesium require a prescription? No. Vitamin B6 and magnesium are both nutritional supplements, not drugs, and may be purchased without a prescription.

Do I need to have a medical testing done to find if extra B6 is needed? No. The best, safest and most accurate test is simply to try the B6/magnesium for a month or so. If you see improvement, your child is one of the 50% who needs extra B6 and magnesium.

I understand that there is a special megavitamin formula for autistic children. How can I find it? Since 1970, the Kirkman Company has made available a megavitamin product, Super Nu-Thera, which contains the vitamins and minerals necessary for placing a child on megavitamin B6 therapy. The formula is available both in caplets and as a powder which may be mixed with applesauce, mashed potatoes, juices, or other foods which the child finds palatable. The powder contains 500 mg of B6 per heaping teaspoon, and adequate amounts of a number of other nutrients. Six caplets equal one heaping teaspoon of the powder. The vitamin treatment costs only a small fraction of the cost of drugs. Since many children resist taking the formula, even when the powder is mixed with food the child likes, the Kirkman Company is planning to place a good-tasting syrup version of the Super Nu-Thera on the market in early 1998 (phone: 888-KIRKMAN; Fax: 503-682-0838).

Why does the Super Nu-Thera formula contain many vitamins and minerals, in addition to the B6 and magnesium? While a single vitamin, such as vitamin B6, may produce favorable results, optimum results are most likely to occur when other nutrients are also provided. Nutrients must form compounds in the body to be effective, and their effectiveness is limited when other nutrients are in short supply. Vitamins differ from drugs in this respect. Drugs operate as blocking agents, and can thus function alone. Vitamins act as facilitating or enabling agents, and thus require the presence of other nutrients. This is why vitamins are so much safer than drugs; vitamins assist the body's metabolism, while drugs interfere with it.

Magnesium is the most important of these supplemental nutrients, because the body cannot properly utilize vitamin B6 without a sufficient supply of magnesium. If the child's diet does not provide him/her with a good supply of this mineral, and it usually does not, magnesium must be provided as a supplement. Vitamin C, the B vitamins and zinc are among the other nutrients which should be given if the B6 treatment is to be safe and effective. While some research studies have reported good results by using from 75 to 1,000 milligrams per day of vitamin B6 along with about 300 milligrams per day of magnesium, it is better to use a carefully formulated megavitamin product. Super Nu-Thera was designed to fill this need.

The Use of Vitamin B6, Magnesium, and DMG

One necessary nutrient not adequately provided in Super Nu-Thera is calcium. Humans need about twice as much calcium as magnesium, but since so many children drink milk, putting additional calcium in Super Nu-Thera might result in their getting too much calcium. If the child does not drink milk, and milk causes problems for many autistic children, supplement the Super Nu-Thera with 500 to 1,000 mg per day of calcium, depending on the child's size and age. There are many calcium supplements on the market.

I also have a child who is hyperactive ("ADHD"). Might the B6 formula help him also? A carefully conducted study by Mary Coleman, M.D. and her associates, published in 1979, showed that when high dose vitamin B6 was compared with Ritalin or a placebo, the B6 was just as effective as the Ritalin and was longer lasting. Of course, the B6 is also cheaper and less harmful than the Ritalin. No one has taken the trouble to try to repeat this study in almost two decades. (Obviously, Ritalin is much more profitable than B6, so why rock the boat?)

What dosage is recommended? Both our research in the US and the French research indicates that, on average, dosages of about 8 mg of B6 per pound of body weight per day, and about 3 or 4 mg of magnesium per pound of body weight per day is about right. However, each individual autistic person is different than the others, so it takes trial and error to find the best dose for each person. For an autistic child weighing 50 pounds, about 400 mg (50 x 8 mg) of B6 and 150 mg (50 x 3 mg) of magnesium would probably be in the right range, but we know of several 50 lb. children for whom only 75 mg of B6 per day was sufficient--so experiment!

Some Further Suggestions

1. It is wise to reduce the sugar, soft drinks and other junk foods in the child's diet. There is ample evidence that these are harmful for all children, whether or not autistic.

186

2. The vitamins should be administered with or after meals in two or three divided doses per day. This provides the vitamins and minerals the optimum opportunity to form proper compounds with other nutrients in the digestive system and bloodstream.

3. The caplets are much easier to use than the powder, if the child will swallow caplets. If the powder is used, it is best mixed with a soft food such as applesauce. It may be mixed with juices, but unless care is taken some ingredients will drop to the bottom of the glass and not be consumed by the child. Many parents mix the powder with partially thawed orange or grape juice that is still "slushy." Try different flavors of juice. The flavored Super Nu-Thera syrup, when available, may solve all of these problems.

4. In many cases behavioral improvement is seen after a few days on megavitamins. In other cases behavior improves gradually, so little change is seen for two or three months. In perhaps 50 percent of the children, the vitamins seem to be of no help, but do not conclude that any given child will not be helped until there has been a 30-day trial.

5. The benefits which are most often observed in autistic children given B6 and the accompanying nutrients are: increased use of sounds, words or speech; improved sleeping habits; decrease in hyperactivity and irritability; better attention span; increase in interest in learning. In some cases, self-stimming, self-injurious, and/or assaultative behaviors have decreased. Vitamin B6 makes the child more normal, in many ways. Other benefits reported have included such indications of improved health as better skin color and complexion, and better muscle tone. Many parents say their child has never been in better health than when on the Super Nu-Thera.

6. If a child is on prescription drugs, most physicians who use megavitamins recommend that the drugs be continued for several weeks after the vitamins have been started. If improvement is observed, a process of weaning the child from the drugs may be initiated. It is often possible for the drug dosage to be cut in half,

and in many cases the drugs could be discontinued. (This must be discussed with the child's doctor. Stopping drugs suddenly can be harmful.)

7. Super Nu-Thera contains a small amount of niacin (vitamin B3). Even this small amount may cause temporary flushing and/or hives in very small children. The flushing is troublesome for a few days, then disappears. It is not harmful.

8. All ages may be helped. Some of the most impressive results have been seen in adults. In Ellman's (1981) study of 16 adults, a 55-year-old responded best.

9. It is suggested that the parents refrain from mentioning the child's vitamin therapy to grandparents, teachers, neighbors or others who have frequent contact with the child. Such people often provide spontaneous comments which are helpful in gaining an objective assessment of the child's response to the vitamins.

10. Super Nu-Thera may be given together with other nutrients, such as DMG. Start with one nutrient, say the DMG, for three weeks before adding the second one. This will help you sort out the different effects.

11. If no improvement is seen in 30 days (usually benefits would be apparent long before that), it may be concluded that the child does not need the extra B6. The Super Nu-Thera should be tapered off and stopped, in that case.
****

Dimethylglycine (DMG), a nontoxic metabolite, and autism
From the Autism Research Review International, Vol. 4, No. 2

DMG is a rather sweet-tasting substance that was described in a recent article in the Journal of Laboratory and Clinical Medicine (1990, 481-86) as a "natural, simple compound with no known undesirable side effects." The article did not pertain to the use of

DMG in autism, but instead described an experiment in which DMG was used to try to enhance the function of the immune system of laboratory rabbits. It worked-the immune systems of the animals given DMG showed 300% to 1,000% better response to infection than the controls.

DMG is readily available in many health food stores. It is legally classified as a food. It does not require a prescription. It is manufactured by several companies, and comes in various forms, most commonly in tiny foil-wrapped tablets about 1/3 the size of an aspirin.

The taste is pleasant and children chew the tablets readily. At about 25 cents per tablet, the cost is minimal, since only one to eight tablets a day are usually taken (eight for adults).

"So far so good," you may be saying, "but what does this have to do with autism?"

In 1965, two Russian investigators, M. G. Blumena and T. L. Belyakova, published a report showing considerable improvement in the speech of 12 of a group of 15 mentally handicapped children who had not been able to use speech to communicate. The children had been treated with a substance variously known as calcium pangamate, or pangamic acid, or "vitamin B15." In addition to enriched vocabulary, the children began to use simple sentences, their general mental state improved, and there was better concentration and interest in toys and games. Subsequent research has shown the essential factor in calcium pangamate to be DMG.

Soon afterward psychiatrist Allan Cott visited Moscow and brought back a small supply of pangamic acid, which he tried on a number of children in his practice, some of whom were autistic. Many of Cott's patients responded in the same way the Russian children had. One mother wrote, "It's the most exciting thing I've ever experienced. He was repeating words and he answers questions now!."

189

The Use of Vitamin B6, Magnesium, and DMG

At about this time pangamic acid, or B15, entered the U.S. market. Chaos ensued. Every manufacturer touted his product as "the original Russian formula." There were at least four different formulas on the market, partly, it is believed, as a result of deliberate deception and obfuscation on the part of the Russians. DMG, in small amounts, was a component of some of the formulas. The FDA stepped in and lengthy legal battles ensued. One outcome is that the term B15 was outlawed. (Although DMG resembles the B vitamins in many ways-it is found in the same foods, for example--there are no known overt symptoms characteristic of a DMG deficiency.)

The significant outcome of the legal battles is that the sale of DMG is now permitted, as long as it is not referred to as a vitamin, and as long as it is sold as a food and not a drug.

I have been following the pangamic acid-DMG situation for almost 25 years. I have mentioned it in some of my lectures, and told parents and professionals about it in conversations and correspondence. Always I would ask, "if you try it, please let me know what results you see, even if no improvement is found."

I am now so firmly convinced that DMG is helpful to a substantial proportion of autistic children and adults that I have decided to "go public" in the Autism Research Review International -to tell people about it freely and openly, so they may try it if they wish.

Some who hear of this boldness may be aghast: "Where are the double blind placebo-controlled scientific studies showing it to be effective in autism?" they will ask. My reply is simple. "There aren't any, and none are needed." There are, of course, numerous double blind non-autism studies of DMG in the scientific and medical literature, using not only humans, but many kinds of laboratory animals, often given very large amounts of DMG. As noted earlier, no adverse side effects have been found with even massive intakes of DMG. (I say "intakes" rather than "dosages" because "dosage" implies that DMG is a drug, which it is not.)

Since no company has the exclusive right to make DMG, competition keeps the price-and profits-down. Thus there is almost no chance that anyone will sponsor a $200,000 double blind study of DMG on autistic children. A parent can buy 30 tablets for about $8.00. That is a sufficient supply, even for an adult given five or more tablets a day, to determine, in most cases, if it will be helpful. If it is felt to be helpful, fine. If not, you have wasted $8.00 (except for the boost given to the immune system).

To help the parents receive unbiased input, I usually tell them to refrain from mentioning to teachers, grandparents and others in the child's environment that DMG is being tried. I have numerous letters in my files saying, "Johnny's speech therapist says he has made more progress in the last two weeks than in the last six months. As you suggested, we had told no one at his school that we were trying DMG."

I am 100% in favor of double blind studies on drugs with considerable potential for harm, such as fenfluramine, Haldol, or the like. However, it doesn't make sense to insist on such refinements before trying a perfectly safe substance such as DMG, apple pie, or chicken soup.

If DMG is going to work, its effects will usually be seen within a week or so, though it should be tried for a few weeks or a month before giving up. In some cases dramatic results have been seen within 24 hours: A Los Angeles mother was driving on the freeway, three-year-old Kathy in the back seat, five-year-old mute autistic son Sammy in the front. DMG had been started the day before. Kathy began to cry. Sammy turned and spoke his first words: "Don't cry, Kathy." The mother, stunned, almost crashed the car.

A similar case: A Texas mother secured her six-year-old mute autistic daughter in the front seat, then, before driving off, turned to tell her husband, "I'll drop Mary at the babysitter's house first." Mary, on DMG for two days, startled her parents with her first words: "No! No babysitter!"

Although speech is the most notable positive change in those children helped by DMG, behavioral improvement is also often reported. One father gave his son one DMG tablet per day without mentioning it to the school. He later requested a copy of the school's detailed record of his son's day-by-day behavioral transgressions. The correlation between outburst-free days and the use of DMG was unmistakable.

An article in the New England Journal of Medicine (October 1982) reported that a 22-year-old mentally retarded man who had 16 to 18 seizures per week on standard anticonvulsants, experienced only three seizures per week while on DMG. Two attempts to remove the DMG dramatically increased seizure frequency.

Last year I sent information on DMG to Lee Dae Kun, Director of the Pusan (Korea) Research Center on Child Problems. He tried the DMG on 39 autistic children, ages three to seven, for three months, with the following (summarized) results:

Benefits seen:

Yes: 31 (80%)
No: 8 (20%)
(Improved speech, eating, excretion, willingness, etc.)
8 children had difficulty sleeping for weeks 1 and 2.
6 children became more active for weeks 1 and 2.

Lee Dae Kun wrote that the parents, usually skeptical, saw the improvements clearly. He concluded that DMG is very beneficial for children with autism, even if it is not a cure.

Information about the use of DMG with older persons is also encouraging. One mother of a 26-year-old who squeezed things (people, TV sets, etc.) very hard when frustrated, tried DMG, quite skeptically, to see if it would stimulate his very sparse speech. It didn't, but brought remarkable improvement in his frustration tolerance. "Even my husband, who was even more skeptical than me, now is a believer," she wrote.

DMG certainly doesn't always help, and it certainly is not a cure, but it is certainly worth trying, in my humble opinion.
If you try it, let me hear from you.

****

Dimethylglycine (DMG) for Autism
Autism Research Institute Publication No. 111

For over 20 years ARI has been hearing from parents who have tried DMG on their autistic children. In many cases remarkably good results have been seen, especially in enhancing speech. In some cases, drug-resistant seizures have been stopped by DMG. (See New England Journal of Medicine, 10-21-82, pgs 1081-82).

There is an extensive research literature on the safety and health benefits of DMG. Many studies have shown that DMG enhances the effectiveness of the immune system, improves the physical and athletic performance of humans and other animals (e.g. race horses) and has, all in all, a very wide range of beneficial effects. It is very safe. I have seen no evidence of any toxic or significant adverse effects. DMG is available in many health food stores in small, foil-sealed 125mg tablets from Food Science Laboratories. Ask for the original Aangamik DMG or for further information from the company, call toll-free at 800-992-8451. (Avoid DMG in liquid or large tablets.) We recommend the foil-wrapped tablets from Food Science Laboratories or the DMG in 125mg capsules offered by mail from the Kirkman Company. Their toll-free phone number is 888-KIRKMAN. From outside the U.S., the number is 503-694-1600.

The Use of Vitamin B6, Magnesium, and DMG

Dimethylglycine is technically classified as a food. It is found, in very small amounts, in some foods, such as brown rice and liver. Chemically and physiologically, it resembles the water-soluble vitamins, such as the B vitamins. The main reason it is not classified as a vitamin is that there are no specific symptoms associated with a deficiency of DMG.

Many parents have reported that, within a few days of starting DMG, the child's behavior improved noticeably, better eye contact was seen, frustration tolerance increased, the child's speech improved, or more interest and ability in speaking was observed.

For a pre-school child, I would start with 1/2 of a 125mg tablet or capsule a day, with breakfast, for a few days, or one tablet a day for a larger child. I would go up, gradually, to one to four tablets a day for a child, and to 2 to 8 tablets per day for an adult. If there is an initial increase in hyperactivity (rare) reduce the dosage. If the hyperactivity continues, the child may be telling you, in effect, that he or she needs more folic acid. Folic acid is a very safe B-vitamin. Purchase some 800 mcg folic acid tablets and give two of these with each 125mg of DMG.

If you try DMG on an autistic child or adult, please write to let us know: how long before effects were seen, what effects were observed in such areas as: behavior, appetite, sleep, speech, alertness, activity level, etc. In 5% or 10% of the cases, there is initial hyperactivity. Let me know if you see any adverse effects (very unlikely).

I am especially interested in receiving notes from parents about comments made by teachers, neighbors, relatives, etc., who were not aware that the child was taking the DMG.

If you are just starting out, I suggest giving the DMG for 2-3 weeks then adding the B6/ magnesium (which should also be started gradually: write to us for publication 39F). When you start a trial of

194

DMG, don't confuse the results by simultaneously starting other vitamins, drugs, or other forms of treatment that might make it difficult to tease out the effects of DMG from the effects of the other things tried. If the child is already taking vitamin B6 and magnesium, or anything else that is helpful, there is no reason to stop taking the B6 (or whatever). The DMG is merely a highly concentrated food. It may in fact improve the effectiveness of the B6.

Dietary Intervention for the Treatment of Autism: Why Implement a Gluten and Casein Free Diet?

by Lisa S. Lewis, Ph.D.

Introduction

When my son was first diagnosed with autism (in 1991) my husband and I were both stunned, and in an odd way, relieved. Relief may seem like a bizarre reaction, but for almost two years we had been dealing with the unknown. It was terribly frightening and we never really knew if we were on the right track. Professionals were of little help. At Sam's three-year checkup I asked our doctor point blank: "Could he be autistic?" At least he was honest. Shaking his head slowly, he replied ,"I just don't know."

With a diagnosis, we had something to grab and run with. We both hold doctorate degrees in Anthropology, and as a result we were already trained to do research. Without discussing it, or formally dividing up what needed to be done, a division of labor seemed to occur naturally. As I look back on it now, I realize that doing research was our coping mechanism. We didn't have time to cry and ask "Why us?" We sprang into action, devoting ourselves to doing something positive for our son.

My husband, Serge, immediately called a wonderful local organization called COSAC (New Jersey Center Outreach and Support for the Autistic Community) and set up an appointment. There we got valuable information on services available to us, our legal rights, whom we should call and where we should start, as well as a copy of Ivar Lovass's *Me Book*. We signed up for a six week parent training course due to start in a few weeks. Serge began looking into schools and other educational matters. (At that time

Sam was in a half-day, "preschool handicapped" program that was not meeting his needs.) Armed with the information he had gathered, we were ready for our IEP(individualized educational plan) meeting, where we presented a case for moving Sam to a more specialized (and far more expensive!) school.

While Serge was looking into education and therapeutic interventions, I began an extensive search for anything I could find on autism—medical and other interventions, outcome and etiology. Fortunately for me, the World Wide Web was just then "taking off," and I was able to do much of my research without leaving my desk. As a (then) employee of Princeton University, I was able to access anything on-line quickly, and at no expense. I had already learned to use the basic tools of electronic research for my work at the university, but now I really honed these skills to find specific information. I found a lot, and I also found how many other people were out there "seeking." I began extensive correspondence with many other parents, and with some notable professionals too, including (the late) Roland Ciarnello who was running the Stanford University Genetics Research program on Autism. Dr. Ciarnello was a big help, and sent us several his articles when we were looking for specific information.

We combined the results of our research to come up with a plan, which included where to have a good educational evaluation done on Sam, where to send him for speech and occupational therapy and what kind of school to put him in. Our school district was helpful and supportive, and gave us most of what we asked for. Still, we continued to search. At that time, there were few Internet news groups on the subject, and locally we only found "support" groups that stressed coping with the diagnosis rather than research or treatment. After reading much of the literature on the subject we weren't surprised by the focus of these groups. Autism was, after all, described a lifelong developmental disability, intractable to most medical treatment.

Why Implement a Gluten and Casein Free Diet?

When Sam was three, he began having violent tantrums. I had read that many children who were allergic to milk behaved that way. He loved milk and any milk products and consumed lots of milk, yogurt, cottage cheese and ice cream. And why not? After all, I was raised to believe that milk was the perfect food! I never loved it but my mother insisted that a certain amount be consumed every day. But as Sam's tantrums intensified I started reading about allergies, and found that children with food allergies generally craved most, those foods that they should not have.

I removed dairy from Sam's diet, and while he did seem to settle down a bit, there wasn't really a profound difference. I still suspected that something he ate was affecting him, and his pattern of recurrent ear and upper respiratory infections which eventually led to asthma, seemed to indicate an immune system gone awry. We took him to a highly recommended pediatric allergist in Philadelphia. Her tests confirmed that Sam was very allergic to pollens and molds, but she found no evidence of food allergy. That was the end of dietary intervention—for a while.

Two years later, when Sam was five, I saw Dr. Doris Rapp on a talk show. She spoke about environmental allergies and food allergies, which I found very interesting. But then she showed videotapes of children who were given concentrations of foods to which they were allergic. These nice children suddenly became wild animals! Screaming, attempting to hit or scratch, throwing tantrums and worse. Milk was said to be one of the main allergens that produced this response. Wheat was also named as a common cause culprit.

At this, a bell went off for me. In addition to his love of dairy, Sam loved crackers, bread, rolls, pretzels—anything starchy and most foods made of wheat. We had been calling him "Carbo-man" because he so loved these (mostly) *wheat based* foods. I could not help noticing the resemblance between those videotapes, and the behavior I had been witnessing and dealing with in my own son. Though he had tested negative for a wheat allergy, I decided then and there to remove it from his diet.

198

Why Implement a Gluten and Casein Free Diet?

Within three days I began getting notes home from school, saying that Sam was doing beautifully and that his behavior was enormously improved. What had we done? I decided not to reveal the removal of wheat at this point. But two weeks later I was eating a slice of pizza. Sam came by and asked for some. I was watching something on television, and was preoccupied. I mindlessly handed him a slice and only after he was halfway through did I realize what I had done. Oh well, I thought, the damage (if any) was already done.

The next morning when Sam asked for a Pop-Tart® I went ahead and gave it to him. Then I waited. At 4:00 his bus pulled up and even before he was out his aide said, "I hear he had a pretty rough day." I barely looked at Sam, instead grabbing his backpack to find his notebook. As I had suspected, the note was **not** good. During the course of the day, Sam had numerous tantrums, had been extremely aggressive and very unfocused. Only late in the day did he start to come around, telling his teacher "don't write in the book" realizing that I would read of his many transgressions!

From that point on, I explained to his teachers and therapists what we were doing (no more pretzel reinforcers during speech therapy!) I began sending wheat free lunches and snacks, and wrote up a long list of what he should not be given at school.

Though I was completely convinced that Sam was greatly affected by what he ate, I was still puzzled over why he tested negative to wheat and milk allergies. I mentioned this to an "electronic friend" (someone I'd met on the Internet, and subsequently in person) named Jean Jasinski. She recalled reading an article about autism and gluten intolerance. I vaguely remembered something about it too, but couldn't remember the authors or where I had seen them. Bless Jean—she searched until she came up with one article, which she mailed to me. I then was able to find other articles by the author, Paul Shattock of the University of Sunderland in Sunderland, England. Shattock's articles in turn led me to the work of Dr. Karl Reichelt in Norway.

Why Implement a Gluten and Casein Free Diet?

After reading about the research going on in England and Norway, I came to realize that I should have removed all gluten grains from Sam's diet, rather than just wheat. I did this, as well as I could. It was very hard to manage since it was new to me, but I found information about celiac sprue and went from there (more on this below.) I did not see the huge change in Sam that I'd seen after first removing wheat, but this seemed natural to me. I had already removed the grain that had the highest concentration of gluten proteins; perhaps I had succeeding in weaning him from the offensive proteins.

Two years later I found Mr. Shattock "on-line." I sent him e-mail immediately, and so began a correspondence which continues to this day. He and his colleagues have proved tremendously helpful to me.

So many people began asking me for information, that I wrote a twenty-page document on how and why to try this intervention. Before long, I was spending a lot of time and money duplicating the article and mailing it to people. There had to be a better way. At that point, many more people had Internet access from their offices or homes, and the World Wide Web was becoming widely available. Since nearly all requests for the article were coming to me via e-mail, I decided to put this document up on the web. I created a home page, and announced it to the autism world, and what a reaction it has had.

I began to receive phone calls, letters and e-mail from all over the world. From these contacts I met many more parents with whom I began exchanging information. It was from this and references from friends who had read my article, that I made contact with many of the "seeker parents" out in the world.

At first, when I began talking and writing on this topic, I was thought to be something of a "nut." For the last year or so, however, the subject of diet is on "the net" constantly, and even doctors have begun taking it seriously. **It may not cure, and it may not even help all that try it, but it will help many.** I hope the information provided in this book and in this chapter will help you to decide whether or not to try new interventions for your child. I hope that I can provide you with information on why it might be a useful experiment. And if you do want to try it, some information is included that will help you get started.

What IS Gluten? Why Eliminate it From the Diet?

Gluten is a protein found in the Plant Kingdom Subclass of *Monocotyledonae* (monocots.) These plants are members of the grass family of **wheat, oats, barley, rye** and their derivatives. Derivatives include: malt, grain starches, hydrolyzed vegetable/plant proteins, textured vegetable proteins, grain vinegar, soy sauce, grain alcohol, flavorings and the binders and fillers found in vitamins and medications. **Casein** is a phospho-protein of milk, which has a molecular structure that is extremely similar to that of gluten.

In the early 1980's, two scientists noted that the behavior of animals under the influence of opioid drugs such as morphine, was very similar to that of some people with **autism**. Dr. Jaak Panksepp proposed that people with autism *might* have elevated levels of naturally occurring opioids in their Central Nervous System. There are several such naturally occurring compounds. The best known of these are the beta-endorphins which produce the so-called "runner's high."

At about the same time, work by Swedish autism expert Christopher Gillberg showed elevated levels of "endorphin-like substances" in the cerebrospinal fluid of some people with autism. It is particularly interesting that levels are high in those children with autism who are insensitive to pain and those who engage in self-injurious behaviors. Dr. Karl Reichelt found abnormal peptides in the urine of people with autism; these peptides are apparently similar to those found by Gillberg. The Autism Research Unit later replicated Reichelt's findings at the University of Sunderland, under the direction of Paul Shattock.

Why Implement a Gluten and Casein Free Diet?

According to Shattock, "In the urine of about 50% of people with autism there appear to be elevated levels of substances with properties similar to those expected from opioid peptides."
Because the urinary compounds greatly exceed what could be possibly be of CNS origin, it is presumed that they result from the incomplete breakdown of certain foods.

Proteins consist of long chains of amino acids. Normally intestinal enzymes digest them, breaking the bonds that connect the protein's amino acids. Genetic mutations, caused by changes in the DNA, can mean that specific enzymes cannot do their work.

Enzymes are also proteins; they are long chains of amino acids that fold into specific three dimensional shapes. Each enzyme has an active site into which the protein it is designed to digest can fit. An alteration in the gene that codes for a particular enzyme can mean that it folds in new way, and the protein to be modified no longer fits into the active site. "Mutations...can change the chemistry of the body by preventing or altering the way certain enzymes and chemical reactions work" (Comings, 1990).

In this case, an incomplete digestive process would leave amino acids bound into short chains called peptides. If the peptides still have biological activity—that is, if they still function as opioids—they could result in symptoms we see in autism. Most of the peptides would be dumped harmlessly into the urine, but if a portion escapes the gut and enters the bloodstream, they could cross the blood-brain barrier and cause serious neurological problems.

Two commonly ingested proteins are known to break down into peptides that have opioid activity. *Casein*, a protein in cow's and goat's milk, breaks down to produce a peptide called *casomorphine*, and *gluten* from wheat breaks down to form gliadinomorphins. The amino acid sequences of these two molecules are extremely similar, which is why the elimination of both gluten and casein is usually recommended.

Why Implement a Gluten and Casein Free Diet?

If one lacks the ability to break down these proteins appropriately, there must be a strategy for reducing the effects of the resulting opioids to minimize neurological effects. One approach would be the anti-opioid drug "naltrexone." Naltrexone has shown very mixed results, however, and there are some difficulties associated with its administration.(Dr. Shaw's note: See Dr. Semon's chapter for effective dosing of Naltrexone to supplement dietary changes.) Finding the optimal dose has proved difficult, and it is a very bitter pill, which most children will resist taking. A second approach is excluding casein and gluten from the diet.

Many parents have had traditional allergy tests run, and most report that their children are not allergic to wheat or milk. This is probably true. Children who are helped by this diet are generally not allergic in the traditional sense; they are gluten or casein sensitive. According to Shattock, "The results are akin to poisoning rather than an extreme sensitivity such as occurs in coeliac disease or sensitivity to certain food colourings."

Many children suffer an initial bad reaction to the removal of their favorite foods. Often, these children seem nearly addicted to a specific type of food--often consuming large quantities of dairy or wheat products. Some children do very well for a few days, then suffer a regression. According to Reichelt, this bodes well for the success of the intervention. Once this period passes, it is generally followed by a good response. Younger children are more likely to benefit dramatically from this intervention, but adults have also been noted to have improved concentration and communication, as well as lessened sensory scrambling.

When I first learned of this research, Dr. Reichelt was working with many families in his native Norway. This work convinced him of the diet's efficacy. He was the only person that I knew of who had data from tests of these theories, and I wanted to know more. I tracked down a fax number for him and sent him a letter requesting more information. I included my e-mail address in my fax, and was delighted to receive a response via e-mail, in just two days. In this mail Dr. Reichelt said:

"In general we recommend a diet free of gluten and casein for autistic...patients. The reason for this is that opioid peptides from gliadin are almost of the same structure as casomorphins from casein. We also recommend addition of multivitamin with trace minerals and magnesium, cod liver oil and calcium. We usually remove both casein and gluten. Opioids from these proteins are very similar."

He ended with: "Effects of diet if useful, tends to be cumulative. Must be tried for 1 year."

Further Research

Mr. Shattock, along with colleague Dawn Savery, has recently written a paper that brings their work on this topic up to date. At the time of writing, Shattock and Savery had examined urine samples from nearly 1,000 subjects. While little other information about the subjects was collected initially, the study is now more formal and involves the collection of much more detailed behavioral and other information.

The theoretical model on which their study is based remains the same, relying heavily on work by Reichelt and colleagues (Knvisberg and Waring.) To summarize:

> ...autism could be the consequence of the action of peptides of exogenous origin effecting neurotransmission within the Central Nervous System (CNS.) We believe that these peptides result in effects which are basically opioid in nature....The CNS neuroregulatory role which is normally performed by the natural opioid peptides...would be intensified to such an extent that normal processes within the CNS would be severely disrupted.

> The presence of this intense opioid activity would result in a large number of the systems of the CNS being

> disrupted....Perception; cognition; emotions; mood and behaviour would all be affected. ...Many and diverse symptoms by which autism is...defined would result. We believe that these peptides are derived from an incomplete breakdown of certain foods, and in particular, gluten....and from casein.
> --"Autism as a Metabolic Disorder," Paul Shattock and Dawn Savery (1997)

Any time proteins are broken down in the gut, peptides result; they are intermediate compounds which should then be broken down further into their amino acid components. In all individuals, a proportion of these may cross from the intestines into the bloodstream, and hence, cross the blood-brain barrier. However, if the gut is "leaky" then the proportion of improperly broken down peptides that cross this protective barrier will be far larger, with potentially devastating consequences. [See discussion on Phenol sulfur Transferase below.]

Sam's Story

I gave an overview of what we did when our son was diagnosed, but here is a little more background about him, and his family.

Sam is now nine years old, and was diagnosed as PDDNOS, pervasive developmental disorder-not otherwise specified, a form of autism at age three and a half. We believe that his development was normal for approximately the first 18 months of his life, but by the age of two and a half he was in an early intervention program. Country officials who ran this program never gave us a specific diagnosis, saying only that he had "sensory integration difficulties." This is certainly true—he was significantly delayed in motor planning, he had a poor sense of where he was in space he had "tactile defensiveness"—refusing to touch textures such as shaving cream, finger paint or sand. But as I read the little that was available about the subject, it seemed clear to me that sensory integration problems were likely a *symptom* of something else, rather than the cause of his many problems.

Why Implement a Gluten and Casein Free Diet?

By age three Sam was in a multiply-handicapped half-day preschool, and was receiving private speech therapy. Though he had language from an appropriate age (13 months), by two it was far behind that of peers and was characterized by (appropriately placed) echolalic utterances. When Sam was three and a half, a neurologist at the University of Medicine & Dentistry of New Jersey (at Rutgers University) finally confirmed our suspicions that he might be autistic.

At this time we began doing the research outlined previously, and we sought an independent educational evaluation at the Eden Institute in Princeton, New Jersey. A placement more specific to autism was recommended, and Sam was accepted at the Douglass Developmental Disabilities Center (DDDC) for the next year.

Because DDDC is a data based program, we have hard data on what happened when wheat was removed from Sam's diet. After five days, Sam's aggressions had dropped dramatically, from double digits over the course of a five-hour day to an average of 6.1/day. During the month he was on vacation, Sam did not aggress at all. When he returned to school in September, his aggressions dropped further, averaging 2.47/day over the next seven months.

Reduced aggression was not the only change we noted when dairy, wheat and gluten were removed from Sam's diet. For two years we had struggled with Sam's reversed pronouns. We did drills at home, he worked on it at school and with his private speech therapist. Within one week of his dietary change, his use of pronouns was suddenly and completely correct. His attention span increased and he responded more quickly to lessons at school, home and in private speech and occupational therapies. His speech therapist referred to him as her "one-trial learner."

In the spring of 1994, we visited Dr. Sidney Baker of Westport, Connecticut. He placed Sam on a strict with *anti-yeast diet coupled with high doses of the anti-fungal drug Nystatin*. We were told that before seeing any improvement we might first see a regression. Sam did have a regression that lasted for three weeks, with terrible behavior but no loss of previously attained skills. After a few weeks, Sam's behavior normalized and his aggressions gradually decreased to a level of 2.47 day during the remaining school year. I did not see a marked improvement as a result of this treatment, however, which was a disappointment. I later had the organic acids test performed by Dr. Shaw, which indicated that a new trial of anti-fungal medication might be in order. Since the test has been expanded and refined, we will likely do it again and try, if necessary, an antifungal other than Nystatin.

Dr. Baker also ordered extensive testing of blood, urine, saliva and stool. While most were normal, Sam was deficient in eight amino acids, and low in zinc. In order to put Sam's system into better balance, we added a vitamin compound, additional calcium and zinc to Sam's daily regimen.

I later added molybdenum and magnesium, as well as essential fatty acids (evening primrose oil.) At various times I have also experimented with DMG, L-Carnitine, a (milk-free) acidophilus powder, extra inositol, pycnogenol and octocosanol. Since I never saw any benefit from these additions, I have not continued to use them on a regular basis. I do know of many children who have responded very well to some of these compounds, and I retry them on a period basis just in case something has changed in his system that might make them helpful.

Sam's diet and nutritional supplements are certainly not the only things that have helped him. He spent four years at an excellent special school, and attended weekly speech and sensory integration therapy for five years. For two years he wore yoke prism glasses and did visual therapy prescribed by Dr. Melvin Kaplan of Tarrytown, New York. The prism glasses helped Sam to focus his visual attention for longer periods (though this remains a problem) and it also put an end to his habit of looking at the world using primarily peripheral vision (i.e. squinting his eyes and turning his head and looking from the side.)

However, the change after removing wheat was both remarkable and undeniable, as is what happened on the occasions that he accidentally ingested gluten. On several occasions Sam has eaten gluten without our knowledge, and the changes in him were fast and quite marked. In each case we were able to determine what had caused the sudden, and thankfully short-lived, regression.

While I cannot be sure what has helped Sam the most, I do have a daily record of his behavior and many of his utterances dating back to when he was three. I can therefore correlate changes with particular interventions. Because autism is likely a disorder with multiple etiologies, it is doubtful that every person with autism would benefit from this diet. I believe strongly, however, that the approach would help many children. Indeed, in the three years since I first began to write on this subject, I know the diet has helped thousands that I am aware of and no doubt countless others who have never contacted me. **It is certainly worth trying**.

For a child with a limited diet, I would start with lab tests to determine if he is likely to benefit from the diet (see below). All parents of children with very limited diets want to broaden the food choices the child accepts. However, if positive test results show that gluten and or casein could be causing damage to the CNS, changing the diet is critically important. **NOTE: tests will not be valid once the child has had gluten and/or casein removed from his diet for any length of time.**

Because Sam responded so well to a GF (and greatly reduced casein) diet, I feel frustration that more parents have not been willing to try this diet. However, I also know that I am lucky. My son is not a fussy eater, and accepts the various substitutes I provide for him. He can now monitor his own diet to a certain extent, refusing "regular" bread or cookies. He also eats a wide variety of foods, much of it healthful. He is now able to swallow pills, and can take the vitamin supplements I give him without trouble.

Why Implement a Gluten and Casein Free Diet?

Jake's Story

Sam's brother Jacob was born when Sam was three, and we watched his development very carefully. He was only three months old when we had a definitive diagnosis for Sam. I tried to remain calm about his development, but when Jake was nine months old I began to worry in earnest.

Jake showed little pre-verbal development; he did not babble and he made very few sounds. While his pediatrician understood the source of my concern, he maintained that it was far too early to see anything, and that I should just keep a close eye on him. At this same visit, the pediatrician told me that Jake was ready for cow's milk. I was working full time and under a great deal of stress. My own milk supply had waned and to keep him happy I had added formula to his diet. I was thrilled to throw away the breast pump and the nasty smelling formula supplements. I bought some whole milk and Jake drank it with gusto.

Cow's milk, however, seemed to cause an immediate change in Jake. He got fussier and had more stomach upsets. Within a day I knew that this child was not ready for cow's milk. I immediately went back to the store to buy formula. Then, in a moment that in retrospect seems like an epiphany, I bought soy formula instead. Within two days Jake was happier than he had ever been. Within three days he was saying "mamamamam" and "dadadada".

On his first birthday Jake had about ten words; by 15 months he had 200; by 18 months he spoke in sentences. He has continued to develop into an incredibly imaginative, verbally precocious little boy. At five, Jake calls himself a scientist and is fascinated by all sea creatures (especially sharks.) He wants to be an underwater photographer and to make nature films, but agrees that perhaps kindergarten should come first. He was four before he had cow's milk products again, and by that time they had no effect on him so they are back in his diet to a limited extent. In addition to the joy he has brought to his parents, Jake is the best "therapist" Sam ever had!

Did I "save" Jacob from autism by removing a potentially harmful protein at a vulnerable age? Did I save him from some other developmental disability? Of course, I will never know.

Testing for Urinary Peptides

Because modification of the diet is far less invasive or harmful than most interventions, it would seem logical to try this method. Many children with autism, however, have such finicky eating habits that the idea of cutting anything they will actually eat out of their dietary repertoire, strikes fear the hearts of their parents. For this reason, some might prefer to test their child's urine for the presence of the urinary peptides found by Reichelt and others. If there are no peptides found, it is unlikely that the diet would help the child. However, if the peptides are present and are escaping from the gut into the bloodstream, it is believed that they can "mimic" neurotransmitters and thus result in the scrambling of sensory input.

There is only one laboratory in the US (that I know of) that is doing this testing. Because it is part of the lab's research, there is no charge for the testing. Directions for the collection and shipment of the specimen can be obtained by calling Dr. Robert Cade at the University of Florida at Gainesville. Dr. Cade's assistant, Malcom Privette, can be reached at 352-392-8952.

If the test is positive for urinary peptides, you will still not know whether the problem is casein or gluten (or both). Dr. Cade asks that participants also have a blood test done (by another lab and at a cost of approximately $50) which should determine which protein is problematic. Mr. Privette can give you this information too. Blood serum is assayed for IgA and IgG antibodies to the following proteins: gliadin, gluten, lactalbumin, beta-lactoglobulin, casein and ovalbumin.

If you have already tried the diet you will not learn anything meaningful from the urine test. By eliminating gluten and casein from the child's diet, you have removed the source of the peptides. It can take a long time to build them back up to pre-diet (baseline) levels, and this is not advisable, especially if the diet has proven helpful.

Recently, Dr. Cade has had some success with adding prescription strength digestive enzymes to the regimen of children with autism. These enzymes apparently help break down proteins in individuals whose digestive system is not functioning properly. While it may not mean that the child can start eating whatever he or she would like to, it can be one more weapon in our treatment arsenal.

Testing for Celiac Disease

What exactly IS Celiac Disease (CD)?

"Celiac disease (also known as Celiac Sprue or gluten-sensitive enteropathy) is a chronic disease in which malabsorption of nutrients is caused by a characteristic...lesion of the small intestine mucosa. The lesion is produced, through unclear mechanisms, by protein constituents of some cereal grains" (J.S. Trier, 1993.) Traditionally, doctors have suspected celiac disease only when patients show poor growth, extreme gastrointestinal problems and fatty stools. It is now known, however, that many patients with sensitivity to gluten serious enough to damage the gut wall show no such symptoms!

In people who have celiac disease but continue to eat gluten, the intestinal wall is excessively porous; not only are nutrients improperly absorbed, but large molecules which should be contained by the gut wall are not. This could be the way in which improperly digested peptides pass into the bloodstream and then cross the blood-brain barrier. Thus, the speculation that celiac disease is present in some children with autism who would benefit from a gluten free diet is not inconsistent with the opioid excess theory of Reichelt and Shattock.

Various experts on autism long ago dismissed the idea that gluten could be a significant causal factor. However, gluten exists as a

Why Implement a Gluten and Casein Free Diet?

"hidden ingredient" in many foods, medicines and even in the envelope glue we lick. It is possible that children with autism children put on a so-called gluten free diet were inadvertently ingesting gluten in small amounts.

For those with full blown celiac disease, tiny amounts of gluten can be toxic; it is not so far fetched to imagine that in less severe forms of gluten intolerance, minute amounts could also cause harm. When full blown celiac disease is diagnosed, it can take more than a month on a gluten-free diet to see changes; again, it is not far fetched to assume that the same is true for people with gluten intolerance that have different outward symptoms.

It may be then, that early researchers and parents who tried this intervention in the past simply gave it up too soon. Patients with full-blown celiac disease often have terrible symptoms of gastrointestinal distress, fatigue, and failure to grow or gain weight. These kinds of symptoms cannot be ignored, and the diet is changed when the child is relatively young. But it is possible that far less severe forms of CD exist and are, in fact, quite common. If so, they could go undiagnosed for years. Undiagnosed, the toxic effects of the ingested gluten could prove extremely damaging and could cause what is likely to be permanent damage to the central nervous system.

According to an article by Dr. Allessio Fasano in a 1994 newsletter of the American Celiac Society:

> In recent years there has been a noticeable change in the age of onset of symptoms and the clinical presentation of celiac disease. Because the typical symptoms of gastrointestinal dysfunction are frequently absent in older children, the diagnosis beyond the first two years of life is more difficult and often delayed. These cases are now regarded as having atypical or late onset forms of celiac disease.

Rimland and Meyer noted as long ago as 1967 that children with the highest score on Rimland's E-2 Diagnostic Checklist also showed many gastrointestinal symptoms. It has also been suggested that

212

celiac disease is an autoimmune disorder with gluten stimulating increased synthesis of some antibodies in celiac disease patients. Ruth Sullivan noted that "though few children with celiac disease have autism, it seems a disproportionate number of children with autism have celiac. Why?
Does malabsorption of the small intestine prohibit vital substances (like serotonin...) from reaching the brain? If so, why do not all classic cases have celiac? Or do they? (1975)"

A disorder very closely related to celiac disease, and necessitating the same dietary intervention, is a skin disease known as dermatitis herpetiformes (DH). According to the newsletter of the American Celiac Society, "Dermatitis herpetiformes is the skin manifestation of gluten sensitivity and 70-80% of DH patients have coexisting damage in the intestine." In many cases DH sufferers have no outward signs of intestinal difficulty, and yet at least 70% actually do suffer from celiac disease! DH appears as a bumpy rash, usually on the arms, legs or buttocks. It is extremely itchy and may also burn.

Interestingly, Sam had such a rash on his arm and inner thigh. This rash first appeared at approximately age 2 (around the age his autistic symptoms also appeared) and was diagnosed by our pediatrician and two dermatologists as severe eczema. All prescribed cortisone creams but the rash did not improve. It was so itchy that my son would frequently scratch until he bled. We removed all synthetic fibers, dressing him in only 100% cotton washed in soap that had no colors or dyes. Nothing helped.

Then, as mysteriously as it appeared, the rash went away. Around the time that I changed Sam's diet I also began giving him evening primrose oil, which was said to help eczema. I credited the oil and bought several bottles. Then I stopped using it and the rash did not reappear. I now realize that the cause of the improvement was probably not the oil, but rather the removal of gluten from Sam 's diet! Though I cannot have the tests run because he is been off gluten too long) I am convinced that he was likely showing signs of DH, which were unrecognized by the doctors who saw it. [Note: I later realized the importance of evening primrose oil for the essential fatty acids it provides, after reading Leo Galland's excellent book, *SuperImmunity For Kids*. I then reinstated the oil into Sam's daily regimen.]

New blood tests show latent and sub-clinical cases of celiac disease. Because even latent celiac disease will cause damage to the intestinal wall, it makes sense to have these tests run. The relevant tests involve screening the blood for celiac antibodies. The tests are called endomysial IgA, gliadin IgA and reticulin IgA. The blood test can rule out or suggest Celiac Disease. If celiac disease is not ruled out, a diagnosis still cannot be made. celiac disease can only be positively identified via intestinal biopsy. If a gluten free diet has already been implemented, these tests will not be valid. While these tests will not reveal a possible sensitivity to casein, they should certainly be done on children who developed normally for up to two years (and who are thus more likely sensitive to gluten). Not all labs are equipped to run these tests. If a local lab cannot do it, you might want to contact Specialty Laboratories, Inc., in Santa Monica, CA at 310-828-6543

Although no child will willingly donate blood, all four tests can be performed following a single draw. While it is doubtful that all people with autism will turn out to have celiac disease, these tests should be performed to rule it out.

Certainly celiac disease causes a leaky gut; if various proteins are being improperly metabolized, such a gut would provide a pathway into the bloodstream for these peptides. Clearly these tests should be added to the battery that children undergo when a diagnosis of autism, PDDNOS or atypical autism is made.

Intestinal Permeability tests also exist, and should be performed, if possible [see section on the DAN! protocol below.] This test requires a patient to ingest a sweet drink provided by the lab performing the test, then eat nothing for several hours. This is followed by a collection of all urine for the next 24 hours. This test must be ordered by a doctor, and will show whether or not the patient has a "leaky gut." If the child is not toilet trained, a bag (obtainable from your doctor) can be taped used to collect urine at each diaper change.

Phenol-Sulfur Transferase (PST) Deficiency

Preliminary studies by Rosemary Waring, of the University of Birmingham, UK, suggest a particular enzyme deficiency in many children with autism. This abnormality affects the sulfur-transferase system, which is one of the body's major means of detoxification. In a recently published book, Dr. Sidney Baker describes this system very succinctly:

> This system helps us get rid of leftover hormones, neurotransmitters and a wide variety of other toxic molecules. Some such molecules come from our own metabolism, like leftover hormones and neurotransmitters, and some come into us with our food or are made by the germs that live in our intestines (--*Detoxification & Healing; The Key to Optimal Health*, 1997.)

With insufficient PST, individuals have an extremely low capacity to oxidize sulfur compounds. Children with this enzyme deficiency are unable to fully metabolize certain foods and chemicals that contain phenols and amines.

As stated by Dr. Baker, PST is necessary to break down hormones, some food components and toxic chemicals. If the enzyme is deficient, the body cannot detoxify the system—that is, it will be unable to render these substances harmless. Harmful substances that should be metabolized would build up to abnormal levels, substances which include serotonin, dopamine and noradrenaline. Many metabolic processes can be disturbed by phenolic compounds and cause many physical problems that may not have been previously thought connected to autism (excessive thirst, night sweating, facial flushing, reddened ears etc.)

Why Implement a Gluten and Casein Free Diet?

The children most likely to show this deficiency (based on Waring's small sample size) showed normal development for the first 18 months to two years of life, and also show family histories of asthma, skin problems and migraine, as well as sensitivity to foods (especially wheat, milk and salicylates.)

There are some tests that can identify whether an individual has a weak detoxification pathway, however, normal levels have not been established for children under the age of twelve. Dr. Waring has a working test for children, which uses acetaminophen (Tylenol®) as a "probe" for finding weakness in the PST system. Testing does require a 24-hour collection of urine, a nearly insurmountable difficulty if a child is not reliably toilet trained. For more information Dr. Waring can be contacted at: The School of Biochemistry, University of Birmingham, Edgbaston, Birmingham, B15 2TT England. Dr. Waring does not currently have Internet access. Dr. Robert Sinaiko, a San Francisco specialist in Allergy and Immunology, is working on perfecting a test in this country. Hopefully, such a test will be available soon.

Unfortunately, there is no standardized, recommended treatment for PST deficiency. Two approaches may be taken—you can try to *increase* the body's ability to detoxify itself, or you can try to *decrease* the toxic load you subject it too. Neither approach is particularly easy or 100% effective. To quote Developmental Delay Registry Founder and nutritionist Kelly Dorfman:

> Some parents have used diets that remove all known phenol compounds (such as Sara's Diet) to take pressure off the PST...system. While sometimes helpful, these diets are extraordinarily difficult to implement long-term as naturally occurring phenols are in every food with color. Except in extreme cases, a diet reducing toxic load form the most concentrated sources...appears to be the best. That is, reduce juices (or limit to pear juice) and eliminate all artificial colors and flavors.

Why Implement a Gluten and Casein Free Diet?

> Unfortunately, no amount of intervention...can totally unburden PST...enzymes....That is why it is critically important to improve the efficiency of the faulty enzyme system while attempting to lessen the load. Several nutrients may help. They include vitamin C, vitamin E, reduced L-glutathione and N-acetylcysteine. All of the antioxidants (including selenium and bioflavonoids) are valuable for detoxification in general.
> -From *New Developments*, Winter 96-97, a DDR publication.

Autism researchers have been intrigued by the fact that the a PST deficiency can cause the improper metabolism of some neurotransmitters (serotonin, dopamine and noradrenaline.) It has been known for years that people with autism often have abnormal levels of serotonin, as least as is measured in the blood. But the buildup of serotonin may be less significant than another outcome of a PST deficiency—namely, the effect this deficiency would have on the permeability of the intestinal lining.

One outcome of an improperly operating sulfur-transferase system is insufficient connective tissue in the gut wall. Thus, a PST deficiency could be yet another reason (besides Celiac Disease and other gastrointestinal ailments) that the gut wall would be "leaky." As stated above, when improperly metabolized proteins (such as gluten or casein) are able to escape the gut lining into the bloodstream, they can cross the protective blood-brain barrier.

I noted above that my son 's urinary amino acids tests revealed a deficiency in eight amino acids. Five of these are sulfur-carrying amino acids. Dr. Baker informs me, that this is a pattern he sees very frequently in autistic patients. It will be interesting to follow Dr. Waring 's research to determine whether or not there is a relationship between her theories and the deficiencies he finds. Because the sulfur-carrying amino acids are involved in the detoxification of the body of both exogenous and endogenous pollutants, disturbances in these systems indicate disturbed immune systems.

Considering how frequently these children suffer from numerous infections and allergies, this is not an unlikely assumption. In some parts of the country immunological approaches are being taken with some benefits to children with autism, and it is possible that for some the cause of autism may be an autoimmune disorder.

Though it cannot yet be proven, there is good evidence that a diet that eliminates gluten and or casein may indeed be beneficial. In an unpublished (1993) manuscript, Waring and Reichelt state "We think that the demonstrated peptides may be central to the aetiology of the disease. Exorphins not only increase social isolation in animal models, but may cause CNS inhibition of maturation." Another observation is equally intriguing: "...because most bioactive peptides are found in different chain lengths, but with very similar activity, different peptidase defects would cause similar but not identical symptom profiles and peptide profiles." They believe that this indicates that such "effector peptides" would be the "final common path of several clinical subtypes involving different lengths of peptides. It would also suggest that other diseases may show autistic symptoms if peptides are involved, as is seen for coeliac disease."

If you are convinced (or become so after having tests run) that this dietary intervention is worth trying with your child, you have your work cut out for you. Even a very good cook must relearn how to shop, how to plan menus and how to cook.

For many of the children who respond positively to dietary intervention, gluten and casein are not the only problematic foods. Some children react to corn, soy and eggs, in addition to gluten and casein. Some can eat dairy but not gluten. Some can eat gluten, but no dairy or eggs. Dietary intervention is time-consuming and tedious because you must be systematic in determining which foods cause problems for a given child. But if your child responds, it is worth the trouble.

Where to Go for Help with A Gluten and Casein Free Diet

There is a large population of celiac sufferers in this country; they are experienced in food substitutions and can be a great source of information for people trying to avoid gluten. Five organizations that have newsletters containing lots of valuable information are:

American Celiac Society
201/325-8837 (New Jersey)

Celiac Sprue
Association, USA 402-
558-0600 (Omaha, Nebraska)

Gluten Intolerance Group of Florida
Orlando, Florida 32837
Internet: Celiac@ispace.com

Gluten Intolerance Group
P.O. Box 23053
Seattle, Washington
407-856- 3754

Celiac Disease Foundation
13251 Ventura Blvd. Suite #3
Studio City, CA 91604
818-990-2354

The Gluten-Free Baker Newsletter is published quarterly, and gives recipes for sweet and savory baked goods. 361 Cherrywood Drive, Fairborn, Ohio, 45324-4012

If you have Internet Access, there is a **Celiac List**, which has a great deal of useful information. For information on subscribing to this list, send e-mail to **Celiac@ispace.com**. You will also receive instructions on how to access the archived recipes posted over the last few years.

The Autism Network for Dietary Intervention (A.N.D.I.) publishes a quarter newsletter. For more information write to *The ANDI News*, PO Box 77111, Rochester, NY 14617-0711 or send e-mail to **AutismNDI@aol.com**.

Some Good Cookbooks

Because so many people have asked for more details on the information contained in this chapter, I have recently completed a book on the topic. Over half of the book is devoted to actually implementing the diet, and it contains over 100 gluten and casein recipes. See the end of this chapter for more information.

The Gluten Free Gourmet, More From the Gluten Free Gourmet and *The Gluten Free Gourmet Cooks Fast and Healthy,* by undisputed GF Guru Bette Hagman, are all published by Holt. All are **excellent**. Each has over 200 gluten free recipes for bread, cookies, pizza, chicken pot pie, cakes etc. It's also full of advice about adapting regular recipes and what to use as substitutions. If you can buy only one cookbook, make it one of Bette Hagman's.

Other useful and excellent cookbooks include: *Allergy Cooking With Ease* by Nicolette Dumke and *The Allergy Self-Help Cookbook* by Marjorie Hurt Jones. For those who are limiting yeast, *The Candida Control Cookbook* by Gail Burton is a very good source of recipes.

Full of Beans by Kay Spicer and Violet Currie has recipes using beans and bean flour. These "odd" ingredients make wonderfully moist and delicious baked goods. *No-Gluten Children 's Cookbook* by Pat Cassidy is available for $25.50 from RAE Publications, PO Box 731, Brush Prairie, WA 98606. *The Practical Gluten-Free Cookbook* by Arlene Stetzer is available from Main Street Systems (608) 534-6730.

There are MANY others-check bookstores and libraries! For Web surfers, visit www.amazon.com.

Where Do We Go From Here?

Everyone agrees that autism is a puzzle. It seems at times, that all the pieces are black and we are trying to put it together in the dark! Everyone has to do what he or she thinks is best for his or her children, and for their families. For forty years parents have been given false hopes and empty promises. There are still few definitive answers, and there are still lots of promises being made.

I hope that the reader of this book does not believe that special diets fall into this category. I do not believe that dietary intervention will "cure" children with autism (or at least, not very many.) But it can help, and it can help a lot. For those children who respond to dietary changes, the ones who respond the most will likely be the very young ones. The few children who were cured by dietary interventions (i.e. they have been reclassified after an initial diagnosis of autism) were generally started prior to the age of three, and usually prior to the age of two. My son was five, and while he has made tremendous progress, **he is still autistic**. I have even heard from autistic adults, who started the diet in their twenties and beyond. They are still disabled, but it has alleviated symptoms that were always present and thus cleared up some of the "fog" these folks felt they were in.

This diet probably won't help everyone who tries it, but should you decide to try, you must be both serious and scrupulous about it the trial. You must also make sure that school staff, sitters and (especially) grandparents get with the program. Many an effort has been scuttled by a grandma saying "but just a little couldn't hurt, could it?" Or by a disbelieving outsider betting you won't notice if they slip a cookie or a pretzel to your child. **This cannot work unless everyone who comes near your child follows the strict guidelines that you provide.**

But what else should you do? If we all now know (no thanks to the late Bruno Bettleheim) that this disorder is an organic rather than an emotional problem, why has so little been done to find a medical answer? Fortunately, things are changing somewhat. In January of

1995, Dr. Bernard Rimland convened the first Defeat Autism Now! (DAN!) Conference in Dallas, Texas. It was a gathering of serious researchers who want to find a way to help children with autism, now, not in twenty years. A major undertaking of the group was the writing of a medical protocol to be used by physicians who treat autistic patients.

Called **"Clinical Assessment Options for Children with Autism and Related Disorders: A Biomedical Approach,"** it represents a consensus report of the participants. The protocol was written by Drs. Sidney Baker and Jon Pangborn, and approved by all but one of the practitioner participants. It has recently been revised, and includes a list of doctors who are willing to use the protocol.

The Dan! Protocol, as it is called, is available from Dr. Rimland's organization, for a cost of $25.00. It is a somewhat daunting document, but it is very well worth the effort to buy the protocol and go through it with your child's doctor.

No one expects that every parent will do every test in the protocol. But when you study it, you will find those tests that seem most likely to give you important information for your child. It is a valuable document, and I highly recommend that you contact Dr. Rimland's organization, the **Autism Research Institute at 4182 Adams Avenue, San Diego, CA 92116.** Dr. Rimland's phone number is 619 281-7165 and his website is www.autism.com/ari. In addition to the DAN! Protocol, Dr. Rimland's newsletter will keep you up to date on everything going on in the autism world.

I was fortunate to have been one of four parents invited to join in the first meeting of Dan! Since that time, Dr. Rimland has convened another conference aimed at training doctors and informing parents (and more are planned.) One thing that came out of these meetings, is the shameful lack of research money dedicated to autism. Another parent who attended the DAN! meetings decided to do something about this situation and along with her husband, started the **Cure Autism Now Foundation. CAN** is dedicated to raising money for research. Please contact **CAN** at **1-213-549-0500** or electronically at **can@primenet.com** for information on what you can do to help. If you have access to the Internet, visit the CAN web page at **www.confoundation.org**. It is absolutely vital that we all join in this effort!

Sam's Story...Today

Many people write and call me to discuss the issues covered in my original paper on this topic. **Without a doubt, the question I am asked most often is "How is Sam doing NOW?"** There is no simple answer to this question. In general, we are very gratified at the progress Sam has made and continues to make. But there are always "glitches" along the way.

As of this writing, Sam is nine, and is attending third grade at a "regular" district school. He was transitioned into the district gradually when he was almost seven, with a great deal of support and instruction from the staff of his former school. He has a personal aide who was also trained by DDDC staff. Sam does his academic work in a self-contained classroom, and most of it is one-on-one with his teacher or aide. He attends morning meeting, art, music, gym, lunch, recess and other "specials" with his third grade peers.

Sam's attendance at this school requires a lot of patience on the part of school personnel, and a lot of adjustment on our parts. At times we miss the extra attention and support we got as a family from his former school. But Sam is so happy to have peers who respond to him! Though his behavior has been difficult at times (we still struggle with bouts of non-compliance and aggression) his attendance at this school is a great experience for everyone. He is well liked by staff and students. His peers try hard to help and understand him, and my husband worked with them at the start of the year so that they could understand Sam's struggles better. They are proud to help him when they can, and he greatly enjoys his social times. They have benefited from learning that not everyone faces the same challenges in life.

Sam continues to have difficulty with visual processing, and reading remains a real challenge. It is a challenge he is meeting however, and I am encouraged that Sam will read fluently in the not too distant future.

Sam's language is excellent, and he shows that he is able to generalize ideas and skills quite well. He clearly has a "theory of mind" and is improving at abstract thinking. His school provides two sessions of speech therapy per week, and two of occupational therapy. Noting that Sam really needed and benefited from input to his vestibular system(the system controlling balance), his occupational therapist obtained a weighted vest for Sam. He wears it for much of each day, and teachers report it calms him down a great deal.

Now, about those "glitches"...Sam has shown, over the last four years, a troubling and completely predictable seasonal cycle. As late autumn approaches, life seems to become increasingly difficult. By mid-winter we are deep into a funk, which includes an increase in the number of tantrums and extremely difficult behavior. At this time of year, if he is not under medication, he will regress into terrible aggression and to a lesser degree, self-aggression. We have found that a small dose of Risperdal (Risperidone) is necessary to get through this portion of the year. As spring approaches, behavior improves as does Sam's attitude and mood. Last year, I removed the medication during his "up" period, but he really seemed to need it even then. As of now, he is taking this medication and doing very well on it. I doubt very much that we could get through a winter without this chemical help.

Sometimes being Sam's advocate is very hard work, but we are extremely proud of him. Getting along is the world is more challenging for him than I can even imagine. Despite the rough spots, however, he is in general sweet and friendly. He can (and does) charm the socks off most adults who meet him and work with him. To sum up: life goes on, and we all work hard to ensure that he will be the very best that he can be.

A final note: if you have found this chapter interesting and would like to pursue a dietary intervention, please contact **Future Horizons, Inc.** to obtain a copy of my book on this subject, *Special Diets for Special Kids: Understanding and Implementing Dietary Intervention for Autistic Children.* In addition to discussing the topics covered here, it contains many recipes and tricks to get you started.

Future Horizons can be contacted by:

Phone: 817-277-0727
Fax: 817-277-2270
e-mail: edfuture@onramp.net
www: http://www.onramp.net/autism

Or write to them at:
Future Horizons, Inc.
42 E. Lamar
Suite 106
Arlington, TX 76011

References

1. Baker, S.M. (1997) *Detoxification & Healing: The Key to Optimal Health.* Keats Publishing: New Canaan, CT.
2. D'Eufemia, P. Celli, M., Finocchiaro, R., Pacifico, L., Viozzi, L., Zaccagnini, M., Cardi, E., Giardini, O. (1996) "Abnormal Intestinal Permeability in children with Autism". *Acta Paediatrica* 85: 1076-1079.
3. Gillberg, C. (1988) "The role of endogenous opioids in autism and possible relationships to clinical features" in Wing, L. (ed.) *Aspects of Autism: Biological Research.* Gaskell:London, pp. 31-37.
4. Knivsberg A-M et al. (1990) "Dietary intervention in autistic syndromes." *Brain Dysfunction*, 3:315- 27.
5. _____, Reichelt, K.L., Lind, G., Nodland, M. (1991) Probable Etiology and Possible Treatment of Childhood Autism; *Brain Dysfunction*, 4 (6) 308-319.
6. O'Reilly, B. A. and R.H. Waring (1990) "Enzyme and Sulfur Oxidation Deficiencies in Autistic Children with Known Food and Chemical Intolerances. *Xenobiotica*, 20:117-122.
7. Panksepp, J. (1979) "A neurochemical theory of autism." *Trends in Neuroscience*, 2: 174-177.
8. Reichelt, K.L., et. al. (1981) "Biologically Active Peptide-Containing Fractions in Schizophrenia and Childhood Autism." *Adv. Biochem. Psychopharmacol.* 28:627-643.
9. Shattock, P., Kennedy, A., Rowell, F., Berney, T.P. (1990) "Proteins, Peptides and Autism. Part 2:Implications for the Education and Care of People with Autism." *Brain Dysfunction*, 3 (5) 328-345.
10. _____ and G. Lowdon (1991) "Proteins, Peptides and Autism; Part 2: Implications for the Education and Care of People With Autism." *Brain Dysfunction*, 4:323-334.
11. _____ and D. Savery (1997). "Autism as a Metabolic Disorder," Paper presented to the Annual Geneva Centre Conference on Autism. Toronto, Canada.

Managed recovery from autism and ADD: One family's journey

By Pamela Scott

Introduction

My husband and I were in our late twenties when we decided to start a family. Excited about the prospects of becoming parents for the first time, we were totally unprepared for the events that took place which would change our lives forever. We were certain of two things when we planned our new family: we were going to produce great children and they would be loved beyond belief.

Well, we did produce great children--two of them in fact. And they are certainly loved with all our hearts. What we had not planned on, not even thought about for more than a fleeting moment, was the possibility that something would be different about our babies; that they wouldn't develop like other "typical" children. And we certainly could not have predicted that not just one, but *both* of our children would have disabilities. This reality was never part of our dream, our vision, for our family.

Instead of experiencing the joy of watching a child grow and learn, we felt fear and anxiety as we agonized over every developmental milestone that our children did not meet. As we compared our children to our friends' children, we became *angry*. *Angry* that our lives were different. *Angry* that physicians and therapists didn't have the answers to our questions. *Angry* that the services and programs available did not meet our children's and family's needs. *Angry* that we were supposed to just accept our children's disabilities and go on with our lives. Just plain **angry**! But out of that *anger* came the *energy* we needed to fight for our children. We decided to search for *our* own answers, to see what researchers were working on. We decided to find *our* own ways to help our children be the best that they could be. We decided to rely on *our* own judgement of what was right for our family. We decided to not accept the standard form of medical treatment for our children's disabilities. **We took responsibility and control of our family's future.**

With this control and responsibility came extreme skepticism and lack of support from most physicians and therapists. What we proposed in the form of treatment for our children was considered by many to be alternative, extreme, and controversial. Nonetheless, we felt it was our best chance to enable our children to become independent, self-sufficient adults. We were willing to take the risk. It was a risk that would have huge pay-offs if it was successful. And it was for our family. We would have never forgiven ourselves if we hadn't at least tried these interventions: these controversial, alternative treatments. Yes, they took an extraordinary amount of time and effort. And yes, our lives were certainly anything but normal during the initial stages of implementation, but we managed. Sometimes we managed quite well and sometimes not, *but it wasn't impossible.*

I would like to share with you our family's journey. It wasn't easy and there were many times when we doubted our decisions. But our sons who had been diagnosed with autism and attention deficit disorder are entering kindergarten and second grade this year *without* an educational label. They will **both** be in a regular education classroom. They do not require an aide or for that matter an individualized education plan (IEP). My husband and I believe, beyond a shadow of a doubt, that this would not have been possible without **all** of the interventions we chose for our children.

I know all families will not make the same decisions that we did for our children; every family and child with a disability is unique. I also recognize the fact that not all children with autism and attention deficit disorder (ADD **and** ADHD) will benefit as significantly as ours did from these types of interventions. But I do want to encourage you to read carefully the information presented in this book and give it due consideration. *It changed my family's life.*

I would now like to discuss in detail our journey with our first child Alan who had attention deficit disorder and then our second child Taylor who was diagnosed with autism.

Alan

Alan was very blue at birth, which concerned us somewhat, but he recovered quickly once the nurse gave him oxygen. I was able to hold and nurse him shortly thereafter. He spent his first night curled up next to his father on a cot beside my hospital bed. All things considered, the whole experience went relatively smoothly. We were dismissed from the hospital ten hours after the birth of Alan, our beautiful, 8 pound baby boy, ready to embark on our new life as a family.

We knew to expect a lot of crying from the latest member of our family; newborns do that. And we knew that lack of sleep would now be a part of our lives; this was also part of caring for a new baby. What we didn't know, because this was our first child, is that babies typically sleep for more than an hour at a time, that they shouldn't throw up almost as much as they eat, that colic doesn't mean that they scream for hours on end every day, and that they typically don't need to be in constant motion to not cry, at least not for the majority of a twenty-four hour period.

Ten days after his birth, we took our son to the physician's office. We were reassured that all babies cry and were told that our son could possibly have colic. I barely touched on the fact that we were walking, rocking, or swinging our son in an effort to calm him almost all of his waking hours, which were plenty.

I decided not to go back to work at the end of my maternity leave and opted to stay home and care for Alan.

At six months of age, he still wasn't sleeping like we knew he should. He wasn't throwing up any more, but he was drooling excessively.

The constant screaming and crying that resulted in us walking, rocking, swinging, and bouncing him **many hours every day** was replaced by loud vocalizations and constant motion on his part. By six months of age he could navigate a walker anywhere he wanted to go. We referred to him as a very "busy" child. He was never still!

While we knew Alan wasn't like any of our friend's children, we didn't really know how to articulate these differences to the professionals. He wasn't behind in his development, *just different.* We didn't know how to convey to them that there must be some unknown medical reason for Alan's peculiarities. Consequently, we were never referred to the services and supports we needed. We continued to attribute all of his "odd" behaviors and any developmental deviance to a visual impairment, which we were unclear about because our physicians did not give us good information. We allowed his vision to become the scapegoat. It would take the birth of our second son for us to start putting the developmental puzzle pieces together in order to get the intervention both of our children needed.

When Alan was eight months old, he was prematurely given his fourth DPT shot by the clinic nurse. It had only been five weeks since he had received his third DPT shot and there is supposed to be a minimum of eight weeks between vaccinations. I didn't realize at the time that this shot should not have been given. I vividly recall the nurse taking Alan's immunization card and "whiting out" the information that she had logged about this DPT vaccination. I thought she put the information in the wrong place and was making a correction.

One of the problems this *correction* caused was that our son received one too many DPT vaccinations. This fourth vaccination was never logged on his immunization card. It never occurred to us that the nurse had made a serious mistake. Not only did Alan receive a DPT vaccination three weeks prematurely, he also received an extra DPT vaccination eight weeks later because the nurse, covering up her mistake, falsified his immunization card! Quite frankly if I had known of the mistake at the time, I am confident I would not have understood the significance it would make in our son's health. We simply did what we were told and believed everything the medical professionals told us. That *in itself* is amazing given both my husband's and my own personality.

Prior to this, Alan had never run a fever or even been cranky after receiving a DPT shot. But it wasn't going to be so easy for him this time. He went to sleep very easily and early that night, which was highly unusual for him. Concerned because he hadn't put up his typical bedtime fight, I went to check on him after a half hour or so to make sure nothing was wrong. I found him arched back, shaking, and running a pretty good fever. Terrified, I screamed for my husband Bill to come and help me. We sponged him off to lower the fever and the convulsions stopped almost immediately. Alan was now awake, alert, and somewhat cranky.

We called the doctor's emergency number and were asked about Alan's current status. When the doctor learned that he now appeared to be fine and was only running a low grade fever, he asked what fever reducing medication I had administered. I sheepishly told him none. While I certainly kept some on hand, Alan had never needed any due to a DPT vaccination or, for that matter, any illness. I was chastised and told that Alan's convulsions were due to the fever and to administer the fever reducing medication immediately and continue giving it for the next 24 hours. We were asked to bring him in the next day for a full checkup, which we did.

Feeling very guilty and responsible for his reaction, we stayed up for the remainder of the night to keep a close watch on him. We took him to the clinic first thing the next morning. During this visit, they made it **extremely** clear that Alan's reaction was due to the fact that **we** did not give him fever reducing medication. If **we** had understood the vaccine information we received, **we** would have known to administer the fever reducing medication. We were never informed that **they** had incorrectly given our son a DPT vaccination three weeks prematurely. They never even reported Alan's reaction to the proper agencies. This "error" went undetected by us for over three years. I guess the hardest thing to deal with is the fact that the clinic made **us** feel responsible for Alan's fever and subsequent convulsions, when **they** were negligent.

In spite of receiving one too many DPT immunizations and one of those being given prematurely, Alan continued to grow and develop. His development had always been somewhat different and the truth of the matter is, the unfortunate vaccination mistake didn't change any of his *outward* behaviors. *(We now feel confident that these vaccination errors intensified his unusual immune system responses.)*

Alan never learned to crawl but was pulling up and "cruising" by the time he was seven months old. And by the time he was eight months old, he was walking very well and into everything. He had also mastered climbing out of his crib, so bedtime was literally a nightmare. When he did stay in the crib, it was to bounce it across the floor or bang it into the wall. I was going crazy!

The other moms I knew could place their child on a blanket on the floor with a few toys and actually get some things done around the house. But not me! These other moms also had children who took naps. I didn't dare let Alan sleep during the day or we would be up all night, instead of the luxurious three maybe four hours of uninterrupted sleep we were getting. Of course this sleep came after Alan had put up at least an hour and a half worth of protest. It wasn't that he wasn't tired or sleepy; but he just couldn't be still or relax long enough to allow himself to sleep. These horrific sleep patterns continued until Alan was 4 years old. This child had endless energy and we were exhausted.

If nothing else, Alan was consistent. His strong preferences about everyday routines were carried over into his eating habits as well. I had been making my own baby food for Alan, but he was very particular about what he would eat. His favorite food groups, after nursing, were dairy and grains. He enjoyed only a few other foods and this disturbed me somewhat because he was on the low end of all the growth charts every time we went to a well baby visit. I thought perhaps if he consumed a wider variety of foods it would help him to gain weight. How **much** he ate wasn't the problem, he had a sufficient appetite. But his strong attraction to certain foods bothered me.

Alan tolerated the rice and barley baby cereal I fed him, but he loved cottage cheese, American cheese, mashed macaroni and cheese, yogurt, scrambled eggs, applesauce, bananas, and almost any kind of bread or cracker. I had no way of knowing at the time that these very foods were responsible for a large portion of his hyperactivity and sleep disturbances (even though we didn't call it hyperactivity back then). We were unaware that Alan had been plagued with significant food allergies since birth and that a majority of his atypical behavior and development could be explained by these allergies.

I was having a difficult time keeping up with Alan as I entered into my second pregnancy. He seemed to be getting more restless and noncompliant. We attributed this to the terrible two's and the expectation of a new baby. I can remember when the new baby started moving. It was so different from Alan's movement in the womb. While the new baby was gently stirring, I would recall how Alan had *literally* almost broke my ribs a few weeks before delivery! In fact, he had been a very active baby even **before** he was born.

And so, five months into focusing on Alan's needs, I gave birth to our second son, Taylor.

(We would later learn that while Alan did not have elevated fungal metabolites due to yeast, he did have elevated levels of anaerobic bacteria products commonly found in children who have been diagnosed with Attention Deficit Disorder and Attention Deficit Disorder with Hyperactivity.).

Taylor

The first year of Taylor's life, we watched him experience a "typical" development. In doing so, we realized how atypical Alan's development had truly been. Taylor actually played with his baby toys and could entertain himself. He was so much calmer than Alan that when we looked back on Alan's first two years of life, it was hard to believe we had survived.

Taylor continued to grow and become his own little person. He was blossoming. He had a wonderful sense of humor, could follow simple instructions, and by one year of age was able to combine a few words, "mama up, want down, go bye-bye, I love you, want more." And he was proficient at making farm animal sounds upon our request! Like his brother, he was an early walker, mastering this feat at 10 months of age after a short stint of belly crawling.

When he was approximately 10 months old, I stopped breast feeding him (actually he was just not interested in nursing anymore) and was having a difficult time finding a formula he would drink. Against the advice of our *new* family physician, I began to give Taylor whole milk. He just would NOT drink anything else (or so I was inclined to believe at the time).

Within a few weeks of adding whole milk instead of a formula to his diet, he needed a round of antibiotics to clear up an upper respiratory tract infection. This would be the first antibiotic in a long line of prescriptions that Taylor would receive for his **repeated** infections. Though the physician was aware that I was giving Taylor whole milk (occasionally Taylor would tolerate the Carnation Good Start formula), the correlation between the increase in milk products and subsequent infections was never made.

Over the course of the next year, Taylor was sick more often than he was well. We were told he had common upper respiratory tract infections. He looked and felt terrible most of the time. In fact he was sick so often, the physician began writing Taylor's prescriptions to be refilled without an office visit, for our convenience. In spite of feeling ill most of the time, Taylor continued to develop typically, *for a while.*

As you know, when a child doesn't feel well it can be a stressful event for the child *and* the family. It was very distressing to have a toddler who was constantly sick and it began to trouble me deeply that we could not find the cause of Taylor's ever increasing upper respiratory tract and occasional ear infections. The antibiotics being prescribed were becoming less effective, more potent, and quite expensive.

Between 10 months and 22 months of age, Taylor received 7 rounds of antibiotics. He began developing dark circles under his eyes and a constant wheezing sound in his chest. At diaper changes, we began noticing that his urine had an odd musty smell to it. He began to have consistent loose stools that often contained mucous, but it was not diarrhea. His genital area would be **VERY** red at times and as soon as his diaper was loosened at changes, he would grab his reddened genitalia. (Dr. Shaw's note: all of these symptoms are characteristic of intestinal yeast overgrowth.)

A significant sleep disturbance was emerging as well. He started having difficulty going to sleep and began waking up at least four times in the night shaking and crying pitifully. He would literally *gulp down* one or two glasses of water as fast as he could and then fall back asleep. He didn't seem to urinate sufficiently for the amount of fluid he took in either. He started to ignore our requests and stopped following simple commands. He became very cranky, tired, and agitated most of the time. We thought he was starting the terrible two's somewhat early when, in fact, *he was changing in a different way.*

Between taking care of a sick toddler who was up several times a night and trying to keep up with a child who slept very little and was extremely energetic *(hyperactive)*, I was beginning to feel

235

overwhelmed again. I knew in my heart of hearts that something was going on with my children, I just couldn't put my finger on it.

While Alan was making definite progress in many areas of development, we still had areas of concern about other aspects of his personality. He just never sat still and played appropriately with toys. He was constantly in motion: running, rolling, spinning. He was frequently making this odd "p-shoosking" sound. He had also begun to ask us questions repeatedly. (*We would answer his question and two to five seconds later he would ask it again. He would continue asking, sometimes to a point of breakdown, his and ours.*) He was grinding his teeth down to nothing and compulsively biting the skin around his nails. He was obsessive about insisting on sameness in household routines and he was becoming very disruptive. He felt the need to empty **everything** in a closet, toy box, drawer, cabinet, whatever, into a pile in the floor. It didn't matter if you were visiting someone else's home either; if the urge came over him, it was done.

In addition to this, he was becoming aggressive toward his brother. I couldn't leave Taylor unattended in the same room with Alan for fear he would hurt him. It wasn't that he didn't love his brother or get enough one-on-one attention from his father and I either. (This had been suggested to us several times when we would discuss our concerns with family, friends, and professionals.) Alan simply couldn't control himself. He was having trouble listening to us at home and his preschool teachers were having difficulties getting him to following directions at school as well, even though he was an incredibly bright little boy.

I recall visiting with a friend from church one day about Alan's behavior. It was immediately after he had consumed a cup of red fruit punch in Sunday school. I never purchased this brand of punch, preferring 100% juice. Alan was *literally* climbing the walls within 15 minutes of drinking it. Needless to say, we hurried home from church. By the time we got home, Alan was extremely agitated. He started rolling on the floor and making odd vocalizations. He was unable to focus and could not control his emotions. Fortunately, my friend had heard about the dyes and preservatives in foods causing these types of adverse reactions in some children and shared this information with me.

This was news to me and I was skeptical. I was also desperate to find answers about my son's behavior because I didn't feel like an effective parent. I decided to put this newfound knowledge to the test. Not believing food could actually cause this type of a reaction, I purchased the same brand of punch Alan had that day at church. I gave it to him for lunch. Our afternoon was not pleasant!

Once again, he exhibited the same type of reaction: rolling on the floor, odd vocalizations, agitation, and emotional distress. I was clearly shocked that food could cause my child to behave in such a fashion. With that seed being planted, I began to wonder about what else food could do to effect behavior and health. Could there be a connection between Alan's strange behavior and other foods? Could Taylor's chronic illnesses be allergy related?

I didn't have to wait long before I had my first opportunity to visit with our family physician on this topic. Taylor had developed yet another infection. This time when I went to the physician's office, I was armed with a list of questions regarding food allergies and illnesses. I was told Taylor's chronic infections had absolutely **nothing** to do with food allergies. All children catch several colds their first two years of life which easily lead to the secondary infections Taylor was experiencing. I was also told that food dyes were safe and did not in any way affect behavior in children. END OF CONVERSATION. At least with him anyway.

I didn't feel confident pursuing the matter any further and left with yet another prescription for antibiotics. I thought his response was a little too emotional and the finality with which he made his claim somewhat disturbing. One thing was for sure, Alan would **not** be ingesting any fruit punch or other foods that contained colors or dyes even if the physician believed there was not a connection between food, allergies, and behavior!

Taylor's development was typical up until he was 15 months old, with the exception of the constant infections. Since his birth, we had the good fortune to participate in a Missouri Department of Education Program called "Parents as Teachers". The program assigned us a parent educator that came to our home for routine visits. The parent educator distributed parenting and educational materials, administered a developmental screening, and documented the findings. Taylor met or exceeded all expectations on each of these screenings until he was 17 months old.

During this particular home visit, the educator asked me about imitation, or the emergence of it, in Taylor's play. I really had to think hard to remember if I had seen him doing anything like that in awhile. I couldn't confidently answer her question. At 17 months of age, this type of play should be developing and she told me to watch for it over the coming summer. This was in May and her next scheduled visit would be in the fall, when the school year started. We would not have to wait that long to discover that Taylor was not on track.

My inability to confidently answer the educator's question tormented me. I began to mentally go over Taylor's development and note the changes in his behavior. Taylor had certainly started communicating early. He had begun using words and putting them together precociously. But he just didn't seem to have the desire to talk anymore or to participate in our family. When I would mention this to family members and friends, I was cautioned not to compare my children to one another. Meanwhile, Taylor continued to withdraw and I was scared.

By the time Taylor was 18 months old I was becoming increasingly alarmed. While I was watching for him to start imitating in his play, I noticed how differently he had started to interact with his toys. It wasn't the same type of play he had exhibited several months earlier and he would throw an absolute fit if you interrupted him or tried to play with him. By the time he was 21 months old, it appeared to me that Taylor was purposefully ignoring my simple requests to interact. Then I began to question his hearing.

I discussed this with my husband and we felt like it was certainly a possibility worth pursuing. We decided to ask babysitters, Sunday school teachers, friends, and relatives if they had noticed a difference in Taylor's personality. We asked if they thought he was fussy and cranky because he couldn't hear and was having a hard time understanding what was going on. They all agreed that he had become withdrawn, "spaced out", and difficult to manage. And then one of them said, *"Well, I have noticed he doesn't talk much anymore and he seems upset much of the time. He used to be so happy."*

We decided to test his hearing ourselves. We set up a variety of opportunities for Taylor to interact with his family and environment. For one of our tests, we quietly came into the room with a pot and spoon and began to loudly bang it, repeatedly, in close proximity to his head. He was sitting in the middle of the living room floor manipulating his toy cars (lining them up) and HE DIDN'T EVEN FLINCH. He was absolutely lost in his own world. We stood there watching him for a few seconds, waiting to see if he would acknowledge our presence. He did not. I can't begin to tell you how scared we both were. The remaining tests we devised proved to be just as disappointing. I immediately made an appointment for Taylor to see our family physician.

Because we had insisted on the first available appointment, we saw a new physician in the practice. He was a very good listener and legitimized our concerns. He called an ear, nose and throat clinic while I waited and scheduled an appointment with an audiologist for the following morning. He agreed that we needed to investigate a possible hearing loss.

Surprisingly, Taylor cooperated nicely for the audiologists. They placed him in a high chair in the middle of the testing booth. He turned on cue every time he heard a sound. He "passed" all their tests. I was confused. I discussed, *in detail*, my concerns about his hearing. I was told he had scored within normal limits on all their tests and they hadn't found anything out of the ordinary. They recommended I wait a month and discuss my concerns with our parent educator through the Parents as Teachers program. (I had filled out an extensive patient history.)

I boldly refused this advice and **insisted** on a visit with the ear, nose and throat (ENT) specialist (otolaryngologist). I needed a *physician's* opinion on Taylor's hearing. While I was scheduling this appointment, I learned that the clinic had a speech pathologist on staff and requested an appointment with her as well. If Taylor wasn't communicating anymore, maybe she could help us figure out why. Fortunately, the ENT doctor and speech pathologist agreed to work us into their schedule that afternoon.

That afternoon my husband and I took Taylor to the clinic for his preliminary evaluation with the Speech Pathologist. As she observed Taylor and began to ask us questions, we had the realization that something **very** serious was going on. After she had gone over all the forms and questionnaire we had filled out, we were asked to wait in the reception area so she could consult with the ENT doctor.

The ENT doctor was a compassionate man who listened intently to our concerns and fears. He observed Taylor manipulating toys and tried to interact with him repeatedly. He looked at us with genuine anguish as he shared the speech pathologist's findings and his own conclusion. Their findings indicated that something other than his hearing lay at the root of our concerns. They were both sensitive to our feelings and very understanding. (We weren't accustomed to this.) He suggested that Taylor see a pediatric neurologist **immediately**. There was only one specialist of this nature in our area and because he was new, his schedule was full. Though the ENT had tried to get us in the following day, we had to wait a week for the appointment. Needless to say, it was an unpleasant week for our family.

Suspecting your child's development is out of the ordinary and having those concerns validated by a specialist is terribly frightening. We had wholeheartedly anticipated that the ENT would find the cause of Taylor's mysterious behavior to be linked to a hearing loss.

Since you don't see neurologists for anything remotely routine, we were very nervous about the appointment. Because we were so afraid and didn't have a clue what to expect, we filled our time by examining Taylor's development. We began by polling all the people involved in his life. We talked about their answers and shared our own observations. Then we compiled a list of all the changes that had occurred in Taylor's personality and development over the past few months. The list was quite extensive.

1. Lack of language or any verbalization
2. Loss of previously used words and phrases
3. Severe sleep disturbances
4. Constantly tired, cranky, and unhappy
5. Spaced out
6. Dark circles under his eyes
7. Spinning himself for an unusual amount of time per day
8. Chronic infections
9. Possible hearing loss
10. Unusual play with toys
11. Resistance to human interaction
12. Developing a weird gait while walking
13. Toe walking
14. Teeth grinding
15. Odd change in hair color and texture
16. Unaware of his environment and the people in it
17. Purposefully putting himself in tight places (i.e. between the wall and refrigerator, and under couch cushions)

18. Excessive thirst at night
19. Lining up his toys
20. Avoidance of eye contact
21. Putting his body at odd angles to look at things
22. Prolonged temper tantrums
23. Clumsiness (previously he had been very well coordinated)
24. Musty odor to urine
25. High tolerance for pain

Shocked by the number of items our list contained, we realized how serious Taylor's situation was. We had never sat down and analyzed his development before. It was clear he was regressing. Feeling intimidated, we asked Bill's mother to go with us to the neurologist for moral support. In the meantime, we began searching medical books and looking on the Internet for possible solutions to the symptoms Taylor was experiencing. Autism was the word that kept cropping up.

Our encounter with this particular neurologist was the best and worst thing that could have happened to our family. Despite his poor bedside manner, the visit started off typically enough with him looking over Taylor's file. He read our family doctor's report, the ENT doctor's report, and the speech pathologist's report. He asked a few questions (some of them we found quite odd) and made an inflammatory remark about the speech evaluation. We were then moved to an examination room where he tested Taylor's reflexes, tracked his eye movement, and watched him walk.

I cautiously brought up the subject of autism and asked if he felt this could be at the root of Taylor's regression. I was told (in a very condescending manner) that children who have autism were very different from our son and that autism was evident from birth. Because of our recent research into Taylor's regression, I knew this was not totally accurate, but I wasn't sure how to respond.

In a manner you would use to tell someone their child has a cold, he informed us of our son's suspected misfortune. *"It doesn't look good for Taylor,"* was his first statement. The three of us were dumbfounded. "What do you mean, it doesn't look good?" I asked.

He proceeded to tell us that Taylor had a neurodegenerative brain disease, that we would have to do extensive testing to determine which disease it was, and that these diseases were incurable.

I pressed on, "What do you mean, incurable? Will he die from this disease?"

His response was even more shocking *"Yes. It could take 18 months or 18 years depending on which disease it is. But you better hope for 18 months, because the pain and suffering are unbearable."*

I was numb. I could clearly see that my husband and mother-in-law were as astonished at this remark as I was.

We assumed he found something conclusive in his examination of Taylor that would give him the confidence to make a statement like this. "What causes this disease?" was our next question. Another offensive response: *"It's genetic. Let's just say that it is unfortunate that you and your husband met and had children."* Terrified, I asked the next question. "If it's genetic will it affect our other son?" His answer: *"Once we determine which disease Taylor has we will have to test Alan. Chances are he will acquire this disease as well."*

Feeling the crushing weight of the world, we sat in silence, in disbelief. He told us we would need to have blood tests done immediately to determine which neurodegenerative disease we were dealing with. It would take six to eight agonizing weeks before we could expect to have the test results back. Since these were rare diseases, not all labs were equipped to administer the tests. The blood would have be sent to laboratories in several states.

243

Physician's orders in hand, we made our way to the hospital laboratory.

The two months of waiting were a nightmare. I remember thinking how nice a diagnosis of hearing impaired or autism would sound in comparison to being told you were going to lose one and quite possibly both of your children to a hideous disease. We stumbled through the days and cried through the nights as our lives came crashing down around us. We poured every ounce of energy into interacting with Taylor. We refused to watch him leave us without a fight.

Remembering the speech pathologist who had been so compassionate and understanding, we decided to give her a call, to take a chance. We knew full well that if Taylor had one of these neurodegenerative diseases, a speech therapist would be of no help. We asked her to start coming to our home twice a week. My husband and I wanted to know how to communicate with the son we were losing. With reservation, she accepted the challenge. It was one of the best decisions we ever made.

The day for answers finally arrived. We had prepared ourselves as much as we could for the news. When we entered the neurologist's office, it was evident that his tone and demeanor were somewhat different from our initial visit. He wasn't quite so abrasive and egotistical. Almost begrudgingly, he informed us that all of our son's tests were normal. (The urine organic acid test done initially was done at a laboratory that did not check for byproducts of microorganisms). He couldn't answer any of our questions except to say that if he were in medical school and Taylor's history was presented as a case study on an exam, he would have failed the exam had he not proceeded in EXACTLY the same manner in which he had.

The neurologist wanted us to see a child psychiatrist. He said he had spoken with her about Taylor and that she would be the appropriate professional to help us. When I called to make an appointment, I was told what the visit would entail, how long to expect to be there, and the cost. When I asked about the specific developmental tests mentioned, I was told that these were the standard tests administered when diagnosing autism or pervasive developmental disorder. I WAS FURIOUS! I thanked the receptionist for her time and promptly canceled the appointment.

I have since learned that the child psychiatrist is a competent, well respected professional. But I wasn't about to see a professional recommended by the neurologist who so condescendingly informed my family that Taylor's regression had NOTHING to do with autism.

Diagnosis of autism
Knowing that because of this misdiagnosis we would always and forever get a second medical opinion on anything remotely serious, we scheduled appointments for Taylor to be evaluated by our local regional center (the state agency responsible for diagnosing and providing services to individuals with developmental disabilities) and a team of neurologists at a University Autism Clinic. We went through all the testing and questions and watched with agony as Taylor failed to comply with their requests. They were all in agreement: late-onset infantile autism. It became Taylor's official diagnosis.

Intervention
The diagnosis of autism was **easy** to take after believing your son was going to suffer a slow, agonizing, painful death. So, while Bill focused on meeting our growing financial demands due to the necessary therapies *(by working three jobs)*, I focused on educating myself about autism.

Taylor had been participating in speech therapy for over a month when he was officially diagnosed. Immediately after receiving a confirmed diagnosis, we added small group speech therapy (at a local university communications disorders lab), occupational therapy (with an emphasis on sensory integration), and in-home behavior management. Initially, the only one-on-one therapy Taylor received outside the home was occupational therapy and we changed this to in-home as soon as possible.

Though Taylor seemed to be benefiting from these interventions, we knew he was going to need something more if we wanted to get our happy little boy back. I was fortunate enough at this time to come across work by Dr. Bernard Rimland and Dr. Ivar Lovaas. I soon realized that we should consider a nutritional approach as well as an intensive one-on-one program.

The occupational therapist that did Taylor's initial evaluation was intrigued by my comments on a dietary approach. She shared with me information about a family she worked with whose child was diagnosed with autism. *Some* of this particular child's autistic behavior was directly related to the food allergies he struggled with. While a diet did **not** cure this child, the results were remarkable. The occupational therapist arranged for me to visit with this family who was willing to share their experiences with an elimination diet (which helps detect hidden food allergies)and other allergy interventions. I was grateful.

As a direct result of my conversation with this wonderful family and my own experience with foods causing adverse reactions (Alan and the red fruit punch), I decided to start with a dietary/nutritional approach. While I was reading one of Dr. Rimland's papers regarding the removal of certain foods from the diet and the positive effects it had on some children with autism, I noticed a one-line statement about Candida-related autism. My interest was piqued. I knew first hand that a round of antibiotics could cause a vaginal yeast infection and I decided to look into the matter since Taylor had certainly had more than his fair share of antibiotics.

I first learned everything I could about yeast and its possible effects on the body.

It seemed logical that Taylor's loose, mucous-containing stools were the direct result of a yeast overgrowth. It also seemed logical that the redness around his anus and in his genital area, which we thought was a diaper rash, was actually a yeast rash that was causing an intense itching feeling. It could also explain his urine's musty odor. I read that a yeast overgrowth could cause fatigue, which Taylor certainly suffered from.

In one of Dr. William Crook's papers (author of *The Yeast Connection, Tracking Down Hidden Food Allergies,* and many other books and articles on allergies and yeast) he talked about ear infections, upper respiratory tract infections, antibiotics, and their relationship to allergies and childhood behavior. I became confident there was a correlation between Taylor's chronic infections, antibiotic use, and his subsequent regression.

During my quest to learn about yeast, I came across a book entitled *"Dr. McFarland's Anti-Candida Diet".* The book was actually a six month program, divided into phases, to eradicate the overgrowth of yeast using a strict diet and a large number of nutritional supplements. Though the program was designed for adults with yeast related illnesses, it made sense to me and I decided to modify the supplement portion of the plan to accommodate a 24 month old child.

(I would like to note that Taylor began taking Super-Nuthera powder approximately one month before we implemented an anti-Candida diet. His eye contact certainly increased with the addition of this supplement and he didn't have as many tantrums at transitions.)

As I began educating myself on diet and nutrition, it became very clear that Alan needed a diet overhaul as well. He had experienced hives on several occasions (*it wasn't always clear what brought on this reaction*) and he had also begun to have unexplained low-grade fevers, joint pain, muscle weakness in his legs, and migraine headaches. His hyperactivity and inability to concentrate were at an

247

all time high. I didn't think he would benefit from the same anti-Candida diet I had planned for Taylor, *(I was mistaken)* but I certainly felt that he would benefit from having all colors, dyes, preservatives, sugar, and processed foods removed. I devised a separate diet and supplement program for him.

Initially, we were unable to find a physician who would listen to our concerns and help with the allergies we felt both of our sons were tormented by. *(In fact, it took us almost two years before we found such a physician).* Not only were physicians not helpful, but we were told on more than one occasion that food or chemicals in the environment COULD NOT cause the type of reactions we were describing. We were bold enough on one occasion to bring copies of our programs for Alan and Taylor for their approval. What a mistake! We were told to not waste our time, that these alternative therapies were a hoax. Since these same physicians were unable to offer their own treatment plan (other than a pharmaceutical "fix" to help our children sleep), we decided to forge ahead with our plans and implement the necessary dietary and supplement changes.

Feeling extremely apprehensive about undertaking such an enormous task without a formal education in nutrition, I decided to consult with a pediatric dietician. The problem was, we couldn't get an appointment until well after the holidays. We decided to proceed on our own until our scheduled appointment. So approximately one month before Christmas, our family started on a journey that would lead to incredible successes for both our children.

We had developed a great relationship with Taylor's speech pathologist and she was very encouraging. We shared with her all of the information we had gathered and she felt it was certainly worth pursuing. Her encouragement meant everything. We also had the support of a family friend who had been fighting yeast-related illnesses for several years. She proved to be critical in helping us to modify recipes.

It is extremely intimidating to step outside the box of standard medical practice and it is so very **critical** that families receive the necessary supports when doing so. If our own family had not received support from a few key individuals, it would not have been possible for us to manage this type of intervention.

The following diet and nutritional supplement programs we implemented for our children were vital to the successes they achieved.

Anti-Candida Diet

Hormone-free, free-range meats *(You will need to purchase free-range meat from a health food store or a natural food cooperative. Store-bought meat contains the hormones and antibiotics the animals have been administered.)*
Fresh vegetables *(organic if possible)*
Organic brown rice
Filtered water
Spices *(sea salt, pepper, and fresh garlic)*
Expeller pressed canola oil *(Oils in the grocery store are derived through a process using petroleum-based chemicals.)*
Now Brand Pure Vegetable Glycerin *(I used this to "sweeten" Taylor's rice and to add to his supplements so he would take them)*
Hain Safflower Margarine *(DO NOT purchase the "no salt" formula as it contains a preservative that may or may not be from a natural source.)*
Brown Rice Flour Brown Rice Pasta *(There are many brands available at health food stores that contain only filtered water, sea salt and brown rice.)*

This restrictive diet seemed to us to be the most natural approach to killing the yeast we felt was interfering with Taylor's development. Because Candida thrives in a sugary environment, we eliminated not only processed simple sugars, but all sugars (i.e. fruits and fruit juices, honey, maple syrup, brown rice syrup etc.) In our efforts to limit carbohydrates (which the yeast can convert to food to survive on), we had unknowingly removed gluten from Taylor's diet. We removed milk and dairy products because we felt confident they had played a role in Taylor's repeated infections. The diet portion of this program was relatively easy to follow since all processed foods were eliminated. Although it was not complicated, it took a little more time to plan ahead and prepare. Getting him to **eat** the foods was another matter.

Taylor's Supplements

Twinlabs Calquick (NON-DAIRY liquid calcium supplement) *Since Taylor is now able to take his supplements in capsule form, I prefer to use **Nature's Way Calcium**, it contains calcium citrate and malate, it is also dairy free.*

NOW Magnesium (Magnesium oxide in a powdered form) *I now use magnesium citrate or magnesium glycinate in a capsule form that can be pulled apart and added to a food if the child cannot tolerate swallowing pills. Both our children now take their magnesium in a citrate and glycinate form.*

Kyolic Pure Garlic Oil Extract (If your child can swallow pills, you may want to use the capsule form, but make sure it is the formula that does NOT contain whey, which is a form of dairy.) *I would get Taylor to take this by putting it on his pasta for flavoring.* This product is an antifungal agent.

Twinlabs MCT Oil (medium chain tryglycerides with orange flavor added) *In retrospect, I wish I had used the plain formula, it is more versatile.* (This product is broken down in the intestine to form the antifungal agent caprylic acid; see chapter on yeast and antifungal treatments.)
NOTE: If your child can swallow pills, caprylic acid supplements are very effective in killing yeast.

***DO NOT** attempt to pull caprylic acid capsules apart in order to add the powder to food, it is extremely bitter and causes a burning sensation on the mucous membranes in the mouth.*

DDS Acidophilus (DAIRY FREE acidophilus in a powder, they also make a capsule form, it is to be given 30 minutes prior to meals in a small amount of filtered water) **DDS now makes a powdered formula that contains FOS, (fructooligosaccharides). FOS is a natural carbohydrate that effectively promotes the growth of beneficial bacteria such as lactobacillus acidophilus and bifidobacteria in the lower intestine.**(1) *If your child swallows pills, you may want to try Nature's Way Primadophilus Jr, Kyo-Dophilus, and Futurebiotics Acidophilus+. They are all dairy free products. You will need to add FOS individually as these brands do not contain it. Twinlabs NutraFlora FOS powder is an acceptable option.*

NOTE: When taking any form of acidophilus or FOS (fructo-oligosaccharides) it is important to gradually work up to the recommended dosage. Adding acidophilus too quickly can cause constipation OR diarrhea. FOS may initially cause gas and belching. (1)

Twinlabs Zinc (chelated zinc gluconate and zinc picolinate, 30mg) *Taylor now takes zinc in the picolinate form only. If your child cannot swallow pills you can buy a capsule form, pull it apart and add it to food. You may also choose to purchase zinc in a liquid form.*

Super Nuthera (powdered form) *Taylor still takes this supplement in the tablet form.*

Twinlabs Choline/Inositol *At the time Taylor was taking SuperNuThera in the powdered form and it did not contain choline and inositol. I knew the tablet form did and decided to supplement these B vitamins.* **Choline is needed for nerve transmission and**

inositol is vital for hair growth.(1) *Remember, Taylor's hair had changed colors and texture. It really didn't feel like hair at all, it was dry and brittle and when he was having a particularly bad day in regards to his behavior, his hair would literally be standing straight up. It was an unexplainable phenomenon.*

Nutricology MultiMin (multiple mineral supplement)

Natrol EPO (evening primrose oil) Primrose oil contains essential fatty acids (EFAs) which aid transmission of nerve impulses and are needed for normal brain function. EFAs are also beneficial in the treatment of candidiasis.(1)

Schiff CoQ10 (Coenzyme Q10) Is a vitamin like substance that resembles vitamin E, but which maybe an even more powerful antioxidant. It is also called ubiquinone. It plays a crucial role in the effectiveness of the immune system, it is beneficial in treating candidiasis, and it has the ability to counter histamine and therefore could be valuable to allergy and asthma sufferers.(1)
Getting Taylor to take all of his supplements was not an easy task. We developed a schedule and he took his supplements before and after every meal and at bedtime. It has been three years and nine months since we started using nutritional supplements and **what** he takes and the **quantity** has changed **considerably.** He is now able to take all of his necessary supplements with his breakfast and evening meal.

Alan's diet was not nearly as restrictive as Taylor's and was originally based on the *Feingold Diet.* The *Feingold Diet* addresses not only food allergies and sensitivities, but the relationship food **additives** play as well. We eliminated **ALL** preservatives, colors, dyes, and processed foods from Alan's diet. In addition, we had to eliminate many typically healthy fruits and vegetables. While this diet made a *marked* improvement in his behavior, we were still missing a critical piece of the puzzle. He took the following supplements while he was on this diet.

For more information about this diet contact:
The Feingold Association of the United States
P.O. Box 6550, Alexandria, VA 22306
(703) 768-FAUS

Alan's Supplements

Natrol Kids Companion (chewable multiple vitamin)
Nutricology MultiMin (multiple mineral supplement)
Natrol EPO (evening primrose oil)
Nature's Way Citronex (grapefruit seed extract)
Schiff Pycnogenol (pinebark)
Schiff CoQ10 (Coenzyme Q10) Is a vitamin like substance that resembles vitamin E, but which maybe an even more powerful antioxidant. It is also called ubiquinone. It plays a crucial role in the effectiveness of the immune system, it is beneficial in treating candidiasis, and it has the ability to counter histamine and therefore could be valuable to allergy and asthma sufferers.(l)
Nature's Way Primadophilus (multiple strains of probiotics, i.e. acidophilus)
Twinlab Zinc 30mg(chelated zinc gluconate and zinc picolinate)

These diets will seem severe and too difficult for many families to adhere to. We decided on them for a variety of reasons.

In Taylor's case we had heard about using Nystatin to kill yeast overgrowths. We had even talked to a couple of families who had children with autism who had been using Nystatin successfully for several months. The problem was, when the child went off the Nystatin, the autistic symptoms returned. We didn't like the idea of a long term use of **any** pharmaceutical and decided to try a "natural" approach with garlic oil, Lactobacillus acidophilus bacteria, and MCT oil first. Everything we read about yeast and Candida outside of *"mainstream"* medicine **insisted** on modifying the diet **and** using nutritional supplements.

In regards to Alan, we had learned that even fresh fruits and vegetables could cause adverse affects in individuals who are sensitive to salicylates. Salicylates occur naturally in many healthy foods and are found artificially in the colors, dyes, and preservatives used in so many of our processed foods. They can also be found in unsuspecting toiletries; mouthwash, toothpaste, etc.(2)

All things considered, we didn't feel like we had a lot of options. We were losing our youngest son to autism and our oldest son was beginning to experience unexplained physical illnesses. In the process of losing Taylor, Alan had begun to have migraine headaches. At first we thought it was due to the stress our family had been through as a direct result of Taylor's misdiagnosis. Then Alan began to experience low-grade fevers. Sometimes the fever was accompanied by muscle weakness in his legs and joint pain, other times not. At about this same time he also started to have hives. The diets just seemed like the right thing to try.

Implementing the anti-yeast diet and dealing with the yeast die-off reaction
Once we made the commitment, everything just seemed to fall into place. Researching and planning these interventions for our family was simple compared to the actual implementation! We had no idea how much skepticism and resistance we would encounter-- not from our children *(although they weren't too cooperative in the beginning)*, but from family and well-meaning friends. We even had our own doubts and it was particularly difficult when Taylor experienced the die-off reaction *(Herxheimer reaction)* after only one day on the diet. We had read about this effect, but we were in no way, shape or form, ready to experience it.

We had decided beforehand that NO MATTER WHAT, we would NOT go off the diet for at least ten days. By mid-afternoon the first day, I was ready to quit. Taylor had been extremely agitated and upset at his entrees for breakfast and lunch and Alan wasn't any too happy either. While the speech therapist was trying to interact with a very tired Taylor, I went to check on Alan. To my astonishment, he was sitting at his table coloring, **inside the lines**, something I had NEVER seen him be able to do. He was always either too busy to sit still or he would scribble wildly all over the paper. I decided to stick to my guns about the diet.

Taylor refused to eat ANYTHING the first day of the diet. We had anticipated he might be stubborn about some of the dietary changes, but we certainly didn't expect him to refuse everything. We made sure he drank an ample amount of filtered water, but that didn't alleviate our concerns about his well being.

He actually went to bed early the first night of the diet, which frightened us considerably. For the past six months he had been fighting sleep horribly and at one point, he was sleeping one to three hours in a 24 hour period and *not all at one time*. The dark circles he had developed around his eyes were even more pronounced after only one day on the diet and he looked terribly pale. We were convinced we were somehow harming our little boy.

The following day didn't prove to be any better. Taylor was extremely lethargic and just lay on the couch for several hours, doing nothing. He had a thick greenish-yellow discharge in the corners of his eyes this day, and for several days thereafter. I prepared and offered him his "new" foods but he didn't have the energy to move, let alone eat. So another day went by and Taylor consumed NOTHING but filtered water.

By the end of the third day, I was in tears. Taylor was still experiencing flu-like symptoms and I was convinced we were killing him. When Bill came home *(working three jobs, we barely got to see him anymore)*, he was able to coax Taylor into eating a few green beans and a couple of small pieces of meat. Taylor had NEVER eaten meat that wasn't processed (i.e. ham, meat sticks, lunch meat, and hot dogs) and I couldn't believe Bill had been able to get him to swallow it. Things were looking up.

By the fourth day, he started eating *some* of his new foods. He still wasn't thrilled with his options, but each day got easier as he slowly began to accept his new diet. The supplements were a little trickier. He soon realized, however, that we were just as stubborn as he was on this issue and he gave up fighting. (There were many days I spent the majority of my time getting him to swallow his supplements.) About ten days into the diet, Taylor's energy level returned.

The tide begins to turn
Everyone who was involved in Taylor's therapy noticed a major difference IMMEDIATELY upon the implementation of the diet and antifungal supplements. We new we had made the right decision. While the diet and antifungal therapy certainly did **not** cure our son's autism, it helped him in many significant ways. His eye contact was increasing and his tantrums were lessening in frequency and severity. He was certainly not as spaced out anymore, and he was able to pay attention and focus more on the *people* in his environment.

After only one month on the diet, his allergic symptoms were vanishing and he looked so much healthier. His dark eye circles were almost non-existent, he wasn't wheezing anymore, and he didn't have the chronic running nose. We decided it was time to forge ahead and add the next component: an intensive, one-on-one, 40 hour per week, home-based program.

Home-based Program
It took us two months to devise a plan that would meet Taylor's needs and not totally disrupt our lives (our so we thought). We had already established a solid foundation of therapeutic intervention for Taylor. He was receiving speech therapy (both one-on-one and group), occupational therapy (with an emphasis on sensory integration), and Bill and I were working with a behavior management technician from a local agency in an effort to learn how to *consistently* and *effectively* handle Taylor's tantrums and non-compliant behavior.

I had the privilege of talking to Dr. Bernard Rimland about the incredible improvement Taylor was making simply by manipulating his diet and adding nutritional supplements. He suggested I talk with a colleague of his who had a child with autism. Through my discussion with her, I learned about the book *Let Me Hear Your Voice*, by Catherine Maurice. It is an incredible book that I used as my guide in setting up Taylor's program. I had already read *The Me Book*, by Dr. Ivar Lovaas, and was aware of the studies that had been conducted using a discreet trial method of teaching (ABA-- applied behavioral analysis). The results of the studies were impressive and we decided to implement this type of teaching technique into Taylor's program.

Because of Taylor's group therapy, I had the advantage of knowing a few professors and many graduate students at the university. It was relatively easy to convince them to participate in our program. Many of them had personally witnessed Taylor's improvement at the onset of the dietary intervention. The key component that was missing was someone who would commit to helping me write and implement a program specifically for Taylor.

We decided to ask the behavior management technician that we already had a relationship with. We fully expected to have to beg her; Alan and Taylor weren't the easiest children to work with! She gladly accepted the invitation and would later prove to be the cornerstone of Taylor's program. Without her loyalty, commitment and dedication, I am confident my children would NOT be where they are today.

The following program changed periodically over the 17 months of its existence. For the most part, we were able to keep the core group of therapists that initially began working with Taylor. Of course, college students graduated and moved on and a few needed to quit because Taylor was so difficult to work with, at least in the beginning.

Therapy Schedule

Occupational Therapy	**2-3 hours per week**
Speech Therapy *(one-on-one)*	**3-5 hours per week**
Speech Therapy *(group)*	**3 hours per week**
Discreet Trial Training *(aba)*	**up to 10 hours per week**
Community Integration	**10 hours per week**

(We had serious problems with Taylor's behavior in public places)

Graduate Students   **up to 12 hours per week**

(To insure Taylor was constructively involved in an appropriate activity at all times)

Even though Taylor's behavior had greatly improved simply by modifying his diet, it was clear that he still needed to "catch up" in his development. He wasn't attempting to initiate communication and was content to be left alone for as long as we would allow (usually to line up his toy cars or blocks).   At times he would still become extremely agitated if we tried to interact with him.

His resistance strengthened with the utilization of discreet trial training. He put up such a fight during these therapy sessions that we were questioning our decision to use this method of teaching. It took well over a month for him to settle down and start to make progress. At the time, his progress seemed painstakingly slow, but in reality it was quite fast. This portion of his program, which was initially very uncomfortable to witness, was an integral part of his success.

Six months into the anti-Candida diet and three into the home-based program, Taylor was doing so well that we began to add foods back into his diet. We chose not to give him dairy products (we suspected they were at the root of his repeated infections) and substituted soy milk and soy cheese. We didn't see any major changes. We then **gradually** added grains (i.e. wheat, cereal, pasta, etc.). Once again we didn't see any major changes. *(I want to note that Taylor had not been ill since the first few days of the anti-Candida diet!)*

With the exception of Alan drinking cow's milk, both boys were now on the same diet. Difficult as it was, we were very motivated to follow this diet to the letter, knowing how much it had improved our children's lives. Taylor was beginning to speak, his breakdowns at transitions were continuing to lessen, and his tantrums were becoming almost nonexistent. Alan was much more in control of himself. After being on the diet for a little less than two years, we were able to gradually discontinue Taylor's home program. He still received speech and occupational therapy but the emphasis was shifted to interacting with children his own age. He was still having difficulty with this.

Even though both boys had made remarkable improvements, they were far from having typical development. They both still had trouble focusing and paying attention to task. They could be extremely impulsive and emotional and at times they were very compulsive and obsessive.

And so we continued to plod along, pleased that the boys were doing better, but still feeling like there was something we were missing. It was about this time I read Lisa Lewis's article on *Understanding and Implementing a Gluten and Casein Free Diet.*

I realized while reading Dr. Lewis's article that we had made a grave error when we added the soy products (they contained casein) and grains (they contained gluten) back into Taylor's diet. I also realized that this could be the missing ingredient in Alan's intervention as well. Determined to find answers, I called our family physician and asked him to order the blood and urine tests. (I had to argue with him over which laboratory we needed to send the specimens to.) A few weeks later we had our results.

The results were conclusive, not one, but *both* children had **extremely** elevated IgG antibodies to not only gluten, gliadin, and casein, but also to ovalbumin (egg). We swiftly removed all offending foods and basically went back to the anti-Candida diet with a few fruits added.

259

We expected to see the boys immediately improve with this removal of troublesome foods and were very disappointed when they didn't. They both developed skin rashes and Taylor even started getting hives that ranged from the size of peas to quarters on his scalp and forehead.**(Note by Dr. Shaw: These rashes are extremely common when withdrawing from gluten- and casein-containing foods according to Dr. Karl Reichelt in Norway.)** Their bowel movements changed to very loose stools and they complained of stomach aches. These symptoms persisted for 6 weeks and were very intense. Agitated would best describe their disposition and aggressive their behavior during this period.

Since we knew without a doubt that the proteins in grains and dairy products were problematic for our children, we decided to stick it out. (I am not sure we would have had the fortitude to continue, if we hadn't had the test results to remind us why we were doing it.) It was one of the more difficult times we experienced. We had been accustomed to continual progress (even though it wasn't fast enough for us) and this seemed like such a setback. Taylor, who had never been hyperactive, was becoming so and Alan was out of control. We had read in Dr. Lewis's article that it could take as long as a year to see any positive results after removing gluten and casein from the diet and we hoped we wouldn't have to wait that long. While there wasn't ever a regression in any skills they had mastered, both boys got *much worse* behaviorally for **several** months. They became extremely agitated and cranky. We encountered quite a lot of skepticism from some family members about the effectiveness of this "crazy" diet.

While I was out in the community, I ran across another mother with a child who had autism. She knew about my children and I began sharing with her our latest experiences with gluten and casein removal. She told me about Dr. William Shaw, a researcher in Kansas City, who was doing urine organic acid testing to determine the levels of abnormal fungal metabolites in children with autism and attention deficit disorders. She had ordered the test for her daughter.

260

Although her daughter had taken antibiotics on only one occasion, she had elevated levels of fungal metabolites. I knew we had to order the test for our boys. I began to wonder if Taylor might still have a yeast problem, even though he had made such incredible progress, and I wanted to assure myself that yeast wasn't the culprit in any of Alan's difficulties.

We were excited to learn that we didn't need to make a doctor's appointment to order the test, (our doctor just needed to sign the release) and that the urine organic acid kit would come directly to our home. We sent for the kits, administered the tests, and waited anxiously for the results. We were very surprised to learn that the children's test results were so similar!

Taylor's urine organic acid results performed in Dr. Shaw's lab showed increased tartaric, possibly of a fungal origin and **both** Taylor and Alan had increased dihydroxyphenylpropionic-like compound of possible anaerobic bacterial origin in their urine. I didn't know what to make of the test and called Dr. Shaw to discuss the results. He was very helpful and after going over the boy's tests with him, I decided to make changes in their supplement program. The most significant finding this test revealed was that both children had high levels of byproducts probably derived from the Clostridia family of bacteria. *(I can only imagine what Taylor's test results would have been prior to the anti-Candida diet.)*

The following day we began increasing the number of probiotics (i.e. Lactobacillus acidophilus) the boys were taking. Gradually we worked up to 15-20 billion organisms a day, or 15 to 20 capsules, depending on which brand we were using. We were trying to replace the anaerobic bacteria, probably from Clostridia bacteria, with "good" bacteria. We continued using this high dosage for six months and then slowly backed down to 5 billion per day which is the dosage both boys are currently taking.

Even with all the progress the children were making, we began to wonder how long we could continue to live on such a restricted diet.

261

If you indeed call it living! We heard about an *immunotherapy* with *enzyme-potentiated desensitization* (**EPD**, see chapter on the immune system) and decided to pursue it. We found an environmental allergist in the Kansas City area who used this form of allergy treatment in his practice and we made an appointment.

Behavioral effects of food allergies and EPD therapy
After three days of testing to determine if the children qualified for the EPD allergy treatment, I was ready for the "nut" house. What we found was that both boys were not only allergic to ALL the foods we tested, but also to animals, molds, pollens and chemicals. Their reactions to the testing ranged from "passing" out, uncontrollable screaming and crying, hitting, spitting, licking other patients, and running wildly around the office, to falling asleep. If I had not been there, I never would have believed that corn, chocolate, apples, peanuts, wheat, molds, etc., could cause this type of reaction. In fact, I lived it and STILL find it hard to believe!

We decided to have a few more tests run to identify digestive abnormalities, possible PST enzyme dysfunction (see chapter by Lisa Lewis, Understanding and implementing a gluten and casein free diet) and vitamin and mineral deficiencies. What we learned was beneficial and it helped to explain why the diet and supplements were helping our children. Although we felt EPD might be advantageous for our children, we didn't look forward to anymore restrictions being placed on the way we lived our lives.

After many discussions, we finally made up our minds to start EPD the following month. Preparing for the shot every eight weeks was (and is) a lot of work and the three day diet you must adhere to is anything but tasty. We adjusted the children's supplements, because it is critical to follow the EPD supplement schedule in order to maximize the benefits of the shot. After six months of the EPD allergy treatments and nine months after the removal of gluten and casein from the diet, *both* boys started making *incredible progress*.

Alan began excelling in school. The learning difficulties he experienced (mainly, dyslexic tendencies and inability to retain information) had more to do with his allergies. Alan was finally able to pay attention and do age-appropriate work. His hyperactivity, unexplained fevers, migraine headaches, hives, joint pain, and muscle weakness have been almost totally alleviated. *He has been on EPD for 17 months now and has received 8 injections. He has had only two unexplained headaches and one instance of muscle weakness since starting EPD. Prior to EPD, he would miss three to five days of school a month because of these complaints.*

Recovery from autism

Taylor stopped **all** formal therapies and was able to attend a typical preschool program, with minimal difficulties, 33 months after starting on the dietary and nutritional intervention program. They were NOT told of his "PREVIOUS" diagnosis of autism. He passed his kindergarten screening this past spring with flying colors and is excited about school. Dietary infractions can still cause him to have adverse reactions, but they are minimal and short-lived. He has friends he has made ON HIS OWN and they regularly call him and invite him to play. *Taylor has also been on EPD for 17 months and has received 8 injections.*

We are still gluten and casein free and we plan to continue the EPD treatment as long as necessary. *(Fourteen months into EPD, we decided to give the boys a shot of B-12 with their EPD shot to see if it would enhance its effects. It certainly seems to be making a difference.)* Currently, we can stretch the time between the children's shots to almost ten weeks without too many symptoms occurring. These symptoms can range from irritability to the inability to control emotions. It is our hope that through EPD, we may some day be able to add gluten and casein back into their diet, at least in limited amounts. But if not, their allergies caused by other foods and environmental factors *should* be eliminated. Only time will tell. While our diet is certainly different from most and children shouldn't have to swallow umpteen supplements a day, it is worth the sacrifice. It is the reason our children have **"recovered"**.

The rest of our story

It has been a little over seven years now since my husband and I became parents. Most of those years we have spent trying to figure out a way to enable our children to lead healthy, productive lives. Many times, the very people who were supposed to provide us with support were the ones who put the biggest obstacles in our path. We learned to count on each other.

Researching and implementing the interventions we chose for our children took so much of our time and energy (not to mention money), that as I read our contribution to this book I am amazed we made it.

Alan and Taylor were certainly worth all our efforts. They started school a few days ago and as I watched them get on the school bus one morning and wave good-bye, I realized how fortunate our family was.

We were able to plan the strategies and interventions we chose for our children because we happened to come across the right information at the right time. It shouldn't be like this. **All** families should have access to the same information as we did, so that they may have the opportunity to **choose** interventions that could drastically affect the quality of their children's lives. **All** children with autism and related disorders deserve the chance to **RECOVER**. I hope that my contribution in this book will make the way easier for other families.

Chances are if you try any of these interventions, things may get worse before they get better. Don't give up. I remember wanting to quit hundreds of times. But every time I hear Taylor playing with a friend, or watch Alan draw one of his intricate pictures, I thank God I didn't.

References
1. Balch J. and Balch P. Nutritional Healing. Avery Publishing Group, Garden City Park, NY. Pgs.7-8,10,37,39,1990.
2. Feingold B. Pure Facts. Feingold Associations of the United States, Alexandria,VA.Pgs.1-2,1976.

Following a different path. A child's documented recovery from autism
by Karyn Seroussi

I wish that there was more public awareness about the early symptoms of autism. Too many of my sentences seem to begin with the words, "when I look back," or, "in retrospect..." I know this is all too common among parents of autistic children.

Even if I did know what I was seeing, even if a scarlet "A" had appeared on Miles' forehead, I still wouldn't have gotten any useful advice from my pediatrician. This is a disorder in transition, its etiology only beginning to be understood. No one walked up to me and announced that Miles' early developmental differences were treatable with changes in his diet. His diet, for heaven's sake! Who would have believed something like that?

When our son Miles was born, in December of 1993, he was a cranky baby. Not colicky, just crabby and unpredictable. He never settled into a routine, he spit up so much that I had to change my shirt after nursing him, and he didn't like to be held when he was tired; he preferred to cry himself to sleep. We never knew when he'd wake up again though, he could sleep for half an hour, two hours, four hours, or longer, if we were really lucky. This went on for months.

I endured the nursing for 12 weeks and then switched Miles to soy formula. My pediatrician seemed surprised that I chose soy. When I told her that there were a lot of allergies in my family she gave me one of those looks that clearly said, "if you say so." I remember feeling slightly embarrassed, but I knew that milk was a common allergen, so why take chances?

Miles did better on the soy formula, although his nights were still terrible. He was one of those autistic children whose social and language development was normal for the first year or so before they regressed, and we had no way of knowing that we would ever be facing a problem greater that our own sleep deprivation.

At eleven months old, our little boy was getting ready to walk. He said "cat" and "fish," and liked to play peek-a-boo. He smiled at us when we played with him, waved "bye-bye" and clapped hands.

When he was almost twelve months old, at his doctor's suggestion, we switched him to cows' milk and it seemed that nothing changed. Then the ear infections began, one after another. The first one was accompanied by a rash on the scalp, face, and neck. I went back to the doctor. Something viral? A case of Roseola? She gave him antibiotics and told me to stop using fabric softener. My faith in her began to ebb. The rash had coincided with the fever. It didn't occur to me at the time that the problem might be related to cow's milk, but I knew it wasn't a matter of laundry. The flushed cheeks persisted, on and off, for months, while Miles was put on a prophylactic dose of amoxicillin for his recurring ear infections.

A parent knows when something is wrong, even when it can't be put into words. When a child learns language, his gains should be progressive. On the day that Miles had tubes inserted in his ears, at fifteen months old, he used the word "fish" for the last time at the aquarium in the doctor's waiting room. A month later, he no longer clapped hands or waved "bye-bye." Contrary to the otolaryngologist's assurance that Miles' language would now "explode," more than ever he appeared to be deaf.

One day, exhausted and late for work, I began to weep in the regular pediatrician's office. I told her that I didn't think she was taking my concerns seriously. I needed to know what *caused* this constant illness that was making our lives were so difficult. She told me, sarcastically, that "parenting can sometimes interfere with our work schedules." I then did the smartest thing I ever did as a parent. I scooped up my son and found a new doctor.

The new pediatrician didn't know much about developmental delays, but she agreed to help us find out what was going on. With the exception of something she called "chronic non-specific diarrhea," Miles was physically normal but he was an odd kid. He had a very long attention span for certain activities, and resisted interaction. Ignorant of the symptoms of autism, I described him as "in his own world." I again expressed my concern that he didn't have any expressive or even receptive language. I had noticed that he didn't recognize the word "cup," which was his favorite thing in the world. In fact, he drank so much milk that for financial reasons we had to restrict him to about 70 oz. of milk per day - over half a gallon! The doctor was concerned that Miles had lost the few words he had learned. She gave us a referral to a speech pathologist and a child psychologist.

On July 12, 1995, I found myself in the emergency-room at midnight. Miles had a high fever and febrile seizures, only eighteen hours after his DPT inoculation. Were the two related? The doctors didn't know. As he lay limply in my arms, exhausted from two hours of screaming, Miles gazed into my eyes for a long, long time. I marveled at his gaze - he seemed to be recognizing me for the first time. How could that be? I realized how odd it was that I found his scrutiny to be unusual. When had he stopped making eye contact?

At nineteen months old, he was seen by a developmental pediatrician. There was a word for what Miles had: autism. We began to see the horrible truth of the diagnosis. Miles would sit in the sandbox for forty-five minutes pouring the same cup of sand, or putting together and taking apart the same two pieces of a toy. He never pointed to objects or brought us toys to look at.

Our lives began to seem as though they were spinning out of control. When my husband and I realized the implications of this diagnosis we could barely function.

Then I read somewhere that a child was misdiagnosed with autism because of a milk allergy. His mother, Mary Callahan, had written a book, describing this as a "cerebral allergy". I was skeptical, but I went to the library for a book about allergy and it mentioned the possible link between ear infections and milk. It also mentioned that children sometimes crave milk if they have an allergy to it. Then my mother-in-law reminded us that my husband had begun to talk at three after she took him off milk products.

One morning I put down my library book, Doris Rapp's "Is This Your Child," and called Alan, my husband, at work.

"Honey, do we still have any soy formula, or did we give the last few cans away?"

We removed dairy from Miles' diet when he was 20 months old.

Surprisingly, he accepted the soy formula and the rice milk I found at the supermarket. We didn't know what would happen but there was no mistaking his reaction to this change. On the first night, tired whining replaced the familiar sound of screaming. The next day, for the first time ever, we awoke to the sound of Miles playing in his room. His crying was greatly reduced that day, and he made more eye contact than he had made in a month. The unfamiliar sound of babbling made us realize how little vocalizing Miles had done. Our babysitter was not immediately told about the reason for the change and she remarked emphatically about the differences in him.

When Alan came home from work on the third day and watched Miles reluctantly participate in a game of "Ring Around The Rosy," he made a pronouncement: Miles was to have no more dairy. No milk, no butter, no casein, no whey, no way.

The developmental pediatrician listened patiently while we raved about his improvement in the two weeks since he had stopped having milk. She agreed that he did seem to be doing well in some areas and suggested that we find an aggressive treatment program for him. However, her diagnosis was still autism. We later discovered that she had heard about this connection before, from "crackpot" parents and researchers, but said nothing to us at the time. She seemed to be taking us seriously, however, since my husband was a research scientist with a Ph.D. in chemistry. She simply agreed that if the diet seemed to be helping, it couldn't hurt to continue.

At 21 months, I noticed that when Miles had a cup of soy formula before his nap he woke up cranky and had small tremors for a few seconds. I restricted him to rice milk. We saw a neurologist at this time who listened attentively to my opinions and asked if I could give Miles some milk and soy, and then try to document any behavioral changes on videotape. Based on his observations he seemed amazed that Miles had been diagnosed with autism, and was skeptical about the original diagnosis. I could see why, since Miles had improved so much, especially in the area of social interaction. I could not bring myself to do what he had asked and give milk to Miles, however. We knew what we were seeing, and his progress was too important to us.

We had implemented a home-based behavioral program to which Miles was responding well, and he began attending a special nursery school four mornings per week. We agreed that these were a factor in his recovery but we knew they would not have been effective while Miles was drinking milk. In one month, Miles had gained over six months in his fine motor skill evaluation, and lost several points on our (his parents') application of the CARS test, indicating a reduction in autistic behaviors. He was rapidly gaining spontaneous appropriate language and social skills, his eye contact was now almost completely normal, he pointed to everything to learn its name, he brought us objects just to share them with us, and he watched his sister carefully for new cues about behavior.

We looked for a sympathetic allergist. Some other parents of autistic children recommended one who agreed that some foods can affect certain children even when they do not show a classic allergic immune system response. He was somewhat helpful. Miles had a reaction to some molds, but only a very minimal reaction to foods, among them egg, corn, wheat, soy, oats, and fish. There was no reaction to milk or rice. I was surprised - why would Miles have such a problem with milk if he did not have an allergy to it?

The doctor explained that he believed there were two types of allergy. In the primary type, symptoms such as hives, swelling, or difficulty breathing were common reactions. I remembered that my nephew had such a problem with peanuts - my sister had to keep an epi-pen(a source of the drug epinephrine to inject in the case of a severe allergic reaction) with him at all times. In the secondary type of allergy, a different part of the immune system seemed to be affected, and the response to such allergens could be headache, diarrhea, disorientation, irritability, or even depression or hyperactivity. He suggested a rotation diet.

A rotation diet is based on the principle that one can eat allergenic foods every four days or so with a lesser reaction then if one ate them every day. In addition, after three days without the food, one was more aware of allergic reactions when it was introduced.

I sat down at my computer and wrote up a weekly schedule of foods that Miles could eat - from a list that already seemed to be rather short.

During the rotation diet, we noticed that Miles definitely no longer tolerated soy. Chinese food gave him hives (soy sauce) and soy formula gave him a severe diaper rash. We also found that corn in any form made his diarrhea worse. We already knew that citrus, grapes, and most fruits gave him a rash, (which was true of our daughter at that age), so we were running out of food choices. To top it off, Miles was very picky about food tastes and textures.

Still, our biggest question was still unanswered: why was Miles getting better from autism after the removal of dairy from his diet?

In November we had a behavioral consultant from California take a look at Miles. He agreed that he had a lot of autistic characteristics and some autistic-like delays, but admitted to being baffled by his social behavior.

270

Following a different path

When we explained about the dairy he said he was mystified, and suggested that we look into galactosemia and other metabolic disorders.

I bought a modem and got on the Internet, hoping to find more information. Within 48 hours I was bombarded with the news about casein/gluten intolerance and autism. I was overwhelmed.

To be taken seriously and to discover that Miles shared his case history with others was breathtaking. Parents like Lisa Lewis and researchers like Paul Shattock made it easier for me to understand that the problem might be caused by the improper breakdown of milk and wheat proteins into opiate-like neurotoxins. Paul suggested removing gluten from Miles' diet. Gluten is a protein found in wheat, oats, rye and barley. It was abundant in all of Miles' favorite foods, and I was horrified to discover that wheat is added to most packaged products as a filler, or to keep foods from sticking together. The prospect of starting a gluten-free diet seemed daunting, but it would be worth it if only to stop the diarrhea. I joked, via e-mail, that if Miles had a formed stool I would buy Paul a bottle of champagne.

We took Miles off gluten in November, when he was twenty-three months old, or so we thought. After a few days I realized that the Rice Krispies I had been giving him contained barley malt - a no-no. Then, within twenty-four hours of removing that food, we were amazed to see his bowel movements normalize.

Miles' gastroenterologist was mystified. He had been given the gluten/gliadin antibody tests and did not prove positive for celiac disease, and yet she saw him improve after the removal of gluten. She had even seen his diapers beforehand - an odious mass of sickly-smelling slush. I later found out that many autistic children seemed to have a form of celiac disease without testing positive to the gluten antibody test. When they were further tested with a small-bowel biopsy, they were usually diagnosed with celiac disease based on their flattened intestinal villi and gut permeability.

Shortly thereafter, without really understanding why, we started giving Miles low doses of nystatin. One of the parents we knew told us that it had helped her son, but was unsure about the reason. After ascertaining that the drug seemed safe, we asked our doctor for a prescription. During this time, his "postural insecurity" greatly improved. Later, after hearing Dr. Shaw speak at a conference and understanding about the Candida theory, I wondered about that. Was the lack of balance caused by the gluten or the yeast? I couldn't say, but Miles soon began to climb stairs on two feet and to try using a seesaw. He lost the drunken gait that had characterized his movement for so long. He remained on nystatin for over two years, and continued to take probiotics such as acidophilus and bifidus.

After a few weeks, we tried a "multiple food elimination diet." This meant that we cut Miles' diet down to the very few foods that seemed the least likely culprits: kosher chicken, potatoes fried in canola or safflower oil, white rice, and tapioca, and then added new things back, one at a time.

We soon discovered that other foods also gave him loose stools, such as eggs and pear juice. By the time we had tested every food at least twice for physical or behavioral reactions, Miles was reduced to the following diet: rice, potatoes, chicken, pork, sesame seeds, macadamia nuts, teff, arrowroot, and tapioca. Within a few months of his being on the diet we discovered that the removal of the other foods had made him even more sensitive to them. Corn was bad and soy was worse, but even the smallest trace of gluten would result in several days of marked regression and diarrhea.

At that point we became very careful, almost fanatical about Miles' diet. If we accidentally dipped a spoon from the pot of wheat pasta into the pot of rice pasta, we threw away the entire batch and started again. Everyone in the household, including our three-year-old daughter, learned to wash their hands after touching bread. Miles had a separate toaster, a separate shelf in the pantry, and sat at the end of the table where crumbs were less likely to fly from our hands.

Our friends and family might have thought us crazy, but we believed that the fact that we were doing the diet 100% was important to his success. We knew other children who responded to the diet whose parents weren't as careful, and their progress was often uneven. Miles' growth continued to soar.

Although we couldn't swear by it, three daily tablets of DMG seemed to improve his language function; he seemed somehow "clearer." At twenty-eight months, he began using three-word combinations. By two and a half, he had a mildly rote manner of speaking, but his sentences were longer and more meaningful, such as "look Mommy, I see a slide." His voice had a sing-song quality to it too, still residual from the autism, but he was highly motivated to communicate.

Miles had finally discovered his sister, only eighteen months older and eager for a playmate. They began to play games of imagination, such as "zoo," "dolls," and "dinosaurs." His imaginary play began as a replay of the same scene, usually involving a carnivorous dinosaur attacking everyone else. As the months went by, however, he took great pleasure in longer and more complex storylines which were always changing. There arrived a day when his sister began to let him take the lead in the play because his ideas were so exciting and different.

By the time Miles was three, his evaluation revealed that he no longer qualified for special education services. In fact, his language tested at a level over eight months above age level. Socially and developmentally, the teachers in his "integrated" classroom found him to be one of the most advanced in the class.

If his special-education teachers were skeptical about my use of the diet at the beginning of the year, they certainly were not by graduation. They had all seen the dramatic changes in Miles, as well as having seen the frightening deterioration that followed the rare occasions when they slipped up and let him get hold of a stray pretzel or cookie. One of them told me that she had never seen a child recover from autism before, and that she would always tell other parents of autistic children to try the intervention.

Another of his teachers told me that after twenty years of working with autistic students, she didn't want to work with any children whose parents refused to at least try the diet. On the days when Miles ate a problem food such as corn, she could always tell without being told, and would pronounce her session with Miles "an utter waste of time." Two of her students, Miles and a younger boy named Bobby who was following a similar path, had opened her eyes to a whole new avenue for recuperation.

The regular nursery school class that he attended twice a week was a good indication of Miles' functioning; he was very well-liked by the other children, who liked to do "whatever Miles was doing." These were "typical" children, and I was pleased to see how well he fit in on the days when it was my turn to assist in the classroom. His teacher assured me that he adapted very well to the rules and routine of the classroom, and was surprised by my anxious questions when I came to pick him up, such as "how did things go today?"

Because of the toileting delays typically associated with autism, potty training had seemed like such a long shot that we didn't push it. We were shocked to hear the toilet flush one day and see Miles walk out of the bathroom with a dry diaper in his hand. A few days later, after dragging me excitedly to the bathroom, Miles pointed out his first bowel movement. Afterwards, as we walked into the living room, Miles took my hand and said, "Mommy, I'm so proud of myself!"

At three and a half, Miles was so different from the child he had been that the past year seemed like a displaced memory, or a fragment of a movie about someone else's life. He was a charming, loving, intense child with an impish grin and a great imagination. He adored his family, readily made new friends, loved to swim and draw pictures, and insisted on picking out his clothes and dressing himself. He expressed himself well and even had a rather sophisticated sense of humor.

Following a different path

Our only reminder of what seemed like an impossible past was Miles' limited diet. He did not have potty accidents so we got a little bit adventurous with new foods, but Miles still had problems with the same list that he had reacted to as a baby. Stomach aches and diarrhea were the usual result, with occasional headaches or trouble sleeping. Although several people suggested EPD (Enzyme Potentiated Desensitization) injections to widen his diet, we decided to wait until Miles was older.

Miles is in a regular school now, with no problems whatsoever. He knows what he can eat, and is very cautious about touching other people's food. If I give him something unfamiliar, he asks, "Is this okay for me?" Miles is a good sport about it - he says "yay, French fries!" like a child who is not seeing them for the fourth time that week. We are resigned to the fact that he may never be able to eat casein or gluten, and that his diet may always be as limited as it is today. However, he gets enough protein and carbohydrate, he is supplemented with vitamins, minerals, calcium, essential fatty acids and amino acids, and the level of his functioning is so good that this seems a small price to pay.

I am one of the lucky parents, I know that. When I start my sentences with "when I look back," I can finish them with thoughts like, "it was a good thing we got such an early diagnosis," or "thank goodness for the Internet." Early intervention was the key for our little boy. Not just treatment of his symptoms, but the treatment of his immune system and the cause of his problems. Miles was young, and his nervous system had not sustained enough permanent damage to impair him for life.

Do I think that every child will respond as well as he did to the diet? Of course not. I have only seen three others in the past two years, all of them under three years old. But hey, that's four children in my city who do not have autism and that ain't bad. In addition, I have seen dozens of older children whose functioning improved well beyond their parents' expectations with the implementation of this diet, and that seems to me to be as good as a million dollars worth of special education.

My advice to parents is to look to the cause first, and treat the symptoms later. Find out as soon as possible if you can strengthen your child's immune system and improve his functioning. A gluten and casein-free diet, vitamin B6, MCT oil, DMG, and essential fatty acids are several safe things to try. Definitely test and treat for yeast and anaerobic bacteria, since it is so prevalent in autistic children and may be causative to the other problems. It doesn't matter how old they are - Donna Williams didn't discover dietary intervention for her own autism until she was in her twenties, and it greatly reduced her anxiety and improved her ability to function and interact with others.

It used to break my heart when I saw a young child with autism, perhaps one that craved milk the way Miles did, and his parents told me that they did not want to try a dietary intervention. I would knock myself out pestering them and explaining it to them, but finally learned that people won't try new things unless they're ready. Unfortunately, a developing brain is not always that forgiving - certain behaviors are meant to be learned during certain stages of development.

For the sake of an autistic child who had terrible diarrhea, I once even found myself begging his mother to take gluten from his diet. I actually used the words, "please, I am begging you." It was very uncomfortable, and I felt embarrassed when she said no. Two years later I found out through a mutual acquaintance that he had been diagnosed as "failure to thrive," and she finally tried the diet with great success. I tried to imagine how awful she must have felt. It's one thing not to have the information, but another thing entirely to have it and not try it out because of intimidation or fear of the unknown.

Perhaps some of my frustration comes from my own fear of what might have happened if we had not pursued the course we did. I suspect that with my own arrogance and skepticism, if my doctor hadn't told me to, or if I hadn't discovered this for myself, I might not have tried the diet based on hearsay.

276

Another thing I've learned is that there is still a lot to know about the biological processes that lead to the symptoms of autism. I have spent a long time formulating theories which make a lot of sense to me until the next conference I attend, the next parent I speak with, or the next research paper I read. I suspect that Miles' vaccinations either introduced a virus that started the problem, or else aggravated his already unstable immune system. I strongly believe that the liberal amount of antibiotics he was given either triggered or contributed to the outcome. All I can say for certain is that a breakdown in the immune system certainly does seem to be involved, as well as the abnormal production of substances which are clearly not present in the urine of normal test subjects, and which can disappear after implementation of a gluten and casein-free diet.

Therefore, tempting though it is to assure parents of newly diagnosed autistic children that I have all of the answers, I usually just share Miles' story, or give them a copy of a paper I wrote, entitled "Frequently Asked Questions About Dietary Intervention For Autism and Other Developmental Disabilities" and lend them one piece of advice before stepping back: try whatever you have to try so that you won't spend the rest of your life wishing you had started sooner.

Frequently Asked Questions about Dietary Intervention for the Treatment of Autism and Other Developmental Disabilities

by Karyn Seroussi
Disclaimer: The following is not medical advice. All changes to your child's diet should be supervised by a physician or a qualified nutritionist.

Q: I don't think my child has allergies, or that allergies could cause autism. Why should I try removing foods from his diet?
A: Although parents have been reporting a connection between autism and diet for decades, there is now a growing body of research that shows

277

that certain foods seem to be affecting the developing brains of some children and causing autistic behaviors. This is not because of allergies, but because many of these children are unable to properly break down certain proteins.

Q: What happens when they get these proteins?
A: Researchers in England, Norway, and at the University of Florida have found peptides (breakdown products of proteins) with opiate activity in the urine of a high percentage of autistic children. Opiates are drugs, like morphine, which affect brain function.

Q: Which proteins are causing this problem?
A: The two main offenders seem to be gluten (the protein in wheat, oats, rye and barley) and casein (milk protein.)

Q: But milk and wheat are the only two foods my child will eat. His diet is completely comprised of milk, cheese, cereal, pasta, and bread. If I take these away, I'm afraid he'll starve.
A: There may be a good reason your child "self-limits" to these foods. Opiates, like opium, are highly addictive. If this "opiate excess" explanation applies to your child, then he is actually addicted to those foods containing the offending proteins. Although it seems as if your child will starve if you take those foods away, many parents report that after an initial "withdrawal" reaction, their children become more willing to eat other foods. After a few weeks, many children surprise their parents by
further broadening their diets.

Q: But if I take away milk, what will my child do for calcium?
A: Children between the ages of one and ten require 800-1000 mg of calcium/day. If the child drinks three 8-oz glasses of fortified rice, soy or potato milk per day, he would meet that requirement. If he drank one cup per day, the remaining 500 mg of additional calcium could be supplied with one of the many supplements available.
Twin Labs makes a chewable calcium citrate wafer that contains no allergenic fillers and tastes like a "SweetTart" candy. Custom-made

calcium liquids can be mixed up by compounding pharmacies (such as Pathway - 1-800-869-9160) using a maple, sucrose syrup, stevia or water base.

There are some very good calcium-enriched milk substitutes on the market. Rice Dream, in the white box, is usually available at the supermarket. Because this brand of rice milk is processed with barley enzymes, there is some concern over whether it will cause a reaction in individuals highly sensitive to gluten. If your child is also on a gluten-free diet, look for other brands of rice milk at your health food store. Darifree, a pleasant-tasting potato-based milk substitute, is available by mail-order (1-800-497-4834.) Soy milk is a good option for some, although many children are allergic to soy.

Q: Is this diet expensive?
A: There is no denying that many of the gluten-free ingredients you will need to keep on hand are more costly than the staples you are used to buying. However, when you order by the case, the above milk substitutes cost about the same as cow's milk. Some parents report that their autistic children were drinking over a gallon of cow's milk per day (about $60/month!) but these same parents were reluctant to switch to rice milk at $1.30/quart.

As with all foods, convenience products such as frozen rice waffles are expensive, but making these from scratch is easy and inexpensive. Bulk rice flour is about 45c/pound, and there are several good gluten-free cookbooks. You'll find yourself making rice and potatoes more often, instead of ordering out. You might even save money.

Q: Isn't milk necessary for children's health?
A: Americans have been raised to believe that this is true, largely due to the efforts of the American Dairy Association, and many parents seem to believe that it is their duty to feed their children as much cow's milk as possible.

However, lots of perfectly healthy children do very well without it. Cow's milk has been called "the world's most overrated nutrient" and "fit only for baby cows." There is even evidence that the cow hormone present in dairy actually blocks the absorption of calcium in humans.

Be careful. Removing dairy means ALL milk, butter, cheese, cream cheese, sour cream, etc. It also includes product ingredients such as "casein" and "whey," or even words containing the word "casein." Read labels - items like bread and tuna fish often contain milk products. Even soy cheese usually contains caseinate.

For more information on dairy-free living, there's a very good book called "Raising Your Child Without Milk" by Jane Zukin. This can be ordered at Barnes & Noble and at Waldenbooks. There is also a very good little book called "Don't Drink Your Milk" by Frank Oski (the head of Pediatrics at Johns Hopkins and author of "Essential Pediatrics.") This book cites the results of several research studies which conclude that milk is an inappropriate food for human children. It is available for $4.95 from Park City Press, PO Box 25, Glenwood Landing, NY 11547, ISBN #
0671228048.

Q: I might be willing to try removing dairy products from his diet, but I don't think I could handle removing gluten. It seems like a lot of work, and I'm so busy already. Is this really necessary?
A: What you need to understand is that for certain children, these foods are toxic to their brains. For some, removing gluten may be far more important than removing dairy products. You would never knowingly feed your child poison, but if he fits into this category, that is exactly what you could be doing. It is possible that for this subgroup of people with autism, eating these foods is actually damaging the developing brain.

Q: Removing both foods at once seems overwhelming, and I'm afraid of my child's reaction. Can I start slowly?
A: Many parents strongly suggest that you try removing dairy first, and then work on planning for a completely gluten-free diet. Gluten can take more effort and some education on your part, and preparation may take

a bit longer. Some physicians recommend doing this diet one step at a time to accurately record the child's response, and to reduce withdrawal reactions. The experts seem to agree that the milk and wheat proteins are so similar to each other that if one is a problem, the other should be removed as soon as possible.

Q: How do I know if this applies to my child?
A: Although there is some peptide testing available, the waiting time for results can be long, and widespread use of a reliable test is not yet available. The researchers agree that this is a very common problem in the autistic population, so a trial period on the diet may be your child's best bet. Although a lab result is more convincing to a doctor, the noticeable improvement many children exhibit will usually persuade even a reluctant spouse to support the diet.

Many affected children who eat a great deal of dairy and/or wheat-based foods will show changes within a few days of their elimination. The diet must be strict.
Many parents have found that their child did not improve until they discovered and removed a hidden source of gluten or dairy. Noticeable changes in eye contact, sociability, and language are one sign that diet is an important issue. Another thing to look for are changes in the child's bowel movements or sleep patterns.

Q: When my child was taken just off dairy he improved greatly, but then he started eating a lot of wheat, perhaps to make up the opiates he was missing. Will I see the same kind of noticeable improvement when I remove gluten?
A: Children who eat a lot of gluten should show an improvement when it is removed. Some parents say that their child's response was more obvious with dairy, and some with gluten. Unfortunately, gluten seems to take longer to disappear from the system than casein does. Urine tests show that casein probably leaves the system in about three days, but it can take up to eight months on a gluten-free diet for all peptide levels to drop. If this intervention is followed by a deterioration or regression (a

withdrawal-type response,) stay the course! It almost certainly means that your child will benefit. This may seem like a lot of work for an uncertain payoff, but in the lifetime of your child it may be the most important step you take.

Q: The only non-dairy, non-wheat foods my child will eat are French fries and chicken nuggets. Are these okay?
A: Chicken nuggets are coated with wheat. Some French fries are dusted with wheat flour to keep them from sticking together. It is a very good idea to get used to checking with your supplier or the manufacturer. Keeping a stack of blank, prestamped postcards in the kitchen is a handy way to check.

The biggest problem with French fries eaten out of the house is contamination of the frying oil with gluten from onion rings and other breaded products. Making fries homemade is a good option. If your child refuses them at first, it may be because of what they're missing! Some parents report that their kids have an uncanny ability to
detect gluten in foods. Since many of the children enjoy salt, salting the fries might make them more acceptable.

Q: What else contains gluten?
A: Wheat, oats, rye, barley, kamut, spelt, semolina, malt, food starch, grain alcohol, and most packaged foods - even those that do not label as such. There is a lot of information on gluten intolerance because of a related disorder called Celiac Disease.

Q: After I removed gluten and casein, I discovered that other foods seemed to be causing a problem, like apples, soy, corn, tomatoes, and bananas. I see irritability, red cheeks and ears, and sometimes diarrhea or a diaper rash. I thought you said that these kids don't have allergies!
A: Many do have allergies, or allergy-related symptoms such as hay fever, asthma or eczema. Sometimes they have problems with foods which are not "classical" allergies, and which won't show up on skin

tests. In this case, a different part of the immune system seems to be involved.

Q: So if these foods are not contributing to his autism, they're okay?
A: Not really. Current research indicates that in a great many cases, autism seems to be an immune system dysfunction. This not only leads to a problem breaking down casein & gluten, but it may also result in a problem breaking down foods which contain phenols (phenol sulfur transferase deficiency,) and an over-reactive response to other allergens.

Often, once gluten is removed, this effect becomes more noticeable, perhaps because the allergens were "masked" by the effect of the gluten. It is also possible that a "leaky gut syndrome," caused by the gluten intolerance, is now permitting other foods to pass through the intestinal screen and into the bloodstream.

For children who respond to this diet, allergens do seem to place further stress on the immune system, and have often been shown to worsen behavior and development.

Q: But my child's immune system seems to be working unusually well - he is rarely sick.
A: What we're describing is not an immune deficiency, but rather an immune dysfunction. Many (although not all) seem to share a history of ear infections and spitting up as babies (possibly milk-related,) or of chronic diarrhea, constipation, or loose stools (possibly wheat-related.)

Other parents note that their autistic children seem to be the healthiest members of the family. In this case, it has been hypothesized that the immune system is too aggressive and ends up turning on the nervous system. This may explain the presence of anti-myelin antibodies in some children, and may also explain why some have immune issues like multiple allergies but do not respond well to dietary intervention.

Q: What causes this problem? Autism seems to be so much more common than it used to be.
A: Researchers are not sure, but it seems likely at this time that many cases are caused by a genetic predisposition or by environmental toxicity, combined with some kind of triggering event that stresses the immune system, such as a vaccination or virus. In several cases, prolonged use of antibiotics seems to have contributed to the onset of the disorder.

Q: So, if I can't give him milk or wheat, and if he has some other food allergies, what do I feed my child?
A: Most kids are okay with chicken, lamb, pork, fish, potato, rice, and egg whites.
Parsnips, tapioca, arrowroot, honey, and maple syrup are usually okay too. French fries from MacDonalds are gluten free (but may contain soy or corn.) Certain white nuts, like macadamia and hazelnuts, are also usually tolerated. Others kids may be okay with white corn, bacon, fruits such as white grapes or pears, beans, sesame seeds, or grains such as amaranth and teff (available at natural foods stores.) There's always something to feed them - even the most finicky kids seem to like sticky white Chinese rice or French fries.

Q: How do I know which foods he's allergic to?
A: Try an allergy elimination diet. For example, keep tomato out of his diet for a few days and then re-introduce it. If you see symptoms, either physical or behavioral, try again in a few days. Try to be systematic, to be certain before ruling out a food. Two excellent resources, which are probably available at your library, are Doris Rapp's book, "Is This Your Child," and William Crook's "Solving the Puzzle of Your Hard to Raise Child."

Q: I'm already worried about my child's nutrition, and his "allergies" are causing me to further reduce his choices. If apple juice and bananas are the only fruits he will eat and he's reacting to them, how is he supposed to get by?
A: Fruit contains water, sugar, fiber, and vitamins. He needs to get these things from other sources.

Q: I thought the "five food groups" were so important!
A: They are, to an individual without food intolerances. But, just as a person who eats a balanced diet might not need to take vitamins, a person with poor nutrition can make up for a lot with a good vitamin and mineral supplement.

Q: So I should be giving my child a vitamin supplement?
A: Absolutely. Poly-vi-sol with Iron is probably okay, or order a gluten-free multi-vitamin & mineral formula from your natural foods store. Kal Dinosaur Chewables are tolerated by many food-sensitive children, and are available with or without minerals.

Because many autistic children have been reported to improve on a regimen of vitamin B6 and magnesium, you may want to order a supplement rich in these nutrients from a compounding pharmacy such as Pathway (1-800-869-9160.) For a 40 pound child, Dr. Bernard Rimland of the Autism Research Institute recommends 300 mg of B6 and 100 mg of magnesium per day. It is likely that in people with a leaky gut, absorption of B6 (which aids in nervous system function) is often greatly diminished.

Q: What else does my child need?
A: There are six basic things a person needs from food: water, protein (and amino acids,) carbohydrates, fats, vitamins, minerals (including iron & calcium.) In addition, food contains certain phytochemical substances which seem to help with functions like disease prevention. It is helpful to consult a nutritionist about the use of supplements such as pycnogenol for any child on a limited diet.

Children who have gone for one year eating only chicken, canola oil, potato, rice, calcium-enriched beverages, and a liquid multivitamin supplement with minerals have had excellent results on nutritional blood tests. You'd be surprised to learn just how unnecessarily varied an American diet is, compared with the diets of other cultures!

285

Q: So how do I know if my child will respond to this diet?
A: The biggest clue is when a child self-limits his diet - especially to milk and wheat. This is no longer seen as a "need for sameness" but as a biological addiction. Children who don't necessarily "self-limit" but who also respond are those who eat an unusually large or small amount of food. Although the former may not recognize the source of the opiates, he knows that eating makes him feel GOOD. The latter may realize that many foods make him feel ill, and tries to avoid eating whenever possible. These "failure to thrive" autistic children are very hard to put on this diet because of their parents' fears, but will usually respond when acceptable substitutes to the non-tolerated foods can be provided.

Other symptoms of food intolerance or vitamin deficiency are dermatitis or extremely dry skin, migraines, bouts of screaming, red cheeks, red ears, abnormal bowel movements, abnormal sleep patterns or seizures.

Q: What's all this I hear about yeast?
A: Candida is a yeast that lives in our bodies in small amounts. It was speculated that in individuals with improperly-functioning immune systems, it could flourish in the gut and lead to a host of problems, including fatigue, sugar cravings, headaches, and behavioral problems.

Q: How do we know if this is really true?
A: We didn't, until recently. Dr. William Shaw in Kansas found unusually high levels of "fungal metabolites" (yeast waste products) in the urine of several groups of abnormally functioning individuals (including people with autism.) His first paper describing this phenomenon was published in the Journal of Clinical Chemistry in 1995 (Vol. 41, No. 8.) He is currently conducting further studies on the effect of anti-fungal therapy on urinary organic acids from children with autism. His test is performed by the Great Plains Laboratory, at 913-341-8949.

Q: So does yeast cause autism?
A: This finding is likely to be just another consequence of the abnormally-functioning autistic immune system. However, it has also been hypothesized that the Candida might aggravate a condition of gut

permeability (the "leaky gut" syndrome) which might let the gluten and casein proteins into the bloodstream before they are broken down, so it may in part be responsible for autistic behaviors. Many parents of children with ADD/ADHD as well as those with autism report that treatment for Candida does improve their children's behavior and concentration.

Q: How do I treat for Candida?
A: One approach is to ask your pediatrician for a course of nystatin, which is a non-systemic (not absorbed into the bloodstream) anti-fungal. Taken orally, it works locally in the gut to fight Candida. This medication is considered to be quite safe, even when taken for several months. For a 25-35 lb. child, ask the doctor for a prescription for nystatin powder (125,000 units per cc) in a stevia base, starting with 1 cc 4x/day. Your local pharmacy probably carries a commercial preparation in a sugar base - this feeds yeast! Again, try Pathway, at 1-800-869-9160.

"Probiotics" such as acidophilus, the natural bacteria found in yogurt, are other Candida-fighters, and are available at the natural foods store in powdered form in the refrigerated section. Some acidophilus preparations are milk-based - be sure to get one that is not! Bifidus works in the large intestine and can be of great benefit. "FOS" is desirable in these supplements, as it feeds the probiotics.

Q: Aren't probiotics the "healthy flora" I've heard about?
A: Yes, they compete with Candida for the sugars you eat. It's the "good bacteria." You may be aware that acidophilus is eradicated from your gut when you take antibiotics.

Q: That's why you're supposed to eat yogurt when you are on antibiotics!
A: Exactly. As a matter of fact, in the 1950's, when oral antibiotics were first prepared for general use, scientists knew about this Candida problem and coated the tablets with nystatin. After a few years, the FDA

decided that the two drugs should be prescribed separately (which they never were) and made them stop.

Q: My friend's child tried nystatin and it made him vomit. If nystatin is so safe, why did he react to it?
A: The child may have experienced a "die-off reaction" to the Candida. As it dies, Candida releases toxins into the bloodstream and can cause nausea, vomiting, or diarrhea. It is likely that Candida was indeed a problem for this child. Your friend should discuss a dosage change (starting with a low dose and working up to a "normal dose") with the prescribing doctor.

Q: My doctor has never heard of any of this and she is extremely skeptical. I'm embarrassed to tell her I'm considering this approach.
A: Skepticism is a good thing in a medical doctor or scientist. However, since there is preliminary evidence to support this safe, non-invasive intervention, it is up to you to educate her, state your wishes, and ask for her support. For a doctor, it is better to wait until all of the data is published in peer-reviewed journals before advocating a treatment. For a parent, it is reasonable to want to help one's child without waiting
for all of the results of the "double-blind placebo" studies. Because this approach does not include any unusual supplements, invasive drugs, or expensive treatments, your pediatrician should be supportive. Explain that you would like to try this for a few weeks, and agree that you will be objective about recording your child's progress while on the diet.

Q: Where can I find support?
A: It is likely that other parents in your area are already aware of this intervention. Forming a support group, or forming a local chapter of Parents of Allergic Children may be a good option. There are also several support groups for the biological treatment of autism on the Internet (search "Autism and Diet,") as well as support for a gluten free diet (search "Celiac Disease.")

Good luck!

For more information about the implementation of a gluten-free diet, visit the ANDI website at http://members.aol.com/AutismNDI/PAGES/index.htm.

For a free copy of the ANDI Newsletter, send mailing address to: Autism Network for Dietary Intervention, PO Box 17711, Rochester, NY 14617-0711, or by email to: AutismNDI@aol.com.

Summing up

by William Shaw Ph.D.

How effective are the nutritional and antifungal therapies discussed in the previous chapters? According to parents of children with autism who were surveyed by Bernard Rimland Ph.D. of the Autism Research Institute, some of these therapies were much more effective than all of the commonly used psychoactive drugs including neuroleptics and stimulants which are commonly prescribed for autism. (These data in Tables 1 and 2 were adapted from Dr. Rimland's published study and are reprinted with permission on the following pages.) The better to worse ratio for antifungal drugs (nystatin and ketoconazole) in children with suspected yeast overgrowth of the intestinal tract is five times higher than the second most effective drug, the psychoactive agent Clonidine (Table1). (The higher this ratio the more effective the drug is rated.) I suspect that the effectiveness of the antifungal agents might be even higher if dietary restriction of simple sugars to reduce yeast overgrowth were employed. Several antiseizure medications were ranked poorly (ratios less than 1.0) based on behavioral response(not on antiseizure effectiveness).All of the stimulant drugs including Cylert, Ritalin, and amphetamine were also rated very poorly. With nutritional supplements (Table 2), high ratios, indicating high effectiveness, were reported for vitamin B-6, DMG, zinc, niacin, vitamin C, calcium, and folic acid.

The idea that autism is made worse or caused by abnormal byproducts of microorganisms and opiates from wheat and milk is not inconsistent with other research findings in autism such as abnormal neuroanatomical findings, abnormal EEG results, and abnormal brain scans. Similar abnormalities were found in the disease PKU even though the primary abnormality is a genetic defect in a single enzymatic reaction. There is no inherent reason that dramatic

Table 1. Parent ratings of behavioral results of drugs

Drug	no. cases	% worse	% no effect	% better	better: worse ratio
Antifungal	208	4	47	49	12.9
Clonidine	118	19	30	51	2.7
Naltrexone	111	19	40	41	2.1
Beta blockers	154	17	49	34	2
Cogentin	47	18	47	35	2
Deanol	169	15	58	27	1.8
Phenergan	48	23	37	40	1.7
Anafranil	102	29	24	47	1.6
Fenfluramine	401	20	51	29	1.5
Tegretol	673	23	43	34	1.5
Lithium	209	24	43	33	1.4
Mellaril	1605	27	38	35	1.3
Buspar	55	27	38	35	1.3
Prolixin	36	33	25	42	1.3
Benadryl	1347	22	52	26	1.2
Depakene	300	27	42	31	1.1
Prozac	206	35	25	40	1.1
Hydroxyzine	247	22	54	24	1.1
Stelazine	348	28	43	29	1
Haldol	804	38	24	38	1
Zarontin	64	30	40	30	1
Tofranil	325	34	34	32	1
Dilantin	841	28	47	25	0.9
Thorazine	763	35	40	25	0.7
Chloral hydrate	90	43	27	30	0.7
Valium	550	34	45	21	0.6
Ritalin	1661	47	27	26	0.5
Cylert	294	46	32	22	0.5
Amphetamine	629	50	30	20	0.4
Phenobarbital	731	48	35	17	0.2
Mysoline	87	53	36	11	0.2

Table 2. Parent ratings of behavioral results of nutrients

Nutrients	no. cases	% worse	% no effect	% better	better: worse ratio
calcium	97	1	41	58	56.0
vitamin C	220	3	48	49	18.2
folic acid	226	3	53	44	16.5
vitamin B-6 and magnesium	2050	5	49	46	9.9
zinc	88	6	44	50	8.8
dimethylglycine	1467	7	52	41	5.9
niacin or niacinamide	49	8	47	45	5.5

biochemical changes in multiple biochemical systems caused by byproducts of microbes or abnormal peptides from wheat and milk. would not be expected to alter brain structure and function.

In PKU, correction of the metabolic defect by restriction of phenylalanine during infancy allows for normal development; retardation occurs if dietary intervention occurs too late. If abnormally elevated metabolites of yeast and bacteria cause autism, then it is reasonable to think that elevations of these compounds would have maximum negative impact during periods of critical brain growth and development. As in PKU, metabolic intervention in autism might only be possible in the early stages of the disorder before the brain has matured. The differences in severity of the disorder and individual differences in symptoms might be due to different combinations of metabolites, how elevated they are, the duration of the elevation, the age at which the metabolites become abnormally elevated, and the susceptibility of the individual developing nervous system to the different microbial metabolites.

Indeed, these differences may even determine *which disease is manifested*. The **concentrations of these microbial products are not trace amounts on the metabolic scale**. One child with autism evaluated in my laboratory had a urine tartaric acid concentration (6000 mmol/mol creatinine) that was nearly 400 times the upper limit of normal (approaching a lethal dose) after the use of multiple oral antibiotics. Many of the concentrations of these microbial compounds found in the urine of children with autism frequently exceed even the concentrations of the predominant mammalian organic acids in urine.

I think that the reason these abnormalities (some of which have been known for decades) have been ignored for so long by almost all of the researchers in the field of metabolic diseases has been the intense focus on finding new inborn errors of metabolism. By definition, abnormal microbial products are not due to a genetic defect in a human biochemical pathway. However, I think that most researchers in the field of metabolic disorders also made the unwarranted assumption that microbial metabolites are metabolically and physiologically inert. Instead, it appears to me that human body and the microorganisms in the gastrointestinal tract are an integrated, interdependent biochemical system within the human body.

Early intervention is key to the treatment of PKU. Children with PKU who are put on the special diet low in phenylalanine have close to normal IQ's while those who are untreated until later in life are impaired. The children of Pamela Scott and Karyn Seroussi who recovered from autism were both started on their therapies at the age of two years. Even this age may be too old for some children. I think that any child under two years old with frequent infections treated by antibiotics is at risk for autism, seizures, and/or ADD and should be tested and treated if abnormal microbial overgrowth is present.

An extensive body of research by Bauman, Courchesne, and others has documented numerous abnormal structures in the brains of children with autism. I wish to emphasize that finding abnormal anatomical structures in the brain **proves nothing about the cause** of these abnormalities. I suspect that some or all of these abnormalities may be due to the toxic effects of the microbial metabolites or the abnormal peptides from wheat and milk just as the drug thalidomide caused abnormal development of the limbs of children exposed to this drug in utero. Saying autism is a brain disease makes just as much sense as saying that the flippers in children exposed to thalidomide are due to an arm disorder; both statements have elements of truth but the oversimplification distorts the complexity of the truth. Studies in which the microbial metabolites and peptides are given to animals should be able to reproduce the symptoms of autism if these compounds cause autism.

The abnormalities that I find in autism are not specific for autism. I have found them elevated in Rett's Syndrome, which is a disorder primarily in girls in which there are some autistic-like behaviors even though it is considered a different disorder. Elevated values have also been found in urine samples of children who have autistic symptoms with Prader-Willi syndrome, Fragile-X syndrome, Tourette's syndrome, Williams disease, neurofibromatosis, and tuberous sclerosis; autistic symptoms are common in all of these disorders. In addition, I have found the yeast byproducts to be elevated in the urine of children with both Down's syndrome and autism; these same metabolites were normal in children with Down's syndrome who exhibited no autistic symptoms. I find elevated yeast and/or bacterial metabolites commonly in seizures, both in adult and child psychosis, in severe depression, and in perhaps 80-90 % of children with attention deficit hyperactivity. These metabolites are also found in some people with hypoglycemia or low blood sugar.

All of my work leads me to discard the prevailing dogma that microbial metabolites are inert in human metabolism.

Based on all of my work and the work of many other researchers, I have developed a theory for autism:

294

Genetic deficiencies of the immune system, inborn errors of metabolism like biotinidase deficiency, adverse reactions to immunizations, or gastrointestinal viral infection from live vaccines impair the immune system and lead to recurrent infections such as ear infections, strep throat, or bronchitis. These infections are then treated with antibiotics.

A yeast overgrowth of the gastrointestinal (GI) tract occurs following the elimination of the normal flora of the gastrointestinal tract. The yeast produces abnormal compounds called gliotoxins and other immunotoxins such as mannan byproducts that are toxic to the immune system and make it weaker. Yeast overgrowth of the intestinal tract may persist in children who are exposed to **any** use of antibiotics as infants, especially if immune deficiencies are also present. Because of immunodeficiency, a child is more likely to be re-infected and be exposed to additional antibiotics until a vicious cycle has been established.

The yeast produce abnormal sugars which may interfere with carbohydrate metabolism or alter the structure and function of critical proteins through the formation of pentosidines. The yeast also produce analogs of the Krebs cycles that inhibit energy production and gluconeogenesis. The yeast also produce enzymes such as phospholipase, which break down phospholipids, and proteases such as secretory aspartate protease which break down proteins. These enzymes may partially digest the lining of the intestinal tract itself. This digestion of the intestinal tract takes place as the yeast cells attach to mucosa lining the intestinal tract. The digestion of the intestinal lining by the yeast and/or viral infection (perhaps from live virus vaccines) causes a leaky gut and may also limit the ability of intestinal cells to produce hormones such as secretin that is necessary for the production of sufficient pancreatic digestive enzymes. Undigested wheat products and other food molecules are more likely to be absorbed from the intestinal tract into the body and elicit an allergic response, a food allergy. Some of these food allergies may manifest as behavioral disorders.

The undigested peptides from wheat and milk react with opiate receptors in the temporal lobes of the brain that are responsible for auditory integration and language and disrupt the functions of this key area. The Candida proliferation also elicits the production of antibodies that cross-react against many of the human tissues including the brain, pancreas and wheat proteins, perhaps leading to atrophy of the pancreas and disruption of key brain functions caused by myelin autoantibodies. Pancreatic atrophy may be associated with further impairment of digestive function with resulting malabsorption and malnutrition. In addition to the yeast overgrowth, there may also be an overgrowth of certain bacteria of the Clostridia family. The Clostridia share one common attribute with the yeast in that they are resistant to many of the common broad spectrum antibiotics used to treat ear infections and Strep throat. The Clostridia probably produces the dihydroxyphenylpropionic acid-like substance and perhaps other neurotoxins that are absorbed into the body and which may also alter behavior.

Implications for gene-searching.
A large amount of money from the National Institutes of Health and other sources has been allocated to various academic centers throughout the country to discover the gene or genes that predispose to autism. If my theory is correct, there would not be a single gene but a whole host of genes, perhaps fifty or even a hundred or more that would lead to increased susceptibility to infection. The current approach is to extract DNA (the chemical basis for our genetic material) from the white blood cells of people with autism, break down the DNA to smaller pieces with enzymes called nucleases, and then separate the pieces by a process called gel electrophoresis. Computers are then used to determine if two siblings from the same family have an abnormal matching band of DNA that is not present in normal people. If my theory is correct, the matching band may very well be different in each family and could result in this information being misread by the researcher since they are looking for a small number of genes. The much higher incidence of autism in males

compared to females naturally led geneticists to suspect that genetic factors influencing autism are linked to the X-chromosome.

Since many of the genes for different immunodeficiencies are linked to the X-chromosome, it would seem worthwhile to focus DNA research on the well-documented phenomenon of immune deficiencies in autism.

Where do we go from here?
Recently, a psychological test called the CHAT test for early diagnosis of autism was developed in England. This test is extremely accurate in predicting autism in children at 18 months of age. No children with a normal CHAT score developed autism while all of the children with two or more major abnormalities in the CHAT test developed autism by the time they were thirty months old. I propose a relatively simple test of the effectiveness of the therapies in this book. Two hundred children with an abnormal CHAT test would be identified. With an incidence of autism at about one in a thousand, approximately 200,000 children would need to be screened. The test is relatively easy to administer, not very time consuming, and could easily be included in a routine well-baby examination with very little expense.

Half of the two hundred children identified as high risk by the CHAT test would receive a low sugar diet and antifungal therapy as appropriate, therapy for Clostridia bacterial overgrowth, gluten and casein restriction, SuperNuthera and DMG supplementation, and food allergy desensitization. Children with immunodeficiency would be treated with gamma globulin and/or transfer factor.

The other 100 children would receive conventional medical treatment. Both groups would get any special training available such as Lovaas therapy, speech therapy, etc, but the therapists would not be told which therapy group the child was in. At the end of one year, all of the children would be evaluated by psychologists who did not know which therapies the children had received. If early biochemical intervention in autism is most effective when started early as in PKU,

297

then the children with the "alternative" treatments would do much better than the children treated with conventional therapies. I propose that these younger children be tested because I suspect that autism is very much like PKU in that the earlier a child is treated, the better the outcome. I have received many reports of benefits of these same therapies in adults with autism and do not want to "write-off" any group of people, but I think our first priority should be an attempt at prevention of any new cases of autism.

There is obviously a tremendous amount of additional work that needs to be done to clarify the best dietary approach used with antifungal therapy; there is considerable disagreement about the best dietary approaches to autism, even among the contributors to this book.

The overuse of antibiotics, especially for recurrent otitis media, needs to be completely re-examined and a large epidemiological study should be undertaken by the Centers for Disease Control to determine how much damage has been caused to our children by antibiotic use. A tax on antibiotics could be used to pay for such a study and other experimental studies on the role of abnormal microbial byproducts in human disease. A large group of infants, perhaps 10,000 or more should be monitored by stool cultures for yeast and bacteria and urine organic acid testing on perhaps a monthly basis for several years to evaluate the association between a wide number of disorders such as ADD, autism, and seizures and abnormal yeast and bacteria overgrowth caused by oral antibiotics.

However, I think it would be a tragic mistake to wait until all data are collected before taking additional action. Sometimes, it is better to act on preliminary findings, when many safe alternatives are available.

Our children are our most precious resource.

Index

Index

Index

Index

Index